# HEAVY METAL

# HEAVY METAL

## How a Global Corporation Poisoned Kodaikanal

AMEER SHAHUL

MACMILLAN

First published in India 2023 by Macmillan
an imprint of Pan Macmillan Publishing India Private Limited
707 Kailash Building
26 K. G. Marg, New Delhi 110001
www.panmacmillan.co.in

Pan Macmillan, The Smithson, 6 Briset Street, Farringdon, London EC1M 5NR
Associated companies throughout the world
www.panmacmillan.com

ISBN 978-93-90742-66-0





1 3 5 7 9 8 6 4 2



Typeset in Adobe Garamond Pro by R. Ajith Kumar, New Delhi
Printed and bound in India by Replika Press Pvt. Ltd.

*To the people of Kodaikanal*

# CONTENTS

## Part III: Unilever in India



## Part IV: Science, Evidence and Reasoning



## Part V: A Poison Named Mercury



## Part VI: Mercury Rising in Kodai

# CAST OF CHARACTERS

**Chesebrough-Pond's Inc, Unilever Plc, Hindustan Lever Limited (HLL), Hindustan Unilever Limited (HUL)**

Douglas Baillie: CEO of Hindustan Lever during 2006–08, who was responsible for changing the name of the company from Hindustan Lever to Hindustan Unilever

Manvinder Singh Banga or Vindi Banga: Chairman of HLL from 2000 to 2010

Sir Robert Augustus Chesebrough: founder of the Chesebrough Manufacturing Company

S. M. Dutta: Chairman of HLL until 1996

A. S. Ganguly: former Chairman of HLL

A. J. C. Hoskyns-Abrahall: Dutch Chairman of Unilever in 1956

Paul Polman: CEO of Unilever PLC from 2009 to 2019

Dr T. Rajagopal: Chief Medical Officer of HLL

M. K. Sharma: Vice-chairman of HLL, who was in charge of the Kodaikanal issue

Prakash Tandon: first Indian Chairman and Managing Director of HLL in 1961

T. Thomas: Tandon's successor as HLL's CEO, who navigated HLL through the Emergency

**Greenpeace India, Greenpeace USA, Greenpeace International**

G. Ananthapadmanabhan: Executive Director of Greenpeace India from 2001 to 2008

Kevin Bridgen: Greenpeace activist, who worked on issues of environmental impact of toxic heavy metals in the UK

Casey Harrell: campaigner with Greenpeace USA during 2002–06

Nirmala Karunan: first employee of Greenpeace in India

Annie Leonard: presently co-Executive Director of Greenpeace USA

David McTaggart: Executive Director of Greenpeace International until 2001

Malini Morzaria: anti-toxics campaigner at Greenpeace International

Samir Nazareth: action team leader at Greenpeace India

Ganesh Nochur: Greenpeace and Narmada Bachao Andolan (NBA) campaigner

David Santillo: head of the Greenpeace Research Laboratory at University of Exeter

Ruth Stringer: researcher at the University of Exeter lab of Greenpeace, who had also surveyed waste stockpiles at the Union Carbide site in Bhopal

Adarsh Varshney: action team leader at Greenpeace India

**Judges and Lawyers**

Rahul Balaji: legal counsel of HUL before the Madras High Court

S. N. Bhargava, Justice (retd): Chairman of the Indian People's Tribunal (IPT) and former Chief Justice of Sikkim High Court

Dushyant Dave: Supreme Court lawyer, who represented HUL at the Madras High Court

A. K. Ganguly, Justice: Chief Justice of Madras High Court, who headed the division bench that heard the ex-workers' case till 2008

Satish Parasaran: legal counsel of HUL before the Madras High Court

Suhrith Parthasarathy: lawyer appointed as the Commissioner by the Madras High Court to implement the settlement

Vaigai Ramamurthy: counsel representing the ex-workers before the Madras High Court

Mukul Rohatgi: former Attorney-General of India, who moved the Supreme Court on HUL's behalf

**Environmentalists**

Claude Alvares: Goa-based environmentalist, who was a member in the Supreme Court Monitoring Committee in 2004–05

Clarence Borel: an industrial worker in the 1930s, who suffered from a form of lung cancer after being exposed to asbestos dust, and initiated the landmark asbestos case in the US

Lois Marie Gibbs: a woman who started the Not In My Back Yard (NIMBY) campaign and ended up fighting with Hooker Chemical Company in the US

Yuyun Ismawati: Indonesian environmentalist who led the fifty Goldman Environmental Prize winners in taking up the Kodaikanal issue with Unilever CEO Paul Polman

Nityanand Jayaraman: Chennai-based environmental activist who initially worked with Greenpeace and had been involved in the Kodaikanal case since 2001

Saleh Mamon: UK-based environmental activist, who raided the Unilever AGM in London

Medha Patkar: environmental activist, who heads the NBA

Pradeep Sharma: civil rights activist and campaigner with NBA

**Local Community**

Gynanasundari Jayaprakash: a local Kodaikanal resident who, after living close to the factory for years, suffered miscarriages and gave birth to two children with congenital defects

Navroz Mody: an environmental activist in Kodaikanal pursuing the mercury poisoning case

Selvi Meenakshi: a young activist who worked for the Palani Hills Conservation Council (PHCC) alongside Mody

**Ex-Workers and their Kith and Kin**

S. A. Mahindran: one of the leaders of the ex-workers' front working alongside Mody; also known as Mahendra Babu

Christopher Martin Colorant: an ex-worker of the thermometer factory, who allegedly died due to mercury poisoning

K. Gopala Krishnan: one of the leaders of the ex-workers' front working alongside Mody

Raja Mohamed: one of the leaders of the ex-workers' front working alongside Mody

Ruby Martin: mother of Christopher Martin Colorant

Ruth Priya: a factory worker in the mercury packing division from 1991 to 2001

Arokiaselva Raja: a worker at the mercury thermometer manufacturing factory, who allegedly died due to mercury exposure in 1997

Ve Paneerselvam Yesudas: a worker at the factory, who allegedly died due to mercury exposure in 1997

**Scientists, Researchers and Medical Practitioners**

Dr J. Arunachalam: Director of the Department of Atomic Energy's National Centre for Compositional Characterization of Materials (NCCCM), Hyderabad

Dr K. Anand: representative from All India Institute of Medical Sciences (AIIMS) in the high court-appointed Expert Committee in 2006

Dr Tapan Chakrabarti: heavy metal remediation scientist at CSIR-NEERI, Nagpur

Dr S. K. Dave: occupational health expert of the National Institute of Occupational Health (NIOH), who was the clinical expert in the high court-appointed Expert Committee

Dr Rakhal Gaitonde: a public health expert, who reviewed the study conducted by the high court-appointed Expert Committee

Dr Mohan Isaac: Professor at the National Institute of Mental Health and Neuro Sciences (NIMHANS) who visited the contaminated site and physically examined thirty workers exposed to mercury in 2002

Dr D. Karunasagar: scientist at the Department of Atomic Energy's NCCCM, Hyderabad

Dr M. V. Balarama Krishna: scientist at the Department of Atomic Energy's NCCCM, Hyderabad

Dr Jayaprakash Muliyil: a community health specialist representing the Christian Medical College, Vellore, and a member in the 2006 high court-appointed Expert Committee

Dr C. S. Pandav: a doctor, who wrote a report on behalf of AIIMS

Dr Mahena Patil: mercury remediation expert from CSIR-NEERI, Nagpur

Dr A. K. Srivastava: Deputy Director and head of Epidemiology division at the Industrial Toxicology Research Centre (ITRC), Lucknow

Tom van Teunenbroek: expert environmental consultant at the Dutch organization Toegepast Natuurwetenschappelijk Onderzoek (TNO)

Dr P. N. Vishwanathan: director-grade scientist at the ITRC (retired), who carried out an assessment for the company in March 2001

### Administrators and Policymakers

Sheela Rani Chunkath: chairperson of the Tamil Nadu Pollution Control Board (TNPCB)

Mallikarjun Kharge: Congress politician and the minister of Labour and Employment in Manmohan Singh's government during 2009–2013

Dr M. Rajaram: Deputy Director of the Directorate General Factory Advice Service & Labour Institutes (DGFASLI)

Jairam Ramesh: Congress politician and the cabinet minister for Environment and Forests from 2009 to 2011

### Media

Sofia Ashraf: artiste from Chennai who performed the viral rap song 'Kodaikanal Won't'

Sarah Hiddleston: the British journalist who wrote an article in *Frontline* about the Kodaikanal case

George Iype: correspondent for the *Associated Press* in south India

Sreenivasan Jain: anchor at NDTV

Dr K. S. Jayaraman: founder of the science division at Press Trust of India and India editor of *Nature*

Rathinan Prasad: photographer turned director, who shot the video for 'Kodaikanal Won't'

Saritha Rai: India correspondent of the *New York Times*

T. E. Rajasimhan: shipping correspondent in 2003 and, currently, Senior Assistant Editor at the *Hindu BusinessLine*

M. R. Subramani: news editor with the *Hindu BusinessLine* from 2000 to 2015

## Organizations

Bombay Natural History Society (BNHS)

Community Health Cell (CHC)

Council of Scientific and Industrial Research–National Environmental Engineering Research Institute (CSIR–NEERI); formerly known as NEERI

CSIR–Indian Institute of Toxicology Research (CSIR-IITR); formerly known as Industrial Toxicology Research Centre (ITRC)

Department of Atomic Energy (DAE)

Directorate General Factory Advice Service & Labour Institutes (DGFASLI)

Environment Protection Agency (EPA)

Global Mercury Observation System (GMOS)

Indian Institute of Technology (IIT)

Indian People's Tribunal (IPT)

National Centre for Compositional Characterization of Materials (NCCCM)

National Institute of Mental Health and Neurosciences (NIMHANS)

National Institute of Occupation Safety and Health (NIOSH)

National Institute of Occupational Health (NIOH)

Tamil Nadu Pollution Control Board (TNPCB)

United Nations Environment Programme (formerly UNEP, now UN Environment)

# PROLOGUE

## A Case against Mercury

IN THE SUMMER OF 2015, A GROUP OF FIFTY AWARDEES OF THE Goldman Environmental Prize, popularly known as the Green Nobel, shot off an indignant letter to the then CEO of Unilever Plc, Paul Polman.

A week prior, Polman had been named the winner of the Champion of the Earth Award by the United Nations Environment Programme (UNEP) – the highest honour bestowed by the UN agency for achievements in the areas of environment and sustainability. The letter sent via email asked Unilever to accept responsibility for the devastation of the pristine south Indian hill station of Kodaikanal in Tamil Nadu, where hundreds of people had been suffering from mercury-related ailments since the 1980s.

Polman felt cornered.

He was to receive the award three days later, during the closing ceremony of the UN's Sustainable Development Goals (SDG) summit in New York – at the same august gathering where a global agenda to eradicate poverty, hunger and gender discrimination by 2030 would be adopted by the UN General Assembly. 'An agenda for people, to end poverty in all its forms – an agenda for the planet, our common home,' as the then UN head, Ban Ki-moon, would describe. At least three of the seventeen goals had direct relevance for Unilever: 'Climate Action', 'Life below Water' and 'Life on Land'.

Polman responded the very next day, conceding some of his company's grave missteps: 'As way of background, this matter began in 2001 when, in breach of our strict operating procedures, we sold some glass scrap containing mercury residue to a local scrap dealer. After becoming aware of the issue, we immediately shut down the factory and launched an investigation. Shortly after, we safely removed and disposed of the waste and machinery.'[1]

This was the first time in the history of Unilever, the fourth-largest consumer goods company in the world, that its CEO had confessed to the company's significant historical lapses – slip-ups that had occurred long before Polman had even joined Unilever.

But what Polman did not optimally address in his response was the large-scale destruction of the unique biodiversity of a fragile ecosystem, locally known as Pambar Shola, similar to the Amazon forests of Brazil, Borneo in Southeast Asia and Madagascar in Africa, where thousands of endangered and near-extinct flora and fauna delicately coexist.

At the same time, he accepted the suffering of over 500 former workers of the now-defunct factory that had manufactured thermometers for almost two decades using a dangerously poisonous heavy metal – mercury. Mercury exposure was known to cause developmental disorders in pregnant women and newborns and also trigger nephrological and neurological disorders, including progressive degenerative disorders such as Alzheimer's disease.

But Polman was still searching for 'evidence of any adverse health impact' on his workers. He wrote back, without conceding any of the scientific, medical and epidemiological evidences available to his company: 'We believe we have acted both responsibly and transparently to address the two main issues: The first concerns the health of our former workers, many of whom – as you say – claim to have become unwell as a result of their work in our factory.' He also referred to the second concern of 'environmental damage within and around the factory site'.

The concerns had presented themselves when the factory was forced to shut down on a morning in March 2001, after members of the local community and the international environmental campaign organization Greenpeace found out that Unilever had been indiscriminately disposing of mercury-laden glass waste by selling it to local scrap dealers. This waste had then travelled across southern India and made it to households in the form of consumables ranging from glass marbles to bulbs and lamps.

On behalf of the Goldman Prize winners, Indonesian environmentalist Yuyun Ismawati quickly rebutted Polman. 'My personal research on Kodaikanal found several publications and reports conducted by various agencies and researchers that [have] shown severe impact of mercury to the communities in Kodaikanal and a high concentration of mercury in the Kodai Lake, moss and lichen in the forest areas. This really refutes your claim and support of the statement that there is no evidence of any adverse impact.'

In fact, there was no dearth of studies on the devastation done to Kodaikanal by mercury pollution. A reputed scientific institute under the Indian Department of Atomic Energy; Greenpeace Research Laboratories at the University of Exeter, UK; a group of doctors associated with India's premier neurological institute, the National Institute of Mental Health and Neurosciences (NIMHANS), as well as studies funded by UNEP's Global Mercury Observation System (GMOS) and the European Commission had all noted and recorded this destruction.

Within two years of Greenpeace revealing high levels of

contamination and environmental damage, Kodaikanal had become one of the most widely studied mercury pollution sites in the world. The studies covered subjects ranging from the health impacts on workers and residents, bioaccumulation of mercury in fish, conversion of mercury from inorganic forms to dangerous organic forms in sediments, air transportation of mercury in the atmosphere and the destructive impacts of mercury on the ecosystem. Many studies found their way into international peer-reviewed scientific journals, while various others were presented at prestigious international conferences and published in books and other publications.

In fact, a public hearing conducted by the independent Indian People's Tribunal (IPT) headed by Justice (retd) S. N. Bhargava, about a year after the closure of the factory in 2002, had documented at least two dozen cases of acute illnesses and deaths among the ex-workers of the factory. The cases ranged from kidney ailments, vascular diseases, neurological and developmental disorders, dermatitis to cancer.

Ruth Priya, formerly an employee in the mercury-packing division of the factory from 1991 to 2001, remembers working on the shop floor without an overcoat, head cover or gloves and going home in her mercury-laden clothes. She would hang them in her closet along with other garments and return to the factory wearing the same set of clothes the next morning.

Towards the end of her career with the company, whenever Priya suffered from headaches and tremors during work hours, the factory management would give her paracetamol tablets. Despite growing up as a healthy child, she would be easily overcome by giddiness and exhaustion after working at the factory for a few years. In 2001, she had twin boys, both of whom displayed deformities at birth. One of them had a cleft foot while the other would gradually suffer from memory loss. With regular medical assistance, however, the children were able to experience a relatively normal childhood.[2]

Arokiaselva Raja, another ex-worker, was faced with an even harsher indictment. He had spent twelve years with Hindustan Lever, leaving in 1997 to undergo medical treatment. His job was to grade and laser-cut mercury thermometers, and screen them on the shop floor. He decided to resign from the company so that he could get himself hospitalized. A few months later, he died at the age of thirty-two.

A non-smoker and teetotaller, Raja began to show some early symptoms of mercury poisoning soon after joining the company. He would have occasional nosebleeds and vomit blood.[3] Each time, the infirmary at the factory would give him over-the-counter pills to tackle the issues.

One day in 1995, Raja developed an extremely high fever with swellings all over his body, especially in his testicles. A detailed medical check-up and consultation revealed that he was suffering from renal parenchyma, a disease that damages the cortex and the medulla of the kidneys – typically caused by the nephrotoxicity of mercury.

His creatinine levels, the prime indicator of kidney damage, kept shooting up during the next couple of months, even though he availed the finest medical treatment with the funds his family could muster by borrowing and mortgaging. Eventually, the doctors advised his family to take him home as nothing more could be done medically, his condition having deteriorated into multiple organ failure. As Raja's brother Sebastian revealed in a deposition before the IPT several years later: 'With limited time left, we finally brought him and even gave him treatment at home but his body would swell up and he would be in terrible pain. Soon he started bleeding rectally and died on 27 April 1997.'[4]

Ve Paneerselvam Yesudas, another factory worker, succumbed to kidney failure at the age of twenty-eight, within five months of Raja's death.

And so the list went on.

The IPT, which first documented the details of the victims, had received submissions from two dozen former workers of the factory as well as the family members of the workers who had died. When a committee constituted in 2011 by the Ministry of Labour and Employment of the Government of India, on the directions of the Madras High Court, contacted the affected workers and the family members of the deceased workers, at least seventy-two victims deposed, narrating their own or their deceased family members' hardships.

S. A. Mahindran, aka Mahendra Babu, president of the ex-workers' union at Pond's (Hindustan Lever) Kodaikanal factory, was himself a victim. Mahindran, who worked in the factory for over six years, until 1989, developed infertility despite being from a family of healthy, fertile individuals. After regularly experiencing nosebleeds and chronic headaches, he left the company at the age of twenty-seven. His andrological issues would be identified much later.

The first death of a factory worker occurred in 1984, Mahindran recalls, a year after the grand opening of the facility to export mercury thermometers around the world. It was a worker named Marimuthu, who died throwing up blood after being taken to the Periyakulam General Hospital, some seventy kilometres from the work site. No one knew the reasons for his death at the time.[5] According to Mahindran, until the closure of the factory in 2001, at least ten workers between the age of twenty-two and thirty-five died while employed by the factory. But if one adds the number of people who died after leaving the company, the total casualties go up to twenty-eight, as per information he submitted to the committee constituted by the Ministry of Labour and Employment. He also disclosed that it was only in 2001, just before the closure of the factory owing to an order from the Tamil Nadu Pollution Control Board (TNPCB), that the workers noticed stickers on the mercury bottles warning against dental, eye, brain and kidney problems as a result of mercury exposure.

'We have never seen the stickers; the company removed the labels (from the mercury bottles before they were sent to the workers in the shop floor),' Mahindran submitted in his affidavit.

In the initial years, perhaps until sometime in 1984, the workers were advised to take a bath before leaving the factory and also to wash their hands with liquid soap before eating meals at the factory canteen. This was in accordance with the guidelines of the National Institute for Occupational Safety and Health (NIOSH), a federal regulator in the United States, from where the thermometer plant had reached Kodaikanal.

The factory had been set up by the US company Chesebrough-Pond's Inc, which sent a used thermometer plant and associated machinery to India in 1983, following the tightening of environmental regulations in the US with the formation of the Environmental Protection Agency (EPA). The factory would drop into Unilever's kitty by 1988.

In the initial years since the establishment of the factory in Kodaikanal, workplace safety was given paramount importance. But the factory would completely change track after the global takeover of Chesebrough-Pond's by Unilever and in India by Unilever's Indian subsidiary, Hindustan Lever. Many other changes would take place after that, the purpose of the company included. Hindustan Lever would get registered as a 'glass manufacturing unit' rather than one dealing with hazardous metals like mercury. This allowed the company to circumvent the problem of having to report the handling of mercury in accordance with India's prevailing hazardous waste management regulations.

All such omissions would come to haunt the company later, when the matter of mercury poisoning would reach the court in 2005 by way of a writ petition filed by the ex-workers of the closed factory. Leading the charges was human rights lawyer Vaigai Ramamurthy who presented a writ, in the absence of provisions in the Indian jurisprudence for class action lawsuits as in the West. It would take another decade for the case to be decided by the High Court of Madras, that too after the parties arrived at an out-of-court settlement upon Polman's intervention.

In 2016, Unilever agreed to a compensation package worth 'an undisclosed sum' for 591 of its ex-workers. It was said to be the second-highest compensation package ever paid by any corporate entity in India, the highest being the $470-million recompense paid by the Dow Chemical Company to the people of Bhopal for its liability in the Bhopal Gas Tragedy of 1984.

There was one more reason for Polman to fast-track Unilever's decision on an issue that had been lingering for over fifteen years. In August 2015, a greenhorn director and an amateur rapper from Chennai had created a music video titled 'Kodaikanal Won't', a spin-off of Nicki Minaj's hit song 'Anaconda' infused with Bharatanatyam and the Tamil folk dance form *dappan koothu.* Soon after the three-minute video released by the NGO Jhatkaa.org went viral, crossing a million views on YouTube, in an instant, Unilever's role in the environmental devastation of Kodaikanal had become a global talking point.

# PART I

# WATERTOWN TO PAMBAR SHOLA

# 1

# WATERTOWN

AN UNUSUAL FEATURE OF NEW YORK STATE'S JEFFERSON COUNTY IS a trail of obsidian water known as the Black River that crisscrosses through the northeastern state before emptying into Lake Ontario. Its source is a massif known as the Adirondack Mountains. The word 'Adirondack' was originally a derogatory term used to refer to the indigenous people of the region, who, unable to farm or store food, would eat tree barks to survive famines and rough winters.[1]

Blackwater rivers, from which the Black River derives its name, are water channels containing decayed vegetable matter from surrounding trees and plants. As the leaves and barks shed by trees decay over time, the decomposed slush containing tannin or tannic acid joins the streams, thus giving such rivers a jet-black colour identical to black tea.[2] Infused with high concentrations of minerals such as aluminium, these rivers tend to be more acidic than their more traditional counterparts.[3]

The Black River flows in a northwesterly direction, separating the Adirondack Mountains on the east and the Tug Hill region to the west. Travelling down all the way to Lake Ontario near Dexter village, about sixteen kilometres west of Watertown, it empties itself specifically into the Black River Bay and Marsh, which are part of the Golden Crescent, located between Cape Vincent and Sackets Harbour, considered by many the largest freshwater bay in the world. Watertown owes both its birth and its name to the Black River.

The city was largely developed in the early part of the nineteenth century, after the Black River canal system was properly established and people began taking advantage of boats and small vessels for ferrying goods from Lake Ontario to the countryside, roughly 200 kilometres inwards.

As corporations began looking for suitable locations to set up factories, Watertown climbed to the top of every company's list. Convenience to move raw materials and finished goods from the hinterlands to Lake Ontario and vice versa certainly held appeal, as did the proximity to the city of New York and the connectivity by road to Washington D.C. Across Lake Ontario was Canada, another growing market.

Soon Watertown established itself as a thriving manufacturing destination.

The Black River, too, provided abundant water resources for industrialization. By the middle of the nineteenth century, entrepreneurs had built paper mills and other major industries, including one that manufactured the first portable steam engine in 1847. Most of these new, upcoming companies selected riverside sites to set up factories, due to the ease with which they could dump waste materials and effluents into the water. The river being black, no one would notice. Thus, the river's name received further endorsement with the growth of the American economy. And the Black River turned blacker.

Watertown's development now took a fast track with considerable revenue flowing into the city administration's coffers. Soon the city would build drainage systems and pavements, invest in public lighting and other amenities. The Watertown city centre would become a point of attraction in the region. Before long, a great civilization began to flourish between the shores of the Black River and the boundaries of Watertown.

In 1888, the Glass Thermometer Company set up shop in the city due to easy availability of water and their ability to discharge mercury waste into the Black River.[4]

The Glass Thermometry Company changed hands (and names) several times, becoming Faichney Instrument Co. in 1920 before being taken over by Chesebrough-Pond's Inc in 1966.[5] In 1988, Unilever acquired Chesebrough-Pond's. Soon after the acquisition, Unilever would dispose of or relocate some of the non-core assets that had come along with the company. It was through this entanglement of mergers and acquisitions that a dilapidated mercury thermometer plant and its associated machinery would be identified and shipped to India in 1983 to the southern hill station of Kodaikanal.

# 2

# CHESEBROUGH-POND'S

IN THE 1860S, A YOUNG NEW YORK-BASED CHEMIST, SIR ROBERT Augustus Chesebrough, noticed some petroleum residue that had accumulated on the rods of some oil pumps. He began investigating it, knowing that workers in petroleum fields and refining factories often used this residue on bruises as the cuts and wounds would dry up soon after its application. As this handy tip began spreading, people started using the material as medication for a number of ailments, including skin rashes and a host of skin infections.

His entrepreneurial spirit encouraged, Chesebrough began producing this residue in his lab. Soon he shifted production to a small 'factory', which was set up at the back of his house. He named the product 'Vaseline', combining '*wasser*', the German word for water, and the ancient Greek word for oil, '*elaion*'.[1]

Chesebrough began selling the product to stores in the area by the 1870s. It soon became known as Vaseline Petroleum Jelly, a name that captured both its parent material and form. It quickly gained the approval of pharmacists and general stores and the sales swelled day by day, boosted by local advertisements. A unique new product on the shelves, Vaseline captured the imagination of common people and medical professionals alike. Enquiries came flooding in from other parts of the country, even from various corners of the world. Since the company's production capacity was starting to reach its limit, new factories had to be established. Almost a household name already, Chesebrough would patent the product in the US in 1872. In 1877, he would be granted a patent in England.

So goes the origin story of a product which would prevail for over 150 years, driving numerous mergers and acquisitions across the continents of Europe and North America. Even today, Vaseline is used to prevent trans-epidermal water loss and is recommended by doctors as a wound care agent after skin surgeries.

Soon offices opened in Great Britain, France and Spain. An exclusive distribution arrangement was reached with one of the megaliths of business, Colgate & Company, in 1873. Petroleum refiners were stunned by the sale proceeds enjoyed by this newly formed company, all through the extraction of a compound from a by-product of the oil refining process. No surprise then that it caught the attention of two shrewd industrialists – John Rockefeller and Henry Flagler, who were running a business empire by the name of Standard Oil.

Rockefeller and Flagler began brainstorming ways to net the promising new kid on the block that was already sourcing raw materials from Standard Oil. Discussions quickly got underway.

In 1881, Standard Oil successfully acquired Chesebrough Manufacturing Company and promptly moved its headquarters from Brooklyn to New Jersey, home to the rest of Standard Oil's offices.

After spending a few decades under the wings of Standard Oil and its steadfast commander Rockefeller, Chesebrough returned to independent operations in 1911, following the US Supreme Court ruling that Standard Oil was an illegal monopoly, thus breaking it into thirty-four smaller entities.[2] This decision would make Rockefeller the richest man on the planet.

Newly independent, Chesebrough started expanding operations by setting up manufacturing plants in Canada and Great Britain. The fledgling company created an array of twenty-five products, most of them petroleum jelly-based personal care items, catering to as many as 120 countries worldwide.

Not far from the centre of these activities, around this time, another chemist named Theron Tilden Pond, leading a modest life in Utica, New York, was building a similar business. Pond had observed that the Oneida tribe in his area had been using an extract from a shrub known as 'witch hazel' to heal all kinds of bruises – from simple boils to fatal burns – very effectively. He tried convincing the tribe's 'medicine man' to join him and help commercialize the extract. Once the man had come on board, they launched it as a product in 1846 under the name 'Golden Extract', referring to the yellow source flower and its hitherto unexploited medical use.[3] By the time Pond died a few years later, the Golden Extract had become a top-selling medicine in the region. Subsequently, the name of the product was changed to Pond's Extract in the memory of the founder.

Pond's was formally incorporated in the US in 1914. By 1933, the company had manufacturing plants in Great Britain and Canada.[4] By the middle of twentieth century, Pond's was selling products in over 100 countries across the globe.

Two companies born within a few hundred miles of each other and in a span of ten years, Chesebrough and Pond's came to be identified as the biggest manufacturers of personal care products in the US and Europe by 1950. Since they were cutting across each other's space and competing on several product lines, the companies soon started seriously sizing each other up. They say people sometimes end up with unexpected bedfellows. In 1950, Pond's chairman Clifford Baker would find a place on the board of Chesebrough.

The two companies decided to explore working more closely and avoid competing in particular geographies. These conversations paved the way for formal merger discussions that would conclude in a complete merger of the two companies in June 1955, giving birth to a new mega corporation known as Chesebrough-Pond's.

# 3

# THE DEATH OF CLARENCE BOREL

FOLLOWING THE 1979 IRANIAN REVOLUTION, OIL PRICES BEGAN soaring worldwide. A significant energy crisis loomed large as the new Tehran regime started slashing production to jack up the price. In the US, a tight monetary policy followed – to control skyrocketing inflation and a consequent all-out recession.

Several companies suffered heavily because of poor consumption and depressed demand. Many began to fail. Across corporations, production was cut down and employees were laid off to control costs, some shutting shop completely. Chesebrough–Pond's, whose top and bottom lines came under severe stress, wasn't spared either.

Almost at the same time, a new change was taking place in the American corporate world – a series of events set in motion by one individual's litigation that would decide the course of corporate ethics in the US and many other parts of the world.

Clarence Borel, an industrial worker since 1936, had worked as an insulation technician in local refineries and shipyards around Texas until he began suffering from serious breathing difficulties. Throughout his early working life and until the mid-1960s, he had maintained good health, except for the odd lung congestion that his doctor attributed to pleurisy. In 1964, Borel was medically examined in connection with an insurance policy, in which the doctor found his lungs to be cloudy. He told Borel that it could be related to his occupation as an insulation worker and advised him to avoid asbestos dust as much as possible.[1]

On 19 January 1969, Borel had to be hospitalized and undergo a lung biopsy. His condition was diagnosed as pulmonary asbestosis. Since the disease was considered irreversible, he was sent home.[2] Soon thereafter, Borel underwent surgery to remove his right lung. The doctors examining his case also determined that he had a form of lung cancer known as mesothelioma caused by asbestosis.[3].

After the diagnosis, Borel decided to reach out to a lawyer named Warn Stephenson. Stephenson, an experienced plaintiff's lawyer, had handled numerous claims for other union workers suffering from occupational injuries or diseases, in most cases claiming damages against employers to compensate for medical expenses and loss of income under the state workers' compensation laws.

In October 1969, Stephenson filed a personal injury suit for $1 million in the Eastern District Court of Texas against eleven firms responsible for manufacturing asbestos and the asbestos-using companies where Borel had worked as an insulation technician. The charges against the companies were of negligence and breach of warranty.

On 3 June 1970, a few months before the judge had opened the jury trial, Clarence Borel died of complications from the disease.[4] And he was replaced by his wife Thelma as the plaintiff in the suit.

The jury returned to deliver its verdict on 29 September 1971, finding Borel guilty of contributory negligence but, more importantly, adjudging that the asbestos manufacturers had violated the Doctrine of Strict Liability and were rigidly accountable for the injuries and death of Borel. For his wife, the jury determined total damages of $79,436 to be paid by the companies.[5] Though the asbestos companies approached the Supreme Court against the appellate court's ruling, the apex court denied their appeal.

Over time, this ruling would become the cornerstone in establishing that corporates could be held strictly liable for their actions under the Doctrine of Strict Liability. It would be subsequently used to hold numerous corporations responsible for their negligent actions of omission and commission.

With this verdict, and a slew of other civil society actions, awareness about the ill-effects of asbestos, heavy metals and pesticides was beginning to grow around the world.

In 1962, the *New Yorker* began publishing American marine biologist Rachel Carson's *Silent Spring* in serialized form. This exhaustively researched, carefully reasoned decrial of the indiscriminate use of pesticides did not exactly make for light reading. Yet it attracted immediate attention and wound up causing a revolution in public opinion.[6]

Published as a book by Houghton Mifflin soon after, it quickly became a bestseller. People had felt alarmed after reading her analysis that 'the common salad bowl may easily present a combination of organic phosphate insecticides' that could 'interact' with lethal consequences to the unsuspecting salad eater.[7]

*Silent Spring*'s role in the history of environmentalism was the same as that of *Uncle Tom's Cabin* in the abolitionist movement. In fact, the Environmental Protection Agency (EPA) could be called, without exaggeration, the extended shadow of Rachel Carson. The influence of her book brought together over 14,000 scientists, lawyers, managers and other professionals across the US to fight the good fight for environmental protection.[8]

As the Borel case proceeded in the Texas courts, the US Congress set out to amend the Clean Air Act of 1963, the first major environmental law of the country, to expand the federal mandate.

This legislation, later known as the Clean Air Act of 1970, provided for comprehensive federal and state laws to regulate emissions from industrial and vehicular sources.[9] Besides laying down rules for the regulation of industrial sources, it also stipulated standards for seven specific air pollutants: asbestos, beryllium, vinyl chloride, benzene, radionuclides, arsenic – and mercury.

The Act set limits for the National Emission Standards for Hazardous Air Pollutants (NESHAPs) emitted by stationary sources, such as factories. These are a category of contaminants known or suspected to cause cancer and other serious health problems, including reproductive disorders and congenital disabilities, as well as adverse environmental effects.[10] The enforcement authority's powers were also substantially expanded.

The adoption of this legislation took place at approximately the same time as the establishment of the National Environmental Policy Act, which in turn led to the creation of the Environmental Protection Agency. The agency was founded on 2 December 1970 for implementing the various requirements included in these Acts[11] and serving the authority role in dealing with the growing environmental pollution. It would do so by heeding the demands and concerns of grassroots movements. In fact, as soon as it was installed, the EPA began seeking details of the status of Hazardous Air Pollutants (HAPs) and NESHAPs from companies across the country, causing some alarm in quite a few boardrooms.

So, when a Congress subcommittee, the Conservation of Natural Resources, began its hearing on mercury pollution with respect to the Enforcement of the Refuse Act of 1899 in July 1971, the Interior Department provided the committee a list of the country's top fifty mercury polluters, along with their daily quantity of mercury ejection and the details of the water body into which it was ejected, as well as the final destination like lakes and ocean. By then, the Department of Justice had already initiated legal proceedings against the ten worst mercury polluters, most of whom were dumping mercury waste into water bodies, some as much as eighteen-plus kilograms per day.[12]

On the list of the fifty worst mercury polluters was a company manufacturing mercury thermometers based in Watertown, New York. Its name was Faichney Instrument Co. and it belonged to Chesebrough-Pond's.

---

Soon after its launch, the EPA undertook a series of activities, starting with a hearing to set automobile pollution control standards in March 1971. The same year it laid down national air quality standards, defined air pollution danger levels and approved clean air plans proposed by several states.[13]

By the time William D. Ruckelshaus was called in to head the FBI in 1973, he had introduced some and overhauled a series of other legislations, including one mandating the clean-up and prevention of oil spills, acid mine drainage and ocean dumping. Under his superintendence, a treaty was signed by eighty countries against the dumping of heavy metals, DDT, PCBs,[14] persistent plastics and radioactive wastes, chemical and biological warfare agents into the oceans. The countries also agreed that special permits would have to be obtained for the usage of cyanides, fluorides and medium- and low-level radioactive wastes.[15]

The EPA also released a 'bubble policy' for regulating air pollution by providing flexibility in meeting emission standards in 1979. This approach meant pollution could be increased at one part of a plant complex and reduced in another, as long as the total did not breach the permissible limit. At the same time, it took a disaster for the EPA to come up with its 'Superfund', meant for emergency clean-ups. On 10 July 1981, a major fire accident broke out in a suburban factory waste dump in Santa Fe Springs, California. The fire started from the chemical waste drum storage unit and resulted in a massive explosion, with debris from the drums landing in a nearby residential area and contaminating a water body that wended through the neighbourhood. In fact, the detritus had spread all the way to the nearby beach after the accident. The EPA ended up spending almost $1.4 million from the Superfund for the initial clean-up. The erring company, Inmont Corporation, negotiated a *quid pro quo* with the agency: they would conduct further clean-up themselves in return for being freed from any liability. The Santa Fe Springs incident turned out to be a test case for the Superfund as the settlement relieved the guilty party from future federal action. Unsurprisingly, therefore, it led to widespread criticism and set a bad precedent.

Thus came the Comprehensive Environmental Response, Compensation and Liability Act (CERCLA), 1980, which initiated actions on a Toxic Substances and Diseases Registry, in addition to assessing liability, fixing financial responsibility in case of accidents and monitoring accident sites even after their closure. The Damoclean sword hung above the heads of all CEOs of firms that had been unscrupulously damaging the environment. Chesebrough Pond's, already struggling under the weight of burgeoning labour costs and industrial unrest at many of its plant sites, had begun to feel the heat at the Watertown plant, where the company had been producing mercury thermometers and dumping industrial effluent into the Blackwater River for almost a century.

A decade earlier, the EPA had noted the mercury disposal at the Watertown site and called for action. But what had gone mostly unnoticed was the emission of gaseous mercury into the pristine air of Jefferson County. So Chesebrough-Pond's identified a new location where they could transport the century-old plant and its machinery.

That place was Kodaikanal, India.

# 4

# KODAIKANAL

THE BRITISH FAMOUSLY HAD AN AFFINITY FOR HILL STATIONS. IN all their colonies, they identified hill stations to set up infirmaries where British citizens and soldiers could recuperate from tropical diseases.

In India, tiny townships crafted from hillside ridges as sanatoriums and convalescence centres for newcomers and the indisposed had, over a period, turned into pleasure retreats for the British. Soon, the hill stations outgrew their purpose as the British realized many locals would go to any length to please their rulers, and so they set up governor's bungalows in the middle of the serene hills.

These were the colonial equivalents of Bath or Brighton – cliquish resorts where young officers, rambunctious ladies, greedy bureaucrats and bored housewives engaged in endless parties and gossip. English poet and novelist Rudyard Kipling writes on the subject in his autobiography *Something of Myself: For My Friends, Known and Unknown*: 'I knew the edge of the great Hills both from Simla and Dalhousie, but had never marched any distance into them. They were to me a revelation of "all might, majesty, dominion, and power, henceforth and forever," in colour, form, and substance indescribable.'[1]

Besides Shimla, Dalhousie, and Wellington in Ooty, the British had also developed hill stations in Darjeeling, Mussoorie, Ranikhet and Nainital, some of India's most popular hill towns even today. Extending the successful concept, they would also build cantonments or military garrisons on hillsides to station the British and the British-Indian Armed Forces.

After Independence, the Indian military forces continued to use these British-style hill cantonments and expand the concept widely. Replacing the viceroys came the ministers and governors of democratic India, who used the hill station chalets to boost their newfound *amour-propre* as the masters of the subcontinent.

One exception was Kodaikanal. Though the British had set foot on these hills very early, building several mansions up the tracks, Kodaikanal had never been turned into a cantonment. It remains a mystery if it was because the British had forgotten to construct one, or that the equally bewitching Ooty was located at almost the same distance from Madras, the regional seat of the British Raj in southern India.

According to available literature, a British Lieutenant named B. S. Ward had scaled the hills and reached Kodaikanal in 1821 to survey the ranges of Palani Hills, of which Kodaikanal is a part. Madurai Revenue Collector J. C. Wroughten and his boss and member of the Madras Presidency, C. R. Cotton, followed him more than a decade later.[2]

Ward's report entitled 'Memoir descriptive of the Vurraghery and Kunnundevan mountains' claims at least 4,000 people were inhabiting the area in well-structured villages.[3] Major J. M. Partridge of the Bombay Army would build a house in 1852, becoming the first European to settle on this hillside. An Anglican church would come up the following year, set up by a group of American and British 'immigrants'.

When the then governor of Madras Presidency visited the hill station in 1860, there were only six bungalows. It took at least about two more years, when David Coit Scudder, an American missionary, reached the hill and settled there, and it would be another fifty years before the fifty-kilometre-long Ghat Road from the plains was constructed. The mist and mystique of the pristine meadows and unfaltering trails of tree covers would add to the mystery of the tapering ghat tracks going up and up on the slippery slopes of massifs.

A solar observatory came up four kilometres from the top of the hill by 1899, after a strong case for photography and spectrography of the sun and the stars using a powerful telescope from a hill station in South India was made by Madras government astronomer Norman Robert Pogson, who had discovered several small planets in another solar system and observed many comets. Kodaikanal was chosen because of its high altitude and dust-free atmosphere. Gradually, most of the work being carried out at the Madras Observatory was shifted to this new one.

By the turn of the century, the new observatory was up and running. The Evershed effect of the sun, a radial motion in sunspots, was first detected at this observatory in January 1909 by John Evershed. This was promptly recalled by *Nature* in 1999 when the post-Independence custodian of the observatory, Indian Institute of Astrophysics, attempted to convert the centre into a convention auditorium to host international science conferences.[4]

Over the next fifty years, Kodaikanal would flourish as a sought-after hill station in southern India, attracting both the British and Americans who wanted to get away from the plains during the summer months and later as a popular holiday destination for India's elite.

# 5

# SILVER SCREEN TO QUICKSILVER

IN THE 1950S, TAMIL MOVIE MEGASTAR M. G. RAMACHANDRAN had smoothly transitioned from an 'acting life' to a 'life of action'. During his acting career, he'd nurtured many fan clubs across the state. MGR would encourage the clubs to meet regularly, support social service activities and intervene in times of natural calamities for relief work and so on. Soon, these clubs developed a well-oiled hierarchical structure akin to a cadre-based political party.

When he transitioned to politics, all he needed to build a mass base was to ask the fan clubs to become units of his newly set up party, and the fans its members. The fans, of course, obliged happily. MGR had wanted to enter politics for a long time, wearing hand-woven khadi attire and even maintaining membership with the Congress party until 1953. As his movie career took off, he joined the Dravida Munnetra Kazhagam (DMK) led by C. N. Annadurai. The party stood for the Dravidian renaissance and, at some point in the past, for an independent Tamil land. A passionate Dravida nationalist, MGR became the glamorous mascot of the party, for which Annadurai first rewarded him with a membership to the Madras Legislative Council in 1962 and then by making him a Member of the Legislative Assembly (MLA) five years later.

Three years after Annadurai's death, realizing he would have to remain content as number two to Muthuvel Karunanidhi, the new DMK chief, he decided to rebel. When he was expelled shortly afterwards, he formed a new political party and named it after his political mentor, Annadurai – Anna DMK. The 'Anna' would later get prefaced by 'All India'.

In the 1977 legislative assembly elections, MGR's party seized the legislative assembly by winning 144 out of the 234 seats, and he became the chief minister of Tamil Nadu. Having realized his dream, he ended his acting career to focus on the development of the state and the prosperity of its people.

Nationally, despite differences of opinion with regional leaders of various political parties, Prime Minister Indira Gandhi had been able to create employment opportunities and develop industries in every state. Even if the motivation might have been to seize non-Congress states from opposition parties, the states benefited from those efforts. In her last term, there were serious efforts towards 'stimulating the private sector through deregulation and liberalising the capital market'.[1] MGR milked this to Tamil Nadu's advantage. Though he was not an advocate of industrialization in his early chief ministerial days, his position shifted substantially towards the end of his career.

After gaining independence, the toughest challenges faced by the country were generating sufficient electricity, producing food for all and creating employment. Prime Minister Jawaharlal Nehru, with a plan to generate 100,000 MW of electricity, had set up the Heavy Electricals (India) Limited, now known as BHEL, to produce turbines and electrical equipment locally. In 1964, the first BHEL plant to produce power boilers would come up in Tamil Nadu on 3,000 acres of land in Tiruchirappalli, south of Madras. In those days, India struggled to find global partners, attract investments and set up its own facilities. However, New Delhi wanted to generate a skilled workforce and create institutions that were able to jump-start the process of identifying technologies for creating food, energy and infrastructure for all. Industries cropped up on their own as well as with foreign collaborations. Some started exporting, while others mostly focused on business within the country.

In the fifties, the investments in chemicals, engineering and the capital goods sectors began to flow, with both the public and private sectors taking on initiatives.[2] By the next big phase, in the seventies, between 1962 and 1971, the performance of the industrial sector had undergone significant changes in size, composition and magnitude between. During this period, the industrial base expanded, and basic and capital goods gained prominence. This change led to a more complex industrial structure, conforming to a higher level of industrialization.[3]

Tamil Nadu was at the forefront of taking advantage of the federal government's efforts. The industrialization of Tamil Nadu received further impetus with the setting up of agencies such as the Tamilnadu Industrial Development Corporation (TIDCO) in 1965 and the State Industries Promotion Corporation of Tamilnadu (SIPCOT) in 1972.

By the end of the decade, Tamil Nadu would emerge as a key industrial hub in the country, thanks to infrastructures such as ports, rail and roads, as well as the early industries and banking systems set up by the British and some visionary schemes of the Government of India.

On a visit to Japan, MGR's faith in the role of the private sector, in close relation with the state, and the greater importance of technology, grew powerful. For the rest of his life, he would remain an admirer of foreign technology. For his part, he welcomed many international companies to Tamil Nadu that could combine investment and technology well. In 1983, one such company set foot in India to manufacture thermometers using quicksilver.

It installed a manufacturing plant at Pambar Shola in the Kodaikanal hills.

# 6

# PALANI HILLS AND PAMBAR SHOLA

IN 1985, WHEN TWO YOUNG BRITISH BACKPACKERS, SEVENTEEN-year-old Tanya Balcar and twenty-one-year-old Robert W. Stewart (aka Bob), took a detour to Kodaikanal from their original itinerary across south India, little did they know that they were about to visit a place which would soon become their home. At the time, the attraction for them had been the pristine, evergreen 'sholas'.

Derived from the Tamil word '*cholai*', meaning grove, the sholas are patches of tropical montane forests found in valleys, intertwining with rolling grasslands in the mountainous regions of southern India. Because of their evergreen nature, and the grasslands and thick forests prevalent in them, these biomes are safe havens for a variety of unique endemic plant and animal species, the existence of many of which are threatened due to poaching and destruction of their habitats.

Many of the species found in the sholas have close relatives only in the similar evergreen forests of Africa, Brazil and Southeast Asia, while many are endemic and restricted to this ecological pocket.

Studies using pollen analysis have shown that the sholas date back to 35,000 years or more. Home to many endemic species of plants, fish, amphibians, reptiles, butterflies, birds and mammals, the area also demonstrates a high endemic nature like the forests in Northeast India and other evergreen forests of the world. As many as thirty-five per cent of the plants, forty-two per cent of the fish, forty-eight per cent of the reptiles and seventy-five per cent of the amphibians living in these rainforests are endemic to the area.

Two dozen tree species had been documented as characteristic of the shola forests.[1] Among them are the Indian mahogany, cluster fig, rusty kamala, bishop wood, *bintangur* and *michelia niligarica*, which is known in Tamil as *kattu shanbagam* and in Hindi as *pila champa*.

The shola forests are uniquely arranged with an upper layer of stunted trees and an understorey of a dense shrub layer. The tree trunks are covered with moss and lichen at the top, with ferns growing underneath in marshy and swampy places. The upper storey is generally described as 'shola trees'. The shola grasslands, on the other hand, are dominated by species resistant to frost and fire, the most common among which is a flowering plant known as country kreat.

Around the time Bob and Tanya arrived at Kodai, montane grasslands – opportunely described as wastelands – were facing severe threat, as its custodians, including the Tamil Nadu Forest Department, were making no income from it. Quietly, more and more of the 'wastelands' got replaced by fast-growing, income-generating species like eucalyptus and acacia, decimating the ecologically sensitive grasslands. The shola tree cover too began shrinking because of the easy human access and the invasion of the plantation tree species.

This became the reason Bob and Tanya never left Kodai. Using their meagre personal resources, they started a shola nursery in the garden of their rented cottage in Vattakanal – three greenhouses with fruit and fuel species for distribution, and hundreds of shola species, many propagated for the first time ever.[2] They worked their way through, first by starting a shola restoration project involving the local youth that led to the formation of the Vattakanal Conservation Trust. The Trust and the duo worked closely with the Forest Department and NGOs like Palani Hills Conservation Council (PHCC) to replace the aging plantations with native shola forest species and evergreen, fruit-bearing trees also found in the islands of Borneo and New Guinea.[3]

Twenty years before Bob and Tanya's arrival, in 1965, a young man named K. M. Matthew had reached Kodaikanal after acquiring a doctorate in the plant taxonomy of Palani Hills, while waiting to be ordained a priest. By establishing the Rapinat Herbarium to work on systematic botany and conservation research in 1967, Father Matthew began his four-decade association with the shola forests. A pioneer in botanical research and conservation across Palani Hills, he would continue his research until his last breath in 2004.[4]

Kodaikanal had been blessed with a number of conservationists, like Father Matthew, Bob and Tanya, who fell in love with the region and decided to dedicate their life to the shola forests. Their work rendered a hope for the survival of the hill station and the extending Palani Hills.

Geographically, the Pambar shola forests are part of the Palani Hills, sixty-five kilometres eastward of the Western Ghats, one of the world's prodigious biodiversity hotspots. With a width of about forty kilometres, these nonpareil woods cover 2,064 square kilometres of hills, shaped off steep cliffs and ridges to a swelling and surging tableland, as low as 1,600 metres (5,200 ft) to over 2,000 metres (6,600 ft) of elevation. The foothills, up to 800 metres of elevation, are covered with 'thorn forests' and bushes and shrubs followed by dry deciduous forests and occasional patches of evergreen, riverine forestlands. These stretches extend as submontane evergreen forests and are trailed and tailed by savannah shrubs up to a height of 1,600 metres. The evergreen patches going up to the lofty heights of 2,000 metres are the outer montane slopes, which are also typified by savannah grasslands and indicate the edges of the shola region. Subsequently, the undulating highland blends with occasional peaks as high as 2,500 metres, covered mostly with grasslands and interspersed with the sholas.

This boundless chain functions as a string of intersecting isles, each with its own ecosystem of flora and fauna and a number of 'hotspots', sites characterized by plant endemism and vulnerability to ecological threat.[5]

The Palani Hills differ significantly from much of the rest of the Western Ghats. Prominently, it lies in the rain shadow of the Western Ghats ranges, where rainfall is scant during the southwest monsoon from June to September. Therefore, the dense, verdant tropical rainforests ubiquitous to the rest of the Western Ghats lowlands are not commonly found here. Often, they are located in a few moist patches along the ravines and in the sheltered pockets of shola forests up to a height of 2,000 metres, where most of the Pambar shola hotspots are also found.

Pambar, a river rising in the Anaimudi Hills on the eastern side of the Western Ghats, flows eastwards, unlike most other rivers of similar origins. This is also where Pambar Shola gets its name, as the region falls on the shadow of Pambar River into which the water from the region drains out.

Besides the Pambar Shola, there are multiple sholas and 'sub-sholas' in and around Kodaikanal, including the Bear Shola, Tiger Shola, Vattakanal Shola, Perumalmalai Shola and Blackburn Shola. Many of these sholas can also be described as sub-sholas of *Pambar Shola.*

The grasslands and sholas, rich with biodiversity, are famously known for various endemic species of plants and trees.

At least a dozen endemic plant species, such as the *Pittosporum tetraspermum*, which is used to treat snakebites, can be found in the hotspots. Other endangered species include *Sonerila pulneyensis,* a delicate succulent herb endemic to Palani Hills, *Hoya wightii ssp. palniensis*, a succulent vine with waxy flowers, *Plectranthus bourneae*, a succulent herb endemic to Pambar shola and *Trichoglottis tenera*, an epiphytic orchid.[6]

As many as fifteen plants have been classified as endemic to the region and a few more share the habitat with the neighbouring Nilgiri and Annamalai hills.[7] Father Matthew had listed 1,758 species as native to the Palani Hills in 1999, and rated forty-six species as vulnerable and fourteen as probably extinct.[8] Other plant species identified to be 'rare' in the area include *Sonerila pulneyensis*, *Hoya wightii ssp. palniensis*, *Plectranthus bourneae*, *Tichoglottis tenera* and *Phyllanthus chandrabosei*.

But the most important of all is the Neelakurinji (*Strobilanthes kunthiana*), which blossoms once in twelve years, with the last flowering having occurred in 2018. Though it blooms across many of south Indian hills, the Sangam Era literature describes its home in Tamil Nadu.

Kurinji Andavar Temple, located in the centre of the Kodaikanal hill station, is a century-old relic dedicated to Lord Murugan and gets encircled by Kurinji flowers once in twelve years. Here, the Kurinji blooming season is celebrated by the locals who consider these flowers to be a symbol of secret love and romance.

It would be here, just a few short kilometres from the temple in the middle of the town, that a mercury thermometer factory would come up and set off a chain of events with sweeping repercussions.

# PART II

# A CATASTROPHE UNFOLDS

# 7

# MADE IN INDIA

IN THE SUMMER OF 1983, A NEW FACTORY WAS BEING SET UP in Kodaikanal at lightning speed. It was to produce mercury thermometers – the kind commonly used in hospitals even in the recent past to measure body temperature, otherwise known as fever thermometers.

During the preceding months, the chief minister of Tamil Nadu, M. G. Ramachandran, had openly railed against the lack of support from the central government in moving the state on the path of industrialization and generating employment. In January of the same year, he publicly criticized the Indira Gandhi government for denying licences to set up industries in Tamil Nadu when approached by companies and accused her of favouring north Indian states like Uttar Pradesh instead.[1] So to avoid further spectacle, the central government had quickly cleared the files and granted the necessary clearances for setting up the hundred per cent-export-oriented unit in Kodaikanal.

Interestingly, the Government of India did not have much of a choice in stamping its approval, as Chesebrough-Pond's had specifically selected Kodaikanal because of its cool weather, which were similar to that of Watertown.[2] Elemental mercury evaporates above the temperature of 24°C, so Kodaikanal, where the average winter temperature is 8°C and the summer temperature 20°C, was ideal. In fact, if the temperature ever rose above the normal levels, leading to the vaporization of the liquid metal, the workers handling it would unknowingly inhale the toxic air.

At a time when the country was craving foreign exchange, a hundred per cent export unit could help bring in the valued US currency. With the central government's approval and the chief minister's full support behind the initiative, even the clearances at the local level moved swiftly.

Around March 1983, the infrastructure of the factory started coming up on a 21.5-acre (87,250 sq metre) quaint plot on St Mary's Road, overlooking the Kodai Lake across the road, in the centre of the town. A rivulet of the Pambar River (approximately half a kilometre to the south) is the nearest water body to the site within the factory catchment area, flowing southwards to the Kumbakkarai Falls about seven kilometres to the southeast, whence it drains eastwards across the Tamil Nadu plain.[3] The sprawling Kodai Lake – the prime attraction of the hill station – is just 500 metres north of the location.

Once the civil construction was almost finished, the non-mercury machinery arrived, followed by the mercury plant and some 35,000 work-in-progress thermometers to train the technicians being hired locally.

The mercury plant dismantled and shipped from the Watertown factory was accompanied by a team of technicians led by Jim Davis, the president of the medical product division of Chesebrough-Pond's. Their objective was to set up the plant, train the local technicians and stabilize the plant operations quickly.

The training started in late November 1983 and was almost completed by the end of December, with both the trainers and trainees working in multiple shifts.

Most of the visitors returned home after the training, in time for Christmas, leaving a few to continue stabilizing the operations. From the new year, production started on a trial basis and, by February, the plant was fully operational. In March, the first shipment, containing four cases of 48,383 thermometers, was dispatched from the plant.

The production process was complex, but it was aided by sophisticated machinery, mostly brought in from the Watertown plant. The stem glass pieces, equivalent to the length of ten thermometers, were imported to India along with bulb glasses and mercury.

The machines neatly cut the stem glasses into individual unit pieces, after which each unit was fused with the small glass bulb at its end. The glass piece melded with the bulb was then filled with triple-distilled mercury in a vacuum, as a small reservoir would form while sealing the open end of the glass. Any trapped air was removed through a series of processes, and the thermometers were then warmed to 41°C to set the scale. Next, they were warmed out to 35°C, before being sent for printing the scale on the surface of the tube, and finally for quality check and certification.

Most of these activities were segregated between mercury and non-mercury areas. For example, the stem cutting, end cutting, bulb forming and other non-mercury operations were carried out using automatic and semi-automatic machines on the 7,120-square-feet non-mercury shop floor.

The filling of mercury in the thermometers was carried out in a cramped 1,350-square-feet room with three exhaust fans to pump out the escaped mercury vapour during the process. The large shop floor was dedicated to other mercury-related work, where up to 25,000 pieces of thermometers went through the top chambering, contracting, air removal, grading, top sealing, scale printing, top making and quality inspection processes in a single day. This 16,720-square-feet area, with various pieces of automatic and semi-automatic machinery that were used by almost a hundred workers, was fitted with twenty-two exhaust fans to sweep out the vapour constantly. In addition, the floor of the hall was kept wet to minimize mercury vaporization.

Separated from the mercury and non-mercury areas was the 720-square-feet mercury distillation chamber, where almost thirty kilograms of mercury – both fresh and recovered – were distilled in a day to be filled inside the cut glass tubes. This chamber was fitted with six exhaust fans. In a similar-sized chamber, the glass scrap was powdered in a crusher and heated in an oven to recover the left-out mercury in it.[4]

All regular and contract employees were provided with uniforms, shoes, goggles, head covers, masks and gloves. The factory also had an area where the mercury zone workers were required to take a bath after taking off their shop floor uniform and before leaving for home, a practice discontinued a few years after operations began.

S. Raja Mohamad worked in the thermometer factory from 1984 to 1989. As the general secretary of the Ex-Mercury Employees Welfare Association later, he would share with a news magazine that the compulsory bathing practice after each shift was stopped soon after the plant was commissioned. Technicians and engineers who accompanied the machinery from the US advised the local recruits to bathe before leaving the factory; but once they had left, by the middle of 1984, the practice gradually came to an end.[5]

During the early days, workers in the mercury filling, distillation and recovery chambers were provided with respiratory cartridges or canisters, as per the NIOH guidelines, to filter out the mercury from the breathing air. In addition, the mercury area was monitored using a Jerome vapour analyser, a handheld device that can detect mercury in the air at very low levels.[6]

Monthly monitoring of the workers' urine samples was used to reassign them to other areas until the mercury levels in their urine returned to near normal. Women workers were not supposed to be assigned to the mercury area, as per the best practices followed by the American parent company.

Since this was an export-oriented unit, there was some gatekeeping for inward and outward movements of raw materials and finished goods. The federal government's customs department set up a post at the factory, as in the case of any unit focused on exports.

The mercury used in thermometers is triple-distilled (99.999 per cent), and its importation requires clearances from India's Union ministries of commerce and finance. The entry of glass or mercury on-site and dispatch of finished products and wastes offsite are carried out upon the certification by the customs official posted at the factory and recorded in the Annual Bond Account.[7]

By the end of the year, the Pond's thermometer factory had become the livelihood of almost 200 locals, besides creating at least another hundred indirect jobs in the hill station.

In the eight months of operations in 1984, as many as 2.8 million pieces were produced and exported. By 2005, these thermometers had reached most parts of the world, including Europe, North and South America and Australia, with a label that read 'Made in India'.

# 8

# A TICKING TIME BOMB

IN 1984, WHILE THE CONSTRUCTION OF THE CHESEBROUGH-Pond's factory was going on at a precipitous pace at St Mary's Road, an unassuming young man in his mid-thirties named Navroz Mody was shifting his base from Auroville in Pondicherry, some 400 kilometres away, to a modest home a few yards from the upcoming factory.

Having worked on watershed management in Pondicherry, he had decided to move to Kodaikanal because of his love for its salubrious climate, virgin forests and his desire to help local farmers and hill communities.

Before moving to Auroville, Mody had been living in Mumbai, where he had been actively involved as an ardent learner and conservator in social and environmental movements. He was one of the founding members of the Bombay Environment Action Group, an early environmental campaign organization based in Mumbai. Many decades on, he continues as an honorary secretary of the group that takes on some of the most powerful corporates, lobbies and the government, both legally and through campaigns.

Mody's tryst with conservation had started early on; he would attend seminars of the Bombay Natural History Society (BNHS), a non-profit founded in 1883 to promote the cause of nature conservation with which renowned ornithologists Salim Ali and Dillon Ripley were associated.[1]

Walking down St Mary's Road every day, Mody would notice the bustling activities at the factory, with people and vehicles rushing to and fro, trucks lining up outside the main gate with materials and carrying neatly packed cartons to the port in Chennai.

Although aware of the dangers of mercury to some extent, he thought that Pond's, a respected multinational company, was surely taking all necessary precautions and following proper safety measures. In addition, he valued the employment generated by the factory which benefited a sizeable number of locals, who badly needed a means of livelihood in a somewhat remote place like Kodaikanal.

It was only around Christmas in 2000 that he first realized the factory was a ticking time bomb. It took him almost sixteen summers to fully realize the perilous impact of the factory on the forests and the town's local inhabitants.

Mody had been deeply engaged in conserving the virgin forests of Pambar Shola, a rare montane extension of the Western Ghats. Along with a set of like-minded individuals, he had started eco-conservation efforts in the winter of 1984, at almost the same time the first thermometer consignment was shipped from the Pond's factory. They formed a discussion group to take stock of the damaging effects of deforestation in general and the destruction of the antediluvian shola forests by poachers and encroachers.

Banding together an informal sub-group called the Palni Hills Conservation Council (PHCC), they brought in ecologists, environmentalists, wildlife enthusiasts and proponents of sustainable development who lived in and around Kodaikanal. By 1985, the council had turned into a formal organization seeking to promote sustainable development in the Pambar Shola.

This was during a time when large-scale encroachment of forest land, destruction of pristine flora and poaching of endangered fauna were peaking in the country. The Indian forest bandit and sandalwood smuggler Veerappan was at the height of his notoriety, poaching wildlife and kidnapping celebrities for ransom across the region and mainly from Erode in Tamil Nadu to Mysore in Karnataka. Conserving endangered flora and fauna required the oversight of civil society and, accordingly, many committed non-profits sprung up along the region.

The PHCC became a protector of Pambar Shola and the extending Western Ghats, a UNESCO heritage site and one of the eight global hotspots of biodiversity.

Before transforming into a busy city over time, the area around the famous temple in Palani used to be in the midst of hills and woods. For the local people and the devotees of Lord Muruga, Palani Hills remains a revered site, especially because in many parts of south India, certain sacred groves are worshipped as an abode of the gods. And so, Mody and the PHCC received tremendous support and encouragement from the local communities and devotees of Lord Muruga, who wanted to protect the 'celestial' forests of Palani.

With the active efforts of the PHCC and other conservation organizations, the fifty-square-kilometre Kodaikanal-Berijam Wildlife Sanctuary was proposed as one of the protected areas in Tamil Nadu, to be given national priority status by the Wildlife Institute of India in the 1990s.

In the early nineties, the Tamil Nadu Forest Department had shared a proposal with the state government to protect much of the Palani Hills, seeking to declare the area a wildlife sanctuary or a national park – a remarkable collaborative effort.[2] The proposal aimed to obtain the 'protected national status' for the forest stretches that were already among the protected areas of the state and to upgrade their International Union for Conservation of Nature (IUCN) status, thus helping improve the habitat and conserve the wildlife. Two decades on, the proposal is still under the Government of India's consideration.

In August 2012, the Tamil Nadu government notified parts of Kodaikanal and the nearby Dindigul divisions of reserve forests to be the buffer zone of the Annamalai Tiger Reserve. This included some 5,000 hectares of the northern slopes of the Palani Hills as well.[3]

# 9

# THE MERCURY DUMP YARD

CHRISTMAS IS A QUIET TIME IN KODAIKANAL. MOST TOURISTS avoid travelling to the hill station in late December because the temperature goes down to around 8°C or even lower. For most south Indians, that is unbearably cold. The sun sets early, and there is a chill in the air. The streets are usually deserted, with very few people visible on the walkways and around the lake after sunset. But it is a good time for the residents, who are able to enjoy the charming Kodaikanal winter. With their fireplaces lit and hot filter coffee brewing, Kodaikanal residents like to enjoy this time of peace and quiet at home and catch up on pending household chores. It was no different for Mody.

Around Christmas in 2000, Mody was looking to procure some cast-off furniture for his humble cottage. During one of his evening walks, someone mentioned a used-goods shop three kilometres down in Moonjikkal. The next evening, Mody walked down to Moonjikkal to the scrap dealer's shop-cum-warehouse. While browsing through the decrepit furniture and old newspapers strewn around, his eyes landed on a sack of broken glass material. On closer inspection, he noticed that on the surface of the glass pieces were droplets of a liquid substance. He spent a while quietly with this heap of glass pieces. It wasn't something he could easily identify. Upon further scrutiny, he realized these pieces were of broken thermometers and he could make out that the droplets on them were the poisonous liquid metal mercury. Drops of mercury were trickling out of the sacks and onto the shop floor. When the shop owner acted evasively upon being asked about the origin of the glass scrap, Mody told himself they must be from a local clinic or hospital. Walking back home pensively, Mody wondered how a hospital or clinic could have disposed of such a large quantity of broken thermometers. But where else could it have come from?

The next day, he instructed one of his PHCC assistants to visit the scrap dealer's shop and assess the quantity of the glass thermometer waste without arousing any suspicion. While discreetly inspecting the store, the assistant realized there was an extension at its rear in the form of a large, thatched shed.

Once inside the shed, the assistant was thunderstruck. There were 'tonnes and tonnes of mercury-laden glass waste', as he would describe to Mody later in the day. Making a quick, rough assessment of the nature and quantity of the waste, he could tell it had been lying there for a long while, as more and more glass scraps were dumped over it.[1]

Mody visited the place again subsequently and tried to engage the shop owner in a friendly conversation as he searched for answers to the multitude of questions swirling in his mind. Who had sold the waste to him? When did he first pick it up? Why was it lying there? How much had he paid for the waste per kilogram? What was its use? Where was it going from here? Were people handling it with bare hands? And so on.

He took it upon himself to investigate. Discreet enquiries revealed a shocking truth. The waste had come from the Pond's factory, by now known as the Hindustan Lever Limited (HLL) company, on St Mary's Road, yards away from his cottage.

In his conversation with the shop owner, Mody had found that the man had no answers to most of the questions; rather he refused to reveal too much information.

By now a picture was emerging in Mody's mind. The company seemed to have been irresponsibly disposing of the glass waste from its factory, probably for the last sixteen years. They were doing it through scrap dealers and by dumping in remote, isolated corners – maybe in the forests, maybe in the stream, perhaps even in the lake.[2]

This is bad, this is really bad, he thought to himself.

His immediate thoughts were about how to handle the situation. There was a strong possibility the mercury waste lying with the scrap dealer could be taken back by the company and destroyed completely without leaving any trail of evidence. He felt a greater responsibility to inform the public in Kodaikanal and beyond about this ticking time bomb without any delay.

The information had to be widely publicized – locally, nationally and globally – so that the company should not be able to eliminate the evidence. He decided to reach out to some good friends involved in environmental issues in the region. One of them was Nityanand Jayaraman, a young engineer who had recently returned to India after spending a few years in Hong Kong as an editor of a trade publication and was working with Greenpeace on issues of environmental exploitation by corporations. Jayaraman was a son of the soil, having been born and raised in Coimbatore and Madurai. Upon completing his engineering, he decided to change tracks and pursue a master's degree in journalism. That had taken him to Ohio University in the US. Upon completion of his degree, he found himself in Alaska, on the fishing boats during the salmon season, and ended up working in the canneries there, separating eggs from the mother fish.[3] During his time at the salmon canneries, witnessing how the fertile eggs had been robbed off from the mother salmons by humans, had made Jayaraman very conscious of the environmental destruction wrought by corporations for profits.

When the call from Mody came, he was busy working for Greenpeace with an international coalition of citizens and environmental and labour organizations to prevent a 118-tonne stockpile of mercury from the defunct HoltraChem chlorine manufacturing plant in Maine in the US from being exported to India. Eventually, the global coalition succeeded in its efforts to prevent movement of the shipment.

Wearing blue jeans and a buttoned-up shirt and sporting a *cause célèbre* ponytail and a thick, black beard, Jayaraman reached the hill station the next day. Meeting him at a local tea shop next to the bus stand, Mody shared what he and his assistant had stumbled upon at the scrapyard. He pulled out a piece of paper from his unusually long cloth bag and they began working out a strategy to expose how mercury was being dumped by HLL at the scrapyard.

The duo chalked out a detailed plan of action: An unannounced protest by a small group of people before the scrapyard had to be organized, without giving any inkling to the scrap dealer or to the company. They decided to take some key media such as the *Hindu* and the *Indian Express* from Dindigul, 100 kilometres away, into confidence. The local media, Tamil newspapers and TV channels had to be tipped off while the protest was ongoing.

However, their most significant predicament was gathering the local people to protest. The company had gained acceptance so deeply among the local people, nobody wanted to go against it for anything. Living in a small town, everybody knew someone working for the company, whether a family member or a friend. Even the local political parties and civil society organizations had all received generous donations for their activities from HLL. Some even ran some small contracts for the company. No one wanted to antagonize a milch cow. Nevertheless, Mody and Jayaraman decided to proceed.

First, they chose a few PHCC volunteers willing to participate in the protest. However, as the news spread, several workers who had left the company on health grounds came around. Next, the family members of some victims who had died in the previous years also offered to join them. The challenge now was to keep the plan under wraps till it had been executed.

On 28 February 2001, a group of about forty people led by Mody marched to the Moonjikkal scrapyard, taking the local people and scrapyard owner by surprise. For about an hour, they sat in front of the scrap store, raising slogans against HLL. As the protest went on, people of the neighbourhood began gathering around them to find out what was going on. These included some passers-by. Pretty soon, there was a crowd of over a hundred people.

Speaking on behalf of Greenpeace, Jayaraman explained to the crowd the dangers of mercury and its impact on humans and on the environment. By now, reporters from the *Hindu* and the *Indian Express* had arrived to cover the protest, too. The local media also arrived at the scene. Many of them had turned up in a few minutes of the protest, some with cameras. There was no commotion; no stampede on the road. Later, the police reached the spot and asked the protesters to disperse. Having conveyed their message, the protesters left the venue peacefully.

The same afternoon, a press release was issued jointly by Greenpeace and the PHCC. The release was cautious enough to not let their actions affect the livelihoods of the factory workers. Its first demand was: 'HLL should immediately end the use of mercury in the Hindustan Lever Thermometer factory and ensure that the livelihoods of workers are not jeopardised due to [HLL's] negligent behaviour.'[4]

The remaining demands included a full investigation into the extent and nature of mercury pollution caused by the factory within its premises, at the scrapyard and in the surrounding environment; the clean-up of the Moonjikkal dump site; accounting for all past waste shipments to other parts of Tamil Nadu; and a probe to assess the damage to the health of current and ex-workers and compensate them for any health impact.

It also asked the regulatory authorities and the government to hold the company criminally and financially liable for the damage done to the workers, the community, the environment of Kodaikanal and the Palani Hills.

The message had gone out to the external world. Loud and clear.

By that evening, the news had reached the executives of the India headquarters of HLL as well as their global bosses.

# 10

# LIQUID METAL EVERYWHERE

MODY HAD BIGGER WORRIES NOW. BESIDES THE MOONJIKKAL scrapyard, where else could the company have dumped their toxic waste from the factory?

They quickly put together an informal core group to execute their next moves. One team tried to reach out to all scrap dealers in the nearby areas, including the ones in Dindigul. Another went searching for dumps in and around the stream, which flowed from the slopes of the factory all the way down to Kumbakkarai waterfall. A third team checked the banks of Kodai Lake and all possible vantage points along the forests.

As anticipated, more such spots were unearthed in the efforts that lasted a week. Alongside the back wall of the factory along the edge of the stream, a large cache of mercury with piled-up broken glass was discovered by the team. One of the main discoveries was a barrel of broken thermometers, from which mercury was spilling onto the soil.[1] This was photographed with great care by a photographer freelancing for some national news magazines.

In fact, the dump behind the factory had been discovered despite the best efforts of the company officials to quietly clear the area soon after the protests of 28 February. The company had dispatched teams of workers to remove any waste quantities dumped in the forest areas, and many of the dumps were quickly cleared with the mercury waste being brought back to the factory premises in the meantime. [2]

The next big task for Mody and team was to speak to the workers of the factory in confidence. Meeting in small groups, they reassured the workers their livelihoods would be protected at all costs. In the event of them losing jobs or the factory shutting down, HLL would be forced to compensate them amply and adequately. After multiple meetings and many rounds of counselling, several workers decided to speak up. The rest, clearly terrified of the repercussions of whistleblowing, stayed quiet, watching the developments as they carried on with their day-to-day jobs.

With some workers on their side and more evidence cropping up, Greenpeace, the PHCC and civil society groups planned their next move – to force the factory to shut down permanently by bringing pressure to the doorsteps.

During the ensuing two weeks, the omissions by the company had become a hot topic of discussion among the local community. It was easier this time around for Mody and the team to convince people to join the protest. Many people who had lost their relatives to unknown illnesses while working in the factory volunteered. A number of employees came out and revealed the health issues they had been suffering due to possible exposure to toxic material. Anger was mounting against the company.

It had become a challenge to control the emotions of the people. A date was fixed for the protest – Wednesday, 7 March 2001. The PHCC and Greenpeace officials took extra precautions to ensure the protest would not culminate into violence. Volunteers were briefed to watch for any unwarranted outbursts and trained to calm down the crowd, if required.

As planned, by 9 a.m. on the designated day, as many as 400 people had gathered in front of the scrapyard. They started to march in the direction of the factory from the Moonjikkal scrapyard. Holding banners and placards, and shouting slogans against the company, they moved in two orderly files, without disturbing the morning traffic. Some volunteers distributed pamphlets in Tamil that described the dangers of mercury to the curious onlookers on the way. A few others kept the files in order.

Upon reaching the factory, the protesters sat in front of the main gate, blocking the movement of vehicles and personnel for almost an hour. The factory manager came out of the building with someone, upon which he was apprised of what was going on. When he attempted to raise his voice, one of the protesters shouted him down.

Most of the reporters, some of whom were arriving from Dindigul, had reached the venue when the protest began formally. Mody explained the dangers of mercury, and how the company had risked the lives of its employees and harmed the natural environment of the town.

Throughout the protest, a group of policemen remained stationed by the side of the road. One of the protesters had brought along a sack full of glass waste from the scrapyard to highlight the extent of damage wrought by the company. Another got entangled in an argument with an executive who was claiming that everything was fine at the factory. As the protest continued, Jayaraman called up HLL's Corporate Communication Manager, Debasis Ray, in Mumbai, using the number available on the company website. After asking several tough questions over the phone, he followed with another set of questions via email. The response came promptly: 'As I told you on the telephone, I once again reiterate that our thermometer unit at Kodaikanal does not send any waste mercury or mercury-contaminated waste outside the factory.' Ray's response went on to say, 'Mercury-containing broken thermometers and ground glass is stored inside the factory, and we recover mercury from them and recycle this for use in thermometer manufacture. Therefore, the unit does not in any way pollute the adjacent habitation.'

The final lines of the email were: 'The factory's operation and its systems for safety and waste handling are completely above board. We do not – neither do we need to – engage in any clandestine practices, as the allegations seem to suggest.'[3]

By eleven o'clock, everyone dispersed peacefully. The print and digital media, both English and regional languages, covered the protest with great enthusiasm. Swinging into action, the Tamil Nadu Pollution Control Board (TNPCB) asked the company for details of its waste disposal practices.

The events unfolding in Kodaikanal had proved that HLL was practising the opposite of what it had claimed in the annual report published in 2000: '[S]uccess requires the highest standards of corporate behaviour towards [our] employees, consumers and the societies and world in which we live'.[4]

On 8 March, HLL issued a statement announcing that production had been 'temporarily suspended' at the factory. Contradicting Ray's email response, it conceded a 'remote possibility that contaminated wastes may have left the factory', blaming it on a 'small human error'. The statement assured that the company would resume operations only after it had 'fully satisfied itself that the factory's continued operation would not cause any hazard to the local environment'.[5]

Within a day, the Greenpeace and the PHCC also issued a press release, which said: 'On 7 March, Hindustan Lever vehemently denied all allegations. On 8 March, they admitted that there is a remote possibility that contaminated wastes may have left the factory. Now they are looking at dismissing the whole thing as the result of a small human error.'[6]

The news spread like wildfire and an arraignment was listed against HLL. While some political parties responded with guarded statements criticizing the company and asked the Tamil Nadu Pollution Control Board to take action, many civil society organizations of the state publicly expressed their anger and supported the ex-workers of the company and the local Kodaikanal groups. An anti-mercury front was taking shape in the state.

On 12 March, the Tamil Nadu Alliance Against Mercury (TAAM) was formed. Its immediate demand from the company was a 'full acknowledgement of the existence of the problem and an unconditional apology for the mercury pollution.'[7] It also asked the state regulator to investigate the allegations levied against the company without any further delay.

The TNPCB acted swiftly, immediately dispatching a group of experts for a spot assessment. The team visited the factory and the scrapyard on 10 March, where they found most of the allegations levelled by Greenpeace and the PHCC to be true. It noted that the company had flouted its licence conditions of storing hazardous waste within the factory premises inside an airtight shed and taking prior concurrence of the TNPC board for waste disposal.[8] The company had also 'not reported generation of mercury bearing hazardous waste to the regulator'.[9] Further, the factory had been registered as a glass-manufacturing company to escape the responsibilities of hazardous waste regulations.

As anticipated, the company surreptitiously tried to move the mercury waste from the scrapyard at night. But the local community led by Mody tipped off the regulator.

On 19 March, a stern warning signed off by the board

chairperson Sheela Rani Chunkath was issued to the company, saying, 'The Board does not appreciate your attempt to remove the mercury bearing waste in such a stealthy manner.'[10]

Concerned about the possibility of health hazards among the workers, on 23 March, the TNPCB gave a direction invoking Section 5 of the Environment Protection Act, 1986, and ordered immediate closure of the unit and disconnection of power supply to the plant.

According to the directive, during the board's spot assessment on 10 March, it had observed that the company had disposed of 5.3 tonnes of glass waste containing mercury to a scrap dealer named Theruvium in Moonjikkal.

HLL admitted to the board that the 5.3 tonnes of mercury-containing glass waste lying at the Moonjikkal scrapyard had indeed originated from its factory. Realizing the regulator had cornered it through the assessment of the scrapyard and recorded its acts of omissions, the company wrote a letter to Greenpeace on 23 March, suggesting it would also track and retrieve other shipments sent to various locations outside the factory.[11]

At the campaign office in Kodaikanal and at TAAM, this admission was assessed as a strategy to allay the roiling emotions and buy peace – the textbook strategy adopted by corporations when caught red-handed. The emphasis of the campaign, therefore, shifted to a demand for 'an unconditional apology', the greatest hurt to a global corporation's brand value.

Addressing a press conference in Chennai the same day, Mody and other leaders of the newly formed TAAM noted that despite multiple demands, instead of issuing an apology, HLL had been downplaying the magnitude of its bad practices. Tired of playing cat and mouse with a powerful multinational company, the leaders reminded everyone of the alarming reality: the truckloads of mercury-contaminated waste that had been shipped out over the last seventeen years by the company would by now be untraceable, spreading across various parts of Tamil Nadu and beyond.

In response, through a press release the same day, HLL said it had already suspended operations of the factory on 8 March and ordered a comprehensive audit, including a review of its glass disposal methods. It also offered to clear the 5.3 tonnes of waste from the scrap dealer's premises.[12]

By now, as the back-and-forth continued between Greenpeace and HLL, with the TNPCB playing the role of an umpire, it was time for the entry of another player – Dames & Moore.

# 11

# GREENPEACE VS HINDUSTAN LEVER

DAMES & MOORE, AN ERSTWHILE AMERICAN CIVIL ENGINEERING company, became widely known in the 1980s for filing a $3 million lawsuit against the Ronald Reagan administration. The firm had sued the government of Iran and certain Iranian banks against their dues, and a district court delivered an order of attachment of the defendants' assets. But following a hostage agreement in 1981 known as the Algerian Accords, the US president issued an executive order nullifying all non-Iranian interests in Iranian assets and thus suspending the settlement claims in return for Iran releasing American hostages. Dames & Moore moved the Supreme Court to have the president's order declared unconstitutional in order to recover its dues. It eventually lost the lawsuit against Treasury Secretary Don Regan, but the company shot to fame across the world as a result of the case.

Dames & Moore had been part of the San Francisco-based URS Corporation since 1999, after being acquired by the company in a $600 million cash-cum-debt deal. It handled various prestigious projects for them, ranging from the 4,200-acre Kennedy Space Centre to the Sellafield nuclear complex in the UK. A Fortune 500 global engineering firm called AECOM would later acquire URS in 2014 after a hedge fund bought a large activist shareholding stake.

As HLL's long-trusted consultant partner, Dames & Moore had conducted environmental impact assessments and similar internal audits of many of its production facilities across India and beyond. It was no surprise then that they were immediately alerted after Greenpeace issued its press release on 28 February about the scrapyard exposé.

After the second protest on 7 March, Dames & Moore agreed to carry out a detailed assessment of the risk and impact on the surrounding environment and workers. And to be fair, the scope of their study acknowledged that glass scrap was being illegally disposed of from the factory to a scrapyard.[1]

A core team comprising engineers, accountants, environmental experts and chemical scientists was dispatched to Kodaikanal, with instructions to remain there until the work was completed. Actively supported by HLL's local team, supervised by its leadership in Mumbai and monitored by Unilever's global office, Dames & Moore finished the task within ten days, preparing a preliminary protocol for recovery and transport of the mercury-laden waste from the scrapyard and for its on-site storage at the factory. The anti-mercury campaigners pointed out that this hasty assessment was intended to pre-empt any harsh crackdowns by the regulator, given the maelstrom of criticism surrounding the company by this point.

Greenpeace and the TAAM reviewed the protocol for the transshipment within a week and suggested some emendations to it on 3 May, which were further reviewed and agreed upon by Dames & Moore's environmental consultant, Dr Tom van Teunenbroek of Toegepast Natuurwetenschappelijk Onderzoek (TNO), an institute for applied science research in the Netherlands. After this the new protocol, in compliance with the NIOSH guidelines, was summarily accepted by the Tamil Nadu Pollution Control Board.

The protocol for the trans-shipment was exacting in its detail: after cordoning off the entire area with the help of the police, a tall cover had to be erected around the facility; the scrapyard floors had to be continuously sprayed with water to prevent generating dust and mercury from evaporating and the mercury in the air, monitored using Jerome vapour analysers; the accompanying soil needed to be cleared out along with the mercury-laden waste. All workers had to be wearing NIOSH-prescribed personal protective equipment such as special suits, goggles, masks, gloves, boots and respirators. Finally, everything would be transported to the factory inside custom-made containers escorted by the police.[2]

Owing to their reservations about HLL's handling of the issue thus far, Greenpeace and the TAAM contacted the TNPCB and sought local involvement in monitoring how the waste was removed and handled beyond the scrapyard.

At the time, the TNPCB was headed by Sheela Rani Chunkath, an upright bureaucrat with very balanced views on this matter. On 9 May, Chunkath formed a nine-member committee, including two members from the local community, calling it the Hazardous Waste Management Committee, or the Working Committee as it became known.[3]

By then, Greenpeace had co-opted Mody due to his active, direct involvement in the case and general commitment to environmental and conservation issues in the region. Therefore, when the TNPCB formed the Working Committee, Mody represented Greenpeace and Selvi Meenakshi, a young green activist who had migrated to the hill station around the time, the PHCC. Besides officials from the regulator and the district administration, the committee also had two members from the chemical industry and one from the

Madras Chamber of Commerce. Conspicuously, no one from HLL had been included.

At their first meeting on 28–29 May inside the Kodaikanal township hall, HLL shared the details of the preliminary assessment carried out by Dames & Moore. The report drawn from the company's 'meticulous records' had some startling revelations:

- Around forty-five tonnes of glass waste had been buried at the factory site in four shallow pits, which the company claimed was mercury-free.
- Mercury in the glass waste was up to six per cent by weight and, despite their best efforts to retrieve it, at least 0.15 per cent of it still remained.
- The company had first started selling glass scrap in 1992; by 2001, at least 98.2 tonnes of glass scrap had been sold off.
- The customer who had bought the entire glass scrap till 1994 was a lamp case-maker in Mysore named MLC Industries.
- In 1998, 11.5 tonnes of glass waste were sold to a dealer in Coimbatore, of which eight tonnes were bought by Philips India Ltd. and the rest by glass marble manufacturers in Bangalore and other places.
- The last sale, of 5.3 tonnes, was to a scrap dealer in Kodaikanal.[4]

This confirmed the worst fears of the local community. Even if these details were to be taken with a pinch of salt, the mercury-laden waste had travelled far and wide – from Mysore to Coimbatore to Bangalore and beyond.

Within the factory, a lot was unfolding. The volume of phone calls to the factory manager from the Indian headquarters in Mumbai had near about tied him to the handset. He was repeatedly asked where the waste had been dumped and to whom it had been sold off. Officials at the Mumbai office were deeply concerned about the fallout of the exposé, as the pressure from its global headquarters grew, and if they had seen the worst of it. Their message was crystal clear: Recover any waste that had gone out of the factory and move it swiftly and discreetly to a secure place inside.

After consulting its various offices, the company decided to retrieve forty-five tonnes of concealed waste from four shallow pits on the factory premises. At the peak of the controversy, this exercise was carried out without notifying the TNPCB, as is mandatory while handling any hazardous waste. For this grave omission, the company would subsequently be reprimanded by the regulator.

On being informed by the factory workers about the breach of rules, Greenpeace wrote to the company. 'Caught on the wrong foot', HLL responded to Jayaraman in an email, implying it had only removed the non-mercury glass waste buried at the factory site back in the eighties. The email failed to mention why the company needed to remove the glass waste at all, if it was indeed mercury-free and harmless.

Those engaged in the unearthing operation would later reveal that contrary to HLL's claims, the waste unearthed had visible quantities of mercury, which the factory workers with years of experience handling it identified instantaneously.[5] Even more worrisome, the workers had been made to dig out the waste without any protective gears or safety measures, despite the possibility of finding mercury-laden waste in the dump.

It was beyond anybody's wildest imagination how many people could have come in contact with the mercury-laced glass as loaders, unloaders, factory workers and consumers of glass marbles, lamps, glass bangles and glass utensils. Nobody knew where all the glass waste could have ended up at and how many kinds of products it could have been used in. Nobody knew how many people had inhaled the mercury-tainted vapour from the leaking glass waste, how many had fallen sick, which water bodies it had been dumped into and where it would have been bioaccumulated by the living organisms, including the fish. There were no efforts to find out how many humans could have consumed it as mercury-bioaccumulated fish either, inhaling it as vapour or ingesting in other forms and ways.

Even as these torpefying details emerged, the urgent priority was to move the mercury waste from the Moonjikkal scrapyard to a safe location. Taking the impending southwest monsoon into consideration, the Working Committee, at a two-day meeting, agreed to schedule the scrapyard clean-up and move the mercury waste to the HLL factory on 20 June.

On the said day, the first signs of daybreak appeared on the margins of the eastern sky heralded by the chirpings of sparrows and finches, as vehicles with men and materials arrived at the scrapyard. Having no prior notice, it was only when a group of men in hazmat suits arrived that the local people were able to surmise what was going on. There they were, with breathing apparatuses and impermeable coveralls, gingerly taking away the material that had been sitting in an open-air scrapyard in the middle of the busiest part of town for five years. Mere metres from the spot that was being treated like a minefield now, vegetables and meat had been regularly sold and devotees of the neighbouring mosque and church as well as the local children had been passing by it daily.[6]

Seeing the workers moving around in hazmat suits and goggles and handling the waste with sophisticated equipment, the locals finally realized the full extent of the danger looming over their lives. In fact, it was also an eye-opener for many of the ex-workers of the factory and the residents of nearby localities who gathered to witness the clean-up on that day.

Drama ensued when the company officials arrived with the consultants by 9 a.m. There was an altercation with the locals which was soon resolved with the timely intervention of the police. Some locals were raising slogans against the company, while others held banners that said 'HLL, CLEAN UP'.

After the scrap reached the factory by afternoon escorted by the police, the company officials tried to prevent the local community, including the members of the Working Committee, from witnessing the weighing process. But the local community was adamant. By then, they were seething with anger at the indiscriminate manner in which the company had been disposing toxic waste everywhere and the inconsistency in its statements about the garbage dumps. The impasse continued for hours until the TNPCB finally stepped in. After hours of stand-off, at the insistence of the TNPCB, the company relented. As it turned out, the scrap weighed 7.4 tonnes and not 5.3 tonnes as per the company's 'meticulous record' – a difference of forty per cent.[7]

The company had insisted all along that only 5.3 tonnes of mercury-laden glass waste had been sold to the Theruvium scrap dealer at a rate of ₹1,250 per tonne. Two months later in August, despite the discovery of 2.1 additional tonnes of mercury waste, Niall Fitzgerald, chairman of Unilever Plc, in his *Hard Talk* interview with BBC's Tim Sebastian, would insist that only 5.3 tonnes of mercury waste had been retrieved from the local scrap dealer.[8]

This significant discrepancy had raised red flags for the community. On verifying the company's other statements and claims through local contacts, they learnt that in fact several illegal shipments of mercury-contaminated glass had been smuggled out of the factory over the past many years.[9]

This incident was the genesis of the community's distrust against the company and its demands for an independent enquiry on the waste disposal, in Kodaikanal and beyond. Ideally, a criminal investigation should have been carried out to trace all the waste shipments, possibly contributing to death and diseases across the country. But this never happened.

# 12

# CHRISTOPHER MARTIN COLORANT

IN 1986, AFTER COMPLETING HIS STUDIES, CHRISTOPHER MARTIN Colorant was looking for a job so that he could take care of his family as well as build a life of his own. When he expressed this wish, one of his distant relatives took him to meet someone working for a company in Kodaikanal. The company produced equipment to treat fever in hospitals – products which they sent to America, he was informed on their way to the official's house. After seeing his educational certificates, the man they were visiting said, 'I can find out ... It seems they are looking for some people in the mercury section.' A few days later, the relative told Colorant he had been asked to go to the factory.

Colorant's heart was pounding when he reached the factory. It was his first interview for a job, and he was excited and tense. He had crossed the factory a couple of times while passing through the area. While waiting in the lobby, he observed the busy but orderly pace of the place. He had never seen a factory from the inside.

'It would be really lucky if I get a job here,' he murmured to himself.

'Christopher Martin Colorant?' Someone ushered him to a cabin a few metres away.

'What kind of work can you do?' the man sitting across the table asked as he sat down, without any introduction.

'I can't think of any,' Colorant replied in Tamil. The man laughed.

'Well, you should. We will hire you as a trainee and teach you what you will do here. You just need to be hard-working and be committed to the company.'

Colorant joined the company soon after and, from then on, the factory became his home. It had given him a job at the age of twenty-two, and that too in his own town. Many of his friends, who were still jobless, envied him. On completing the mandatory training, he was posted in the mercury area, where he switched between the mercury filling, top chambering and contracting sections.

It was all going well until one evening when he felt a choking sensation while filling mercury in the cut thermometer tubes inside the assigned chamber. He stepped out, took a minute to compose himself and returned to work. Somehow he managed to finish his shift by 10.30 p.m.

But the choking and breathlessness returned a few days later, and then again, and again. Soon the frequency of the attacks increased, and he started having these episodes regularly. Halfway through the workday, he would feel exhausted and unable to breathe at all.

He started losing interest in food, not because he didn't want to eat, rather because his appetite vanished. Odd symptoms began to crop up: First it was some localized swellings on his body and then, inexplicable fatigue. His health kept worsening despite his efforts to ignore the symptoms and work through them. By the time he was twenty-five years old in 1989, the situation was so bad, he was forced to formally request through the workers' union for a transfer to the non-mercury area, as he realized his condition deteriorated when he was working in the mercury zone. But the request was denied, and he was told, 'You are hired for the mercury area and were trained on mercury-related skills.'

One day while working in the mercury area, sometime in 1991 or 1992, he experienced a heavy choking sensation, as if something was stuck in his throat. Overcome by nausea, he ended up coughing and throwing up blood. This was when Colorant realized something was seriously wrong with him. He fell to the floor unconscious and was carried to the lobby by his fellow workers. When he regained consciousness, he saw the accounts manager Madan Gopal seated next to him, who told Colorant he was fine after vomiting in the filling room.[1]

Gopal also said they would drop him home since Colorant looked very tired. And he indeed wanted to go home and rest. On the way back in the company vehicle, Gopal told him, 'You need to take rest for a few days and consult a doctor.' Before leaving, he promised to grant a few days' leave so that Colorant could consult doctors and recuperate.

The following day, he got admitted to the Kodaikanal Government Hospital where he was treated for a few days. The physician, Dr R. Balaji, unable to diagnose his illness, referred Colorant to an alternative-cum-modern medicine centre in Tiruchirappalli, around 200 kilometres away, called Dr Isaac Mathuram Memorial Hospital (established in the memory of Dr Ayyathurai Mathuram, one of the area's most notable physicians).[2]

After several rounds of testing and scanning, the doctors at this hospital suggested Colorant's symptoms could be a reaction to mercury exposure, though they did not explain it in medical terms. They probably thought Colorant or his mother Ruby Martin, who could neither comprehend the disease, let alone afford the treatment for it, might panic, as Ruby would tell me later. The note from one of the doctors at the hospital to the company at the time of discharge read: 'Christopher Martin Colorant be advised to work in a non-mercury area'.

By that time, Colorant's vision had deteriorated, causing him to wear high-powered lenses to see things even at a close distance. Back in the factory, he began working in the non-mercury area. Yet again Colorant's condition began to worsen. Maybe the amount of mercury in his body had increased to the extent that his body could no longer tolerate lower exposure in the non-mercury area either. When he began falling down suddenly and found himself unable to get up from bed in the morning, he was once again admitted at the Dr Isaac Mathuram Memorial Hospital for about a month.

As his condition deteriorated and his family could no longer afford the treatment costs, his mother shifted him to the missionary-run Christian Fellowship Hospital in Oddanchatram, ninety kilometres down the hills of Kodaikanal. He remained bedridden there for almost six months under round-the-clock observation. Though he didn't return to normal health, with serious treatment and care his health improved significantly.

Back home, within a few months, his lungs began failing so rapidly that he struggled to breathe and his condition was set to aggravate. This time his mother decided to take him to the Government Rajaji Hospital in Madurai, 120 kilometres away. After a detailed examination, the doctors there concluded that his lungs and kidneys had been irreparably damaged. They also informed Ruby that no treatment could save Colorant's life.[3] After three peaceful months, Colorant breathed his last on Sunday, 2 February 1997.

Throughout her son's illness, Ruby had tried to convince everyone that Colorant's health issues were caused by working in a factory dealing with dangerous chemicals. Most did not pay her any attention and others, laughed at her. After all, it seemed ludicrous that only her son in the entire factory had taken ill from 'the poison'.

Except that there had been more deaths and illnesses among the workers at the factory and their close relatives. It simply hadn't caught anyone else's attention yet. Five years before Colorant, Edward Antony, another worker, had died at the age of thirty-four. After working in the factory for about two years since 1985, Antony began experiencing dizziness, nausea and severe migraines. In 1989, he was diagnosed with an intracranial tumour, which was operated on at the Apollo Hospital in Chennai.[4] Despite the surgery, his condition worsened. A year later, in 1992, Antony would die at the Government Rajaji Hospital in Madurai.

# 13

# URINE SAMPLES

IN THE WINTER OF 2001, I DECIDED TO VISIT KODAIKANAL AFTER reading about the developments in the mercury contamination case since March. My interest was to report on the ongoing crisis for the Agence France-Presse (AFP), the French news agency at which I worked as part of its financial news wire AFX at the New Delhi office, covering business, economic and financial events in the country. As the Indian arm of the Anglo-Dutch Unilever Plc, HLL was always in the catbird seat of the business and financial communities, especially in Europe.

My first visit to Kodaikanal was during my university days over a decade ago. Nevertheless, the time I had spent there was still fresh in my memories. Back then, the pristine hill station had been an astounding sight to behold. I remembered the boundless bends and cambers of the colossal peaks stroked by drifting sleets and mantles of clouds. At times the clouds were so close, it was as if they were playing around; from the middle of the hills, they would zigzag down the dales to the creeks like a silvery creeper. Like everyone who had ever visited the town, I was nostalgic about the 'queen of the hill stations', Kodaikanal's popular moniker. This was another reason I wanted to get involved in the case.

Aided by local friends, I spoke to several people, including workers, company executives, community members, government officials and the scrap dealer. Everyone had the same thing to say: they hadn't expected this kind of trouble from a company like HLL. In fact, a lot of water had flown through the Shola streams to the Vaigai River since the 7 March protests and the 23 March TNPCB order to permanently close down the factory.

The local community had objected to many details in Dames & Moore's report, which they had taken up with the regulator directly, and through the Working Committee. Following their initial assessment and contribution to the removal of the mercury waste from the scrapyard, Dames & Moore was appointed by the company for a comprehensive examination as pressure from Greenpeace, the regulator and the local community built up.

Around this time, Mody and Meenakshi alerted the Bangalore-based non-profit Community Health Cell (CHC), an association of highly skilled medical practitioners. The NGO conducted sessions to help campaign groups study the local health problems linked to environmental issues in scientific ways. Consequently, a team led by Dr Mohan Isaac, an eminent professor at the National Institute of Mental Health and Neurosciences (NIMHANS), India's premier neuroscience medical institution, visited Kodaikanal and physically examined thirty ex-workers who had been exposed to mercury.

Based on its evaluation, the CHC team reported that there was a need to conduct a detailed examination of all the exposed ex-workers to study the effects of mercury on their health. Based on the results, further assessment needed to be carried out for those who showed evidence of mercury poisoning. It also recommended a detailed community survey of the population living around the factory.[1]

As soon as HLL got wind of the CHC survey and the contents of its report, emails started flying between various offices of HLL and Unilever. The company started gathering more information about the doctor and his study. Who was Dr Isaac? Why was NIMHANS interested in this matter and so on?

Soon, HLL's Medical Advisor Dr T. Rajagopal reached out to Dr Isaac. In return for a meeting, Dr Rajagopal promised to share the details of a study conducted by the company's health team on some 255 workers. Intrigued, Isaac agreed.

On 27 November 2001, HLL's medical team comprising occupational health experts and medical advisors met the CHC doctors in Bangalore.[2]

In anticipation of the meeting, the CHC team was fully prepared. Its ten members included some of the best medical experts from the region: Besides Dr Isaac and Ravi Narayan, a renowned occupational health consultant, a physiologist, a neurologist, an endocrinologist, a psychiatrist, a biochemist, a statistician, a community health specialist – from NIMHANS and St John's Medical College, Bangalore – and the director and senior scientist of the Regional Occupational Health Centre, part of the federal agency for occupational health.

As promised, the HLL team shared a study it claimed had been conducted after the factory's closure. It was carried out at a company-organized medical camp attended by the workers and former employees in response to a newspaper advertisement.[3] The hardcore research team from CHC had been looking forward to peer-reviewing HLL's study and thereafter providing feedback on it. However, despite repeated requests before, during and after the meeting, no copy of the study was made available to them.

Nevertheless, based on the notes taken by the team and the details shared by the company representatives at the meeting, they concluded that HLL had carried out a biological monitoring study, not an occupational health monitoring assessment. Biological monitoring in occupational health is the mere detection of chemical substances (biomarkers) in the samples, whereas occupational health surveillance, according to International Labour Organization (ILO), is a continuous systematic collection, analysis, interpretation and dissemination of data for preventing hazards. It also noted that the sample was epidemiologically 'opportunistic', meaning the occupational history had not been adequately considered and the study objectives were unclear based on its attempt to link biochemical parameters with clinical examinations.[4] More importantly, the CHC team found that the study did not correlate its results with the monthly health records of the workers and with the occupational data. The team picked many more holes in the HLL study and recommended further evaluation of the workers, especially for those who were found to have higher levels of mercury in their urine. In more ways than one, its harsh critique served as a wake-up call for the HLL medical team. Challenged by subject experts, the company realized the study could not be taken seriously by the scientific community in its present shape. Therefore, HLL decided to present it at international conferences and get it published in peer-reviewed journals to gain acceptance – shortcuts to gain scientific and peer group approvals.

By the time a group of ex-workers would file a case against the company in 2006, HLL had presented the study at the 32nd International Congress on Occupational and Environmental Health in the Production and use of Chemicals, otherwise known as MEDICHEM, in Paris. It was also published as a paper in the *Indian Journal of Occupational and Environmental Medicine*, of whose editorial board Dr Rajagopal, HLL's medical advisor, was a member.[5] Unsurprisingly, it was published in the journal within a month of the ex-workers filing a writ petition before the High

Court of Madras on 22 March 2006. The published paper read like a corporate promotional material, rather than a peer-reviewed scientific paper, as an eminent scientist commented anonymously. Later, this article would be used by the company as an important piece of evidence to counter the arguments of the plaintiffs in the Madras High Court.

# 14

# THE INDIAN PEOPLE'S TRIBUNAL

WITH NO PRODUCTION AT THE FACTORY SINCE 8 MARCH FOLLOWING the closure order, all 129 workers had been given transfer orders for another factory at Kandla in Gujarat, some 2,200 kilometres away. When the workers had first declined to move to the far-off location, the company followed with a voluntary retirement scheme (VRS) as reparation. Hesitantly, they accepted the offer. According to the Memorandum of Settlement shared by the government of Tamil Nadu, the company claimed that 'All the employees have been paid three months' pay for every completed year of work and an additional lumpsum ranging from ₹65,000 (~$900) to ₹140,000 (~$2000) depending on the job role of the employee through the VRS settlement arrived at before the Deputy Labour Commissioner, Dindigul on November 9, 2001.'[1]

The workers, likely suffering from health issues due to the mercury exposure, were numbed upon realizing that their employer had neither warned them, nor shared any of the risks of working with mercury. So instead of accepting the jobs in Gujarat, all of them separated from a company they had once considered their guardian angel.

In 2011, the Dr Rajaram Committee appointed by the Ministry

of Labour and Employment of the Government of India, on perusing the VRS package details and the documents submitted by the company, concluded that 'the company deliberately wanted to remove these workers from the factory as they had suffered from mercury exposure to the extent that they were not productive to the company any longer and the workers also wanted to leave as they were not able to do the job any longer on account of serious health problems.'[2] This report concluded that the workmen were forced to accept the VRS package since the company had resorted to tactics like transferring them out of Kodaikanal.

On listening to the stories of people directly affected, I had an irrepressible urge to become involved. But I didn't do so immediately. I decided to first observe the scenario unravelling around us and support the local community in whatever way I could.

All this while, the Dames & Moore team was busy working on the second assessment. It had a lot of ground to cover. Activists and the local community refrained that they were, in fact, 'working to cover up' the company's blunders. As part of its detailed assessment, the team also audited the waste disposal practices and the quantity of imported mercury, finished thermometers and mercury in the shipped-out products. It scanned the occupational health data of workers, and the medical history and details of the workers and ex-workers who had died in the recent years. All prerequisites of an environment impact assessment such as the mercury recovery processes, storage practices and regulatory approvals were studied. The report was ready by May 2002. Once it was cleared by the company after further review, the consultant, on behalf of the company, shared a copy with the TNPCB.

The report did not go down well with the regulator. In fact, it did not find acceptance beyond the company. Most of the data in the report covered a period only from 1988, the year the factory was formally handed over to HLL after Unilever's global acquisition of Chesebrough-Pond's. Moreover, there were great variations in crucial numbers presented in the new report vis à vis that of Dames & Moore's own 2001 report. While the 2001 assessment was widely considered more accurate in many areas, a relatively sincere attempt by the consultant to gather information *ipso facto*, the 2002 report read like an effort to water down the impact of mercury poisoning on workers and on the environment. The variations included the quantity of mercury used to fill in each thermometer – a quantity that had remained unchanged over eighteen years – and the total mercury that had disappeared as waste and through air dispersal. There were changes in the waste quantity and the workers' health data as well.

Greenpeace issued a scathing press release in protest. TAAM and the ex-workers wrote to the TNPCB against the company's efforts to whitewash its acts of omission and commission. Frustrated, the community was trying to find other avenues of pursuing justice when one of Mody's friends from Mumbai suggested a judicial forum that had been set up to address the issues of environment and human rights – the Indian People's Tribunal (IPT).

The IPT, at the time, was headed by a retired judicial luminary, Justice S. N. Bhargava, who had served as the chief justice of Sikkim High Court and the chairman of the Assam Human Rights Commission. After doing some groundwork, on 30 June, Mody, representing Greenpeace, and Meenakshi, the United Citizen Council of Kodaikanal, along with an affected worker A. Dhinakaran, held a press conference in Mumbai where they formally requested the IPT to probe the issue.[3] The forum had originally been set up in 1993, after a national conference on human rights, environment and the law attended by over 400 judges, lawyers, environmentalists and human rights activists. It functioned as an alternative forum owing to the judicial apathy towards matters of environment and human rights during those days.[4]

Under the IPT, retired judges of the Supreme Court and high courts would chair panels and study evidence from victims and other involved parties to prepare reports critical for campaign organizations to pursue the cases judicially or by other means. Since its inception, it had attended many issues, ranging from the relocation of rural and tribal communities to construct dams, eviction of slum dwellers, indiscriminate industrial pollution to blatant communal and state-sponsored violence. Over a dozen retired justices of the Supreme Court and high courts would go on to chair the forum, including Justice V. R. Krishna Iyer, whose famous 1975 judgment led to Prime Minister Indira Gandhi declaring the Emergency[5] and Justice Rajinder Sachar, who prepared the report on the social, economic and educational status of Muslims in India.[6]

For the community of Kodaikanal, it signalled a ray of hope. The forum could help probe the issue with high-level judicial scrutiny using legal and scientific methods. The panel in this case comprised Amit Nair, an environmentalist who had worked with the International Atomic Energy Agency (IAEA), the World Bank, the British Department of International Development (DFID) and the Japanese Bank of International Cooperation; Professor Ramakrishnan, who had spent time with the UNICEF and the Swedish International Development Cooperation Agency and had served in various task forces of federal and state governments; along with Justice S. N. Bhargava.

Once convinced of a prima facie case after studying the issue, the panel decided to conduct public hearings on 2 and 3 September at the Boat Club in Kodaikanal. All concerned parties, including HLL, were invited to depose before the panel with proper evidence and sworn statements. It also visited the plant, surrounding forest areas and Kodai Lake to understand the severity of the issue on the day of the hearing. About 160 ex-workers, representatives of TAAM, PHCC, Greenpeace, CHC and a large group of concerned local citizens were in attendance, and all the parties, including the regulator TNPCB, deposed before the panel, but for one – Hindustan Lever Limited.

The company had offered a tour to the panel of the factory and provided copies of the May 2001 Dames & Moore report and the medical surveillance study of 129 workers, but it refused to cooperate with the investigation beyond that. The representatives of HLL even declined to respond to queries from the panel, despite having initially agreed to answer written questions. The panel was left with no choice than to arrive at conclusions based on the two Dames & Moore reports and the medical surveillance report of workers shared by the company, in the absence of any response on many of the discrepancies in these reports and in the hearing and consultation processes with various other stakeholders.

Despite the company's refusal to cooperate, the panel made a sincere attempt to objectively judge the situation, circumspect about arriving at a conclusion. It recommended conducting a more authentic study involving a reputable governmental agency with the expertise and infrastructure to handle a sophisticated sample testing. After perusing various records provided to it and the testimonies of the workers, the panel also observed that the employees had been exposed to severe ambient mercury levels that could cause health implications.[7]

The panel ended its report with an unequivocal statement: 'The ex-workers of HLL thermometer factory suffer from occupational health problems.'

# PART III

# UNILEVER IN INDIA

# 15

# THE SALT-TO-SALON EMPIRE

THE PENNINES, FAMOUSLY KNOWN AS THE 'BACKBONE OF ENGLAND', is a mountain range separating northwest England from Yorkshire and northeast England. It forms the West Pennine Moors across some ninety square miles (230 sq km) of moorland and reservoirs in Lancashire and Greater Manchester. On the lap of the West Pennine Moors twelve miles from Manchester, there used to be a small somnolent town in the nineteenth century called Bolton that was getting noticed because of the booming cotton industry and the related bleaching and dyeing industries in the area. In 1851, a few months after the use of arsenic was regulated and the notorious 'window tax' was abolished by Queen Victoria, William Hesketh Lever was born in Bolton. Because of his father's growing grocery business in Bolton, William was sent to a private school. At age ten, he was shifted to a much-respected school run by the local church, where he continued his studies till his matriculation.

By the time William graduated school, his father's business had grown from retail to wholesale, and he joined the company as an apprentice. Dedicated and hardworking, with a modern worldview, Wiliam Lever liked to make changes and, hence, kept moving from one warehouse to another and one business to another to grow their thriving grocery empire.

Around the same time, the popularity of soap and soap making was soaring around the world. Soap was still a prized product affordable only for the aristocrats and rich class. It was made with animal fat, by boiling tallow with ash or similar materials and used mostly for cleaning dirt and stains from clothes. For the most part till the early half of the century, soap making had remained a household practice. Women would store fat from butchering, grease from cooking and wood ashes over the winter months. In the spring, they would make lye from the ashes and then boil it with the fat and grease in a giant kettle.[1] This soft soap was used during the great monthly washing days, which seem to have been customary for a century after the settlement of the colonies. The household laundry was allowed to accumulate, and the washing was done once a month, going up to once in three months in some houses.[2]

And so, soap companies, small and large, began sprouting all over the world. In the US, Colgate came up in New York in 1807 and Procter & Gamble (P&G) in Cincinnati in 1837; in England, another William, William Hough Watson, came up with a process through which soap could be produced using glycerine and vegetable oils like palm oil instead of animal fat, overcoming the challenges of tallow availability and making soap a universal luxury.

The news spread like wildfire. Hearing about William Watson's invention, William and his brother James Darcy Lever decided to invest in it. They were going to produce bars of cut, wrapped and branded soap and sell it through their father's grocery distribution. With this, the world's first packaged, branded laundry soap, named Sunlight, was launched formally in 1884. Two years after the success of Sunlight, their soap manufacturing company was established as the Lever Brothers. Marking the beginning of a new empire from British soil, with a tagline 'Record reign, Record sale and Record soap,' it was the genesis of an era of personal care – one that continues to rule the world, thanks to the vision of Lever. Much later, the company would describe Lever as 'one of the great pioneers of modern consumerism. He understood the need for innovation, diversification, and adding value through marketing. Many of the values he stood for still have resonance for us as a business today.'[3]

On the other side of the world, the company took many decades to reach Indian shores as an entity, though the products, Sunlight, Lifebuoy and Lux, were being exported to the subcontinent soon after their launch in England. Sunlight was introduced as early as 1888 and by 1895, based on the good reception, the Lever Brothers appointed agents in Bombay, Calcutta, Madras and Karachi to sell its products in the British Indian territories.

This made distribution and sales easier in the region and in 1902, Pears was introduced in India and Lux, in 1905, a few years after their launch in England. The Vim scouring powder reached rich Indian kitchens by 1913. Besides Sunlight, other washing and bath soaps like Lifebuoy, Vinolia, Velvet Skin Soap, Lever's Health Soap, Blondeau and Lullaby Bath Soap were imported and sold by visiting British nationals and the resident British representatives in Bombay, Calcutta and Madras. The only problem was that customers had to make payments in the pound sterling.[4]

It was only after the death of William Hesketh Lever and the merger of Lever Brothers with Margarine Unie, a company formed in 1927 in Rotterdam, that the Lever Brothers arrived in India as a formal entity. The 'Uni' in 'Unilever' of course came from the Dutch firm, whose roots went back even further than the launch of Sunlight. It was well established in the sector of food products, having made it big through selling margarine, a butter substitute made from animal fat.

Margarine Unie had been founded by the middle of the nineteenth century in a village called Oss near Brabant in the Netherlands by Simon van den Bergh to sell butter. Around 1872, their rivals, the Jurgens family, which ran a similar business in their village, had obtained the formula to make margarine from the inventor Hippolyte Mège-Mouriès. Then in an inexplicable twist of fate, Antoon Jurgens decided to visit van den Bergh with a sample of their product.[5]

Van den Bergh replicated the Jurgens' margarine with some external support and defeated their rival in its production and sales. Gradually, it would be replicated by many others. Since the margarine industry was deeply competitive in the Netherlands, in the 1920s, Jurgens and van den Bergh united their companies by joining hands with a third margarine manufacturer in Bohemia. In 1927, the three companies, including Jurgens and van den Berghs, formed Margarine Unie in Holland.[6]

On 2 September 1929, the Lever Brothers and Margarine Unie signed an agreement to create Unilever. But it would be almost a year before the merger and integration were formalized. The businesses initially aimed to negotiate an arrangement to keep out of each other's principal interests of soap and margarine production, but ultimately decided to amalgamate instead.[7] Right before the merger, Margarine Unie formed an Indian company named Hindustan Vanaspati Manufacturing Company and began its production from its Sewri factory in Bombay.

The Hindustan Vanaspati Manufacturing Company had been importing food products from Margarine Unie, mainly cooking mediums, which were then being sold under the brand name Vanaspati, meaning 'king of the forest'. Once the company was registered as Vanaspati in India, it began marketing its palm oil products under the brand of Dalda – a name now synonymous with hydrogenated vegetable oil.

In May 1933, Lever Brothers too filed a formal application to set up a soap factory at Sewri and set eyes on the neighbouring Vanaspati. The Lever Brothers India Limited was incorporated in India on 17 October 1933.[8] This event marked the formal establishment of an Anglo-Dutch empire that would go on to rule the Indian food and Fast-moving Consumer Goods (FMCG) markets, and many others in the world, for decades and still does today.

The new company, with old Dutch values, did not want to colonize the business in India. By 1942, the new management decided to train Indians to take over junior and senior management positions in order to gradually reduce the role of Europeans in the local management. This would go a long way in establishing the company as a truly Indian entity early on. True to its words, the Unilever management would hand over the Indian operations to Prakash Tandon, the first Indian to join Hindustan Vanaspati Manufacturing as a manager in 1937 and, eventually, its first Indian director by 1951. He also became the first Indian chairman and managing director of HLL in 1961.[9] By then, 191 of its 205 managers were Indians.

# 16

# T. THOMAS AND LEVER'S DESI OVERTURES

TOWARDS THE END OF THE SECOND WORLD WAR, UNILEVER WAS rising meteorically as a maker of personal care products globally. It began strengthening its US business by acquiring a tea firm, Thomas J. Lipton Company, and a toothpaste brand, Pepsodent.

Once the war ended, industrial activities and cargo movement regained their lost muscles and many new products started arriving at far-off places like India. One such product was the Pond's cream, manufactured by none other than Chesebrough-Pond's Inc in the US. The year 1947 was a significant one, when India gained independence from the British empire. It was almost eight years before Chesebrough Manufacturing merged with Pond's Inc globally and formed Chesebrough-Pond's, the world's largest personal care products company in 1955. And it had nothing to do with the Lever Brothers or the newly merged entity of Unilever.

In India, Unilever had three entities even after its global merger and integration – Lever Brothers India Limited, Hindustan Vanaspati Manufacturing Company Limited and United Traders Limited. They ran their businesses independently until the companies formally merged in 1956 to form the Hindustan Lever

Limited (HLL). After the merger and restructuring, the company offered 557,000 shares to the Indian public by divesting ten per cent of its total stake in the new firm. The public issue offer was oversubscribed by six times, and 21,623 retail shareholders bought ten-rupee shares at five paisa per share.[1] The entire process was carried out under the leadership of its Dutch chairman, A. J. C. Hoskyns-Abrahall.

The offer was a great success, given that the capital market in India was in a very nascent stage. It would take another year for the Indian government to recognize the Bombay Stock Exchange under the Securities Contracts Regulation Act, where the shares were listed.

During his tenure, Prakash Tandon attempted to make the company appear more Indian than what had been prescribed by its European parents. Given the country's heavy dependence on milk-based products, he initiated a dairy collection and processing centre in one of its most underdeveloped regions, Etah in Uttar Pradesh, 200 odd kilometres from the national capital.

But after a strong welcome, the initiative ran into hot waters. The farmers preferred selling the milk locally for daily cash against staggered periodic payments, so the project was failing to gain popularity. Under the stead of T. Thomas, Tandon's successor, the company combatted this by coming out with another initiative, the Integrated Rural Development Programme (IRDP), which would support the farmers to increase their yield. It would so happen that the Government of India would copy the project's name a decade later for one of its flagship programmes supporting rural families below the poverty line with capital subsidy and complementary low-interest credits in order to generate rural income.

Under the IRDP, HLL streamlined its strategy and changed its ways of working with the local farmers by 1975. Its methods would soon yield results: the supplies of milk began reaching required volume levels and net farmer income from dairy herds began increasing significantly.[2] By 1995, the company would go on to cover over 200 villages under the IRDP programme.

Thomas also successfully navigated the company through the price control regime of the Government of India during the seventies. Following significant escalation in crude oil prices imposed by the Organization of Petroleum Exporting Countries (OPEC) in 1972, the Indian government regulated the prices of an array of products to control the burgeoning inflation that had struck the nation. Because soaps and packaged oil products were part of an artificially managed price control list, wherein the prices of its products are decided by the government, HLL was one of the companies impacted by it. Caught between fluctuating prices of imported edible oil and the domestic price control for the finished product, it was feeling the heat.

Thomas tried to engage with the government at the highest levels. Most officials cold-shouldered him, pointing out that the country was going through a difficult phase and HLL should accept these changes along with the rest of India.

Just when he was losing hope and started turning despondent, Jagjivan Ram, one of the most senior cabinet ministers to whom Thomas had presented HLL's case, gave him an idea: Since the government was concerned about the plight of the common man, he suggested it would be a good idea for the company to come out with a soap for the common man – a *janata* (public) soap at a reasonable price. And the move could help persuade the government to decontrol soaps, he observed.

Thomas took this idea quite seriously and soon, HLL launched a new soap for the janata named Saral.[3] Five decades later, the story of how the company navigated the government-imposed price control would often be recalled as the 'turning point in the history of HLL'.

Thomas would soon meet Dev Kant Barooah, the cabinet minister in charge of the chemicals and fertilizers ministry (under whose ambit fell soaps and detergents), and later Prime Minister Indira Gandhi. Upon meeting Thomas, the prime minister would ask him, 'What will be the price of your janata soap?' Not having prepared for this question, he summarily made up a number by adding fifty per cent to the controlled price of a bar of soap.

'How soon could you restore production to full capacity?' she asked next, worried about the shortage of soaps.

'Immediately,' came Thomas's quick reply.

Within a few days, on 20 September 1974, soap was decontrolled. Interestingly, had the price control continued longer, HLL would have suffered mounting losses and Unilever might have considered pulling out of India as it had done in some African countries.[4]

Then came another challenge. In 1973, Indira Gandhi came out with the Foreign Exchange Regulations Act, under which all foreign companies operating in non-core sectors like luxury goods manufacturing, cosmetics etc. were required to dilute up to sixty per cent of their stake, either by offering to Indians or by expanding the equity base through investment in core sector activities. While most companies of foreign origin had fallen in line, Thomas felt that holding the majority stake was in the interest of preserving Unilever's professional management culture and getting access to global technology.[5] With his relentless efforts at advocating for the company, Thomas succeeded in forcing the government to allow Unilever to retain a fifty-one per cent stake, albeit with some riders: it should have sixty per cent of its turnover from core sectors and activities involving sophisticated technology; and within that sixty per cent, at least ten per cent should come from exports.

HLL took this opportunity to develop technology for processing neem and rice bran oil, and evolved catalyst manufacturing methods at its dedicated research centre established in Mumbai in 1967. It also started manufacturing sodium tripolyphosphate (STPP) at the Haldia port facility in West Bengal, using imported rock phosphate and sulphur. STPP was being imported and was in great demand because of its wide use in detergents and food products.

Thomas's business acumen was on display again when the Monopolistic and Restrictive Trade Practices (MRTP) Act, a new law preventing companies like HLL from expanding their operations at their facilities, came into force in 1970. Setting up new factories to increase production capacity was restrictive for their businesses, so he had to search for a loophole. The company spared no time in moving to a site outside the jurisdiction of the MRTP Act to set up a new facility so that HLL could expand without any curtailment from the Act. The location was in the erstwhile Indian state of Jammu & Kashmir. With the state government rolling out a red carpet for employment opportunities, production of synthetic detergents started at the newly set-up Jammu plant by February 1977, along with a supporting facility in the Kashmir valley. Less than a year later, the Indian shareholding in the company crossed the one-third mark and breached thirty-four per cent. Born to foreign parents, by now the *videsi* company had made great strides to become even more *desi* than the *desis*.

# 17

# MOTHER TERESA AND ASHA DAN

THOMAS WAS ASTUTE IN CULTIVATING LONG-LASTING RELATIONSHIPS with strategically significant personalities. One of these relationships was with Mother Teresa, an association that began in the seventies, long before she received the Nobel Peace Prize in 1979. This would become an alliance HLL would continue to this day and proudly display on all their platforms.

It started with an unplanned visit by Thomas to the Missionaries of Charity in Calcutta while returning from the nearby HLL factory in Shamnagar. He had noticed the 'Missionaries of Charities' signboard at the Lower Circular Road on the way in his visits to the factory. At the Mother House, Mother Teresa explained to him the mission of the organization: that every human life, irrespective of whether they were destitute, poor or abandoned, should experience being loved and cared for before passing on from the world. After listening to her, he asked if there was anything he could do for the Mother and her nuns. After some thought, she asked if Thomas could find a place for the sisters of the Missionaries of Charity in Bombay to stay so they could avoid long commutes to tend to the unprivileged in the city locales.

'It is very difficult to find a place given the business growth and the pressure on housing in the main city areas because of the growing activities,' was his reply.

'You are sent here by God, and he will help find an answer,' she responded.

Many months later, when HLL's godown on Sankli Street in the heart of Bombay was being replaced by multiple warehouses in suburban areas for ease of distribution, Mother Teresa's words echoed in Thomas's ears. He convinced the owner of the property, the brother of the famous Indian cricketer Vijay Merchant, to lease it out to the Mother for her charity work. The owner unequivocally agreed, delighted to be part of such a noble cause. After getting the necessary government clearances, the facility was inaugurated on 8 January 1976 – christened as Asha Dan (Gift of Hope) – for the thirty-five women and children who had been moved from a house in the Vile Parle area to live in. In subsequent years, it would turn into a shelter for the destitute and a care home for HIV+/AIDS patients. HLL would continue its association with the facility and support it. The Asha Dan is now a 72,500-square-feet building owned by HLL, which takes care of its maintenance and upkeep.[1] But the vision to blend the company's mission with that of the Missionaries of Charity and of Mother Teresa was Thomas's.

Around this time, a young journalist working full time in the same city for the *Economic and Political Weekly* – a publication majorly read by researchers and social intellectuals – was metamorphosing into an environmentalist. Actively involved in the environmental issues of Mumbai, he was part of many groups fighting for the burning problems faced by the people and environment – from the lasting effects of Agent Orange, one of the deadly herbicides used by the US in Vietnam, resulting in the deaths of 400,000 people due to cancers and other ailments, to local waste disposal issues in Bombay. He would soon move to Auroville in Pondicherry and eventually to Kodaikanal by 1983, around the same time the thermometer factory was shifted by Chesebrough-Pond's to the hill station, in time to take on HLL when it was caught red-handed, leaving behind a toxic legacy in Kodaikanal.

# 18

# FAIR & LOVELY TO DOVE

ANOTHER ONE OF THOMAS'S ACHIEVEMENTS WAS LAUNCHING A beauty product that continues to generate debate four decades on – Fair & Lovely. The brand reached Indian store shelves in 1978, four years after Unilever patented niacinamide, a melanin suppressor, as its active ingredient. It apparently also contains stearic acid, an ingredient used in soaps and detergents. In 2020, the product's name would be changed to Glow & Lovely after persistent social media criticism against the company following the Black Lives Matter movement in the US, after which Johnson & Johnson halted production of its Clean and Clear product range.

In the eighties, it was not the African-American movement against discrimination but the workers in its factories that troubled HLL. A great departure from the previous decade, the period witnessed an upsurge of trade union movements across India – from Kerala in the south where a Communist government was elected to power in 1957 to West Bengal in the east where the Communist party's Jyoti Basu was elected Chief Minister in 1977 at the end of the Emergency. Trade union movements sprung up in all major industrial townships and cities where textile industries and other medium- and large-scale industries were being established.

It was a consequence of the country's dire need to create more jobs through industrialization, compromising the rural and agrarian development offered by its socialistic ideals for almost three decades. With inexorable population growth and stagnant agrarian income, large-scale internal migration in search of livelihood to flourishing cities began. Primarily inspired by the socialist ideals and Communist successes in certain pockets of the country, trade unions sprouted wherever industries were being established. The spurt in the number of trade unions and their membership could be chalked down to the relentless greed of company promoters, besides the growing awareness among workers and the neglect they had faced from trade unions in some cases.

In the early eighties, India began moving towards market-friendly policies and liberalization, wanting to embrace computerization and automation, especially after Prime Minister Rajiv Gandhi assumed office in 1984. And trade unions were quick to take advantage of the proposals to shift policies towards a market-friendly economy.

The first flare-up was the Great Bombay Textile Strike of 1982. The strike led by trade union leader Dutta Samant had virtually closed down textile industries. It impacted almost eighty textile companies that had been employing thousands of workers in Bombay. Soon the ripples flowed onto the other sectors too. At HLL, an industrial action brought its major manufacturing facility in Sewri to a grinding halt.

In fact, trade unionism had taken roots in HLL factories much earlier. It started in Calcutta, soon after the Communist government came to power. The Garden Reach factory there had witnessed several industrial actions, which were handled by a precocious manager by the name of K. P. V. Menon. He tried to discipline the Bengal Communist trade unions in his Kerala-style of socialism. When they locked him up in his cabin, he patiently sat through days and nights. Eventually, on the third morning, when he was released, he went home and returned in an hour after taking a bath. Apparently, when a union leader had threatened him with a knife, he had retorted: 'You can kill me, but a tougher manager will be in my place the next morning.' He largely succeeded in shutting down the unions with the unstinted support of the management and of the state government at some level. The factory strikes in Garden Reach and Sewri were utilized by the company management to plan contingencies without impacting production – a long-term plan of action, in case of any eventuality. The company also developed a strategy, rather a playbook, to deal with the trade unions. Its focus was on figuring out the root causes of the workers' disenchantment so that a proper plan could be set up to address their concerns early. One of the key aspects of the strategy was to train managers who could effectively deal with the 'troublemaking' workers.

The plan yielded more than desired results. In subsequent years, HLL would transform into one of the most worker-friendly companies in India, witnessing very few industrial actions.

Then came the marketing turf war of Wheel versus Nirma.

The iconic advertisement jingle *'Doodh si saphedi Nirma se aayi'* (Get milky whiteness from Nirma) left the HLL marketers scratching their heads. A company that Karsanbhai Patel, a government chemist in Gujarat, had started to supplement his daily income in 1969 in his hometown of Ruppur, had taken on the most powerful detergent brand in India – Surf.[1] It set off a price war: ₹3.50 per sachet of Nirma was pitched against ₹13 for a sachet of Surf. Nirma went on to eat up the market share of Surf for almost two years until 1987, when HLL finally came up with its counter – a low-priced equivalent of Surf, to cater to the low-income households, that was named Wheel.

In a show of brilliant marketing prowess, HLL roped in Bollywood star Salman Khan, who had shot to fame with the romantic family drama *Maine Pyar Kiya* (1989) to endorse Wheel. On the other hand, Nirma's packaging featured Karsanbhai Patel's daughter Nirupama, who had inspired the name of the brand. It gave the competition a David vs Goliath touch.

Gradually, HLL regained the lost market share and salvaged its punctured ego reasonably. The creation of the Wheel brand using an entirely different business model was a good example of the marketing ingenuity of Hindustan Unilever, as its then chairman Ashok Ganguly would state later.[2] All this while, Unilever kept growing across the world, barring a few minor hiccups in the US. The Sunsilk shampoo was launched in the UK in 1954 with advertising campaigns focused around hair issues. It would go on to release a television commercial with John Barry's iconic score 'The Girl with the Sun in Her Hair', which was subsequently released as a pop single. Half a century later, by 2008, these ads would transform into women empowerment campaigns featuring Madonna, Shakira, Marilyn Monroe and Priyanka Chopra, promoting messages of women gaining better control of their lives.

As newer brands entered the fray, Sunsilk slowly disappeared from the American and Canadian markets in the decades of the twenty-first century, though this had nothing to do with its origins as a European brand. In fact, three years after the launch of Sunsilk in the UK, Unilever had launched the Dove bathing soap in the US market.

The story of Dove, in a way, is the story of Vincent Lamberti, an Italian-American chemist and inventor. Lamberti had developed a simpler and inexpensive process to manufacture a compound that could replace the fatty acids in soap – a breakthrough of sorts in the synthetic bar soap development process in the twentieth century. Unilever marketed it aggressively as a less irritable soap choice for skincare. Lamberti generated 140 patents, for which Unilever magnanimously allowed him to retain the rights. To this day, no one in the history of Unilever has accumulated as many patents. In 2014 the *New York Times Magazine* would feature him on its cover as one of America's outstanding young scientists.[3]

After the launch of Dove, Unilever went on a brand raid spree in the US. Some of its victims were Frosted Foods and Good Humour. Frosted Foods was taken over and transformed into Birds Eye, followed by Good Humour ice creams, a beloved feature of 1950s American culture, which had introduced the chocolate-coated ice cream bar on a stick and sold them from its 2,000-odd ice cream trucks. Lipton Ltd was picked up from Allied Suppliers in 1971 and National Starch was taken over for close to $500 million, the largest-ever foreign acquisition of a US company back then. A facility of National Starch manufacturing functionalized biopolymers would later come up in 1988 in Pondicherry in south India, 400 kilometres away from Kodaikanal.

In the early 1980s, Unilever decided to reposition itself as a manufacturer of personal care and food products. It raided Brooke Bond, makers of PG Tips tea in the UK in its first-ever hostile takeover in 1984. Within two years, it would repeat this manoeuvre in the US with a plan to consolidate its position in the skincare market. The target was now Chesebrough-Pond's.

It so happened that the Chairman of Chesebrough, Ralph E. Ward would contact the Chairman of Unilever United States Inc, Gordon K. G. Stevens, for a takeover after a rival company American Brands Inc had made an unsolicited bid for the firm.[4] In India, Chesebrough-Pond's had been already running its operations. The Pond's cream was one of the top-selling cosmetic products in the country and it was in a league of its own.

The company was also running a manufacturing operation in Tamil Nadu – a mercury thermometer factory in a town named Kodaikanal.

# 19

# THE ₹100 BILLION COMPANY

'Build a better mousetrap, and the world will beat a path to your door.' This is arguably the most legendary quote about invention often wrongly attributed to the nineteenth-century American essayist and poet Ralph Waldo Emerson. Nonetheless, drawing inspiration from it, people continue to design new mouse traps even today! Apparently, more than 4,400 patents have already been issued by the United States Patent and Trademark Office for mousetrap designs, with thousands of unsuccessful applicants, making the mouse trap the 'most frequently invented device in U.S. history'.[1] Coincidentally, this was also the motto of HLL during the last decade of the last millennium.

'How to build a better mousetrap,' S. M. Dutta, the HLL chairman till 1996, would write in the seventy-five-year anniversary issue of Hindustan Unilever Limited titled *Doing Well by Doing Good.* 'That [building better mousetrap] spirit has always prevailed in HUL,' he would recall.[2]

As the dark clouds of price control and closed market regime cleared under the aegis of Prime Minister P. V. Narasimha Rao, assisted by his economist finance minister, Manmohan Singh, in the era of liberalization, HLL's growth rose in volume, in revenue and in profits. The company hit the market with a new goal: 'A million tonnes by 1994,' in 1989, when the company was producing and selling about 450,000 tonnes of products. For the company and its executives, the aspiration to cross million tonnes in five years sustained growth year after year.[3]

HLL focused on organic growth while looking for high value acquisitions from the market. One such target was Tata Oil Mills Company, otherwise known as TOMCO, located near the Sewri factory of HLL in Bombay.

TOMCO was more than an oil company. Incorporated in 1917 by Dorabji Tata, son of the Tata Group founder, Jamsetji Tata, it was listed on the Bombay Stock Exchange (BSE). The company was involved in manufacturing and selling products ranging from soaps and detergents to cooking oils and cattle feed, with production facilities spread across states like Maharashtra, Gujarat, West Bengal, Bihar, Uttar Pradesh, Kerala and Tamil Nadu.[4] It manufactured some popular toilet soaps of the time, such as Hamam, Okay and Moti. And HLL was competing with the company on products like edible oil and cattle and poultry feed brands, which were growing rapidly.

Strengthening its position in some of the high-growth sectors like steel, chemicals and engineering, the Tata Group began identifying the core areas it wanted to focus on, rather than spreading itself too thin. The group felt that TOMCO would not fit into its core business and long-term strategy, so it decided to exit the sector, ignoring its second position in the market.

For HLL, on the other hand, soaps, detergents and edible oil were the core products. Therefore, TOMCO's exit presented a great opportunity – to get rid of a competitor and gain a monopoly in the market. After long, protracted negotiations, the Tata Group sold TOMCO to HLL.

By the end of 1994, TOMCO was completely integrated into HLL's operations based on the agreement signed on 1 April 1993.[5] TOMCO's integration was a difficult process, as was completing the required legal formalities and passing the proposals from the respective companies.[6] It became the most publicized acquisition in Indian corporate history in the last decade of the twentieth century, and led HLL to prey on another target from the Tata stable – Lakmé.

Lakmé Ltd was born out of a request Prime Minister Jawaharlal Nehru had made to J. R. D. Tata – to manufacture beauty products in India as the country was spending precious foreign exchange to import them for women. In 1952, the Tatas would set up a company as a hundred per cent subsidiary of TOMCO. To suit the product portfolio and attract women customers, they chose the name 'Lakmé', the lead character in a three-part opera based on Théodore Pavie's story, '*Les babouches du Brahamane*'. Lakmé, the French name for the Hindu goddess Lakshmi, the goddess of fortune, wealth, fertility and prosperity, is the daughter of a Brahmin priest in the opera.[7] It was set against the backdrop of British rule in India and highlighted the colonial arrogance towards Indian culture and the Hindu religion.

By 1995, HLL had formed a 50:50 joint venture with the Tatas and the company was named Lakmé Lever Ltd. It gave HLL a foot in the door of the Tata Group by marketing Lakmé cosmetics, which was the undisputed leader in Indian beauty products. Within three years, however, the partnership would progress into HLL swallowing Lakmé completely and the Tata Group divesting its remaining fifty per cent stake. The soap- and detergent-making company was now a major cosmetics brand as well, with branches and franchises of Lakmé opening all over the country, and the brand conquering the hearts and minds of Indian women.

Dairy-based desserts and confectioneries came next, with buyouts of ice cream brands like that of Cadbury India, followed by an independent brand, Kwality. The latter would soon metamorphose into Kwality Wall's, a sweetened blend, the Wall's brand having been acquired way back in 1922, jointly by the pre-merged entities of Margarine Unie and Lever Brothers. Other acquired brands like Gaylord-Milkfood would be phased out in subsequent years to focus on Kwality Wall's. But the acquisition of Kissan tomato ketchup by the group company, Brooke Bond Lipton India Ltd (BBLIL), from the United Breweries (UB) group in 1993, was HLL's foray into the foods business. Introduced for British settlers in India by the Mitchell Bros in 1935, Kissan had fallen into the UB group kitty way back in 1950.

Then came the company's most controversial merger: HLL, which was turning in around ₹33.67 billion in revenue, decided to merge with its largest independent subsidiary, BBLIL, pegged at ₹20.74 billion, to form the largest consumer goods company and the third-largest corporate in the country at the time. While both HLL and BBLIL had merged with other companies to add to their existing product range in the past – for instance, HLL with TOMCO and BBLIL with Kwality – since the companies were in completely different areas of business, this merger offered few mutual manufacturing or distribution advantages.[8] But soon after the announcement, the Indian market regulator Securities Exchange Board of India (SEBI) discovered 'unpublished price sensitive information' that HLL had acquired 800,000 shares of BBLIL from the Unit Trust of India (UTI) on 25 March 1996, barely two weeks before the proposed merger had been publicly announced. The subsequent investigations would create a controversy that would take some time for the company to untangle.

Just before initiating the merger, the company had also

launched a product that would take its name to every dinner table in the country – common salt. HLL decided to create a new brand, Annapurna, in early 1995 to expand its empire from soaps and beauty salons to staple foods. Iodine deficiency had been identified as a serious health concern in India, because of which the government had directed use of iodised salt. HLL played a critical role in this initiative with the launch of Annapurna iodised salt.[9] Three years later, the company would expand the scope of the brand by launching a new product line of wheat flour as 'Annapurna Atta', promising 'tasty rotis (Indian bread) as it is made from the choicest of grains, brought fresh from the farms, cleaned thrice and packed in hygienic conditions'.[10]

But while the firm had become a household name in the country by helping people cleanse themselves and their dishes and laundry, it wasn't doing enough to clean up its own backyard. The company had been working on reducing the effluent discharge to water bodies and nearby land from its factories. These efforts, however, were neither serious enough nor supplied with sufficient resources. In fact, eight new HLL factories had been commissioned – three each in Silvassa and Pondicherry and one in Pune and Chiplun in Maharashtra – in the last decade of the previous century. In some of those places, the company was facing serious resistance from the local community regarding the dangerous effluent discharge to their neighbourhood. In a few cases, the state pollution control boards had already begun to take notice.

At this point, a member of the technical team, Vasant Marballi, came up with the idea of 'zero effluent discharge' factories, with the quick support of the company's Chief Engineer, S. Raychaudhuri. Soon a pilot effort was started at Chhindwara in Madhya Pradesh. Despite this commendable effort, even today, HLL is not a completely zero-discharge company. It recycles only a portion of the effluent and sends it back into processing, but uses most of the recycled water for land irrigation purposes, for example, in gardening.[11]

Immediately after the merger with Brooke Bond Lipton, rumours were rife that the next merger would be Pond's India Pvt Ltd, another of its subsidiaries in the cosmetics space. Pond's India had come into HLL's repository as part of the global acquisition of Chesebrough-Pond's in 1984, but it had been operating independently in the Indian market. HLL would quickly deny the rumours vehemently, suggesting 'no synergies'. It had painstakingly created an impression that Lever's personal products portfolio would be led by three different companies in three key segments – Hindustan Lever in dental and haircare products, Lakmé-Lever in colour cosmetics and fragrances and Pond's in skincare products like creams, lotions and talcum powder. This, despite the fact that the company had merged the sales forces of all three companies for the sake of 'synergy'.

Within a year and a half, HLL would merge Pond's India into the mother entity to take its combined turnover to ₹83 billion, through a miraculous somersault. A joint statement issued by the two companies soon after the decision read that the proposed amalgamation would ensure for the group benefits from economies of scale, both in domestic and export markets, and enable it to fund investments required for aggressively building new categories, such as deodorants and other personal care products.[12]

Behind the curtains, work on this merger had been going on for quite some time.

By 1997, HLL had reached an out-of-court settlement with the Reserve Bank of India (RBI) on the contentious preferential allotment issue, thus paving the way for the merger.[13] This merger would help the company cross the rubicon of ₹100 billion (₹10,215 crore in 1998) before the turn of the millennium, thus making it one of the venerable ₹100 billion companies in India.

Characterized by a seemingly insatiable hunger for growth, the company would further cross the milestone of ₹500 billion by 2022 (₹50,336 crore in 2021–22), the first FMCG company to achieve such financial heights in India.

# 20

# THE BANGA ERA

THE NEW YEAR OF THE NEW MILLENNIUM STARTED WITH A BIG bang for HLL and the new chairman Manvinder Singh Banga, better known as Vindi Banga. HLL was the sole bidder for the government's seventy-four per cent stake sale in Modern Foods, a bread company with bakeries in the country's major cities. The Government of India set it up under Modern Bakeries, the country's first bread manufacturer in Madras, in 1965. The deal fetched ₹1.05 billion for the seventy-four per cent divested stake and became the first instance of divestment by a public sector company, setting off a series of sell-offs in subsequent years by the Atal Bihari Vajpayee-led government.

Two years later, the company would pick up the remaining twenty-six per cent for a relatively small sum of ₹440 million. When the business still didn't pick up year after year, despite heavy investments and best efforts, the company branded it as a 'sick unit' a few months into buying the second tranche of stake. The same year, HLL referred the company to the Board of Industrial and Financial Reconstruction (BIFR), an agency the Rajiv Gandhi government set up to revive sick industrial units, as losses kept mounting. In 2006, HLL reconsidered and merged Modern Foods with itself, setting a target of turning it around in two years.[1] But this ambitious objective proved unachievable, and it started looking for a suitor to get rid of the loss-making business. For HLL, Modern Foods would turn out to be an enduring symbol of failure – exposing its inability to bring back a loss-making unit to life. Later, the company blamed systemic failure and the unit's hidebound '*Sarkari*' culture for the fiasco.

For Vindi Banga, Modern Foods would remain one of the two thorns in his side for the rest of his career, the other being Kodaikanal. Both proved costly in his bid for Unilever's CEO position in 2010. He lost the top job, despite having devoted thirty-three years to the company. This boardroom debacle would sink him into anonymity at the age of fifty-five until he would set up a private equity firm with his own funds.

Eventually, a private equity Everstone Group would pick up Modern Foods in 2015 for about ₹2.5 billion, a mere one billion rupees more than HLL had paid fifteen years ago. The deal was struck under the guidance of its global chairman Paul Polman, the man to whom Banga had lost out for the CEO position around the same time his younger brother Ajay Banga became the president and CEO of Mastercard Inc.

At the turn of the millennium, along with Vindi Banga came Project Millennium, which resulted in the Project Shakti and Power Brands. Consultants McKinsey & Co had been working on Project Millennium to prepare the company for its long-term growth in the upcoming decade since the end of the previous decennary. The one-line brief given to McKinsey was to identify a set of projects with future business opportunities, besides identifying the brightest people in the company. And so, McKinsey defined an innovative people-friendly philosophy and a plan to regain HLL's losing glory in recruitments at premier management campuses.

The plan bore fruit soon and HLL replaced its own consultant McKinsey as the preferred employer in day-one recruitments at top business schools. With 'water business' being identified as a great opportunity by Project Millennium, an innocuous rural intervention was planned to test the waters and project the company as a 'water-sensitive organization', which cares for the sustainable and safe use of water. The location identified was the water-starved Khamgaon village in Maharashtra, 500-odd kilometres northeast of Mumbai.

A water recycling pilot project was launched in the village to use recycled water for horticulture and agriculture. It was replicated thereafter in the neighbouring village of Parkhed, jointly with The Energy and Resources Institute (TERI) and the BAIF Development Research Foundation, two key respected non-profits working in the sustainable development space. And it would continue to be replicated in more locations. By 2018, the company would claim that its water conservation and farm-based livelihood initiatives had cumulatively created water conservation potential of over 700 billion litres, additional agriculture and biomass production of over 0.8 million tonnes and generated over 7.5-million-person days of employment.[2]

Once the ground was set to buttress the image of the company as a responsible corporation, especially in the areas of water conservation and access to safe potable water, the company launched its first product in the 'water business', which its research divisions had been working on since McKinsey's recommendations. This was in 2005, five years after McKinsey advised the company to dive into the water purification business. The product was called Pureit. To start with, the economically upward and educated customers of south India were targeted, followed by those in Maharashtra and West Bengal. By 2008, the water purifier was being sold in most parts of India.

The only other player in the market was a company named Eureka Forbes, promoted by the Shapoorji Pallonji group, which had focused on engineering, construction and real estate businesses until then. The Pallonji group's home water purification product range was called Aquaguard. Seeing the immediate success of Pureit, another large corporation began training guns at the new and emerging market segment. One of the Tata group companies, Tata Chemicals Ltd (TCL), would soon take on Pureit with its 'Tata Swach'. Branded as the world's cheapest household water purification system, Tata's entry had threatened the two years of monopoly Pureit had enjoyed.

In December 2009, Ratan Tata, chairman of the $70 billion Tata Group launched the 'Tata Swach' priced at ₹999 ($22), with a promise to bring a yet cheaper model at ₹720 ($16). Having expected this move, in an overnight coup, a day before the launch of Swach, HLL flooded the market with 'Pureit Compact', also priced at ₹999.

The HLL team had, in fact, been working on a low-cost water purifier as part of its innovation programme, so when they learnt of the imminent launch of Tata's rival product, they rushed to bring out theirs first. After that, in a surprise move, they turned their attention to the high-end market, with Pureit Marvella.[3] This heralded the beginning of the war in the Indian water purification market, a sector now projected to cross the billion-dollar mark by 2025.

By 2020, the $400 million market would really heat up, with a dozen players in addition to Hindustan Unilever, Tata Chemicals and Eureka Forbes, such as Ion Exchange, Kent RO Systems, LG Electronics, Luminous Water Technologies, Okaya Power, Panasonic, Whirlpool and so on. And the water market kept boiling, even as HLL kept a close watch. However, it took some time for HLL (by now Hindustan Unilever/HUL) to realize that a watched pot never boils.

An unintended fallout of the 'water war' was the formation of a Section 25 (currently Section 8), not-for-profit company named Hindustan Unilever Foundation. Connected to Unilever's Water, Sanitation and Hygiene (WASH) plan, it promoted a message of 'Water for Public Good' and became a part of various national water conservation and livelihood development measures.

Besides water, another imperceptible opportunity that was being industriously explored since the turn of the century was reaching out to rural women. This too was the outcome of Project Millennium. Calling it 'the goal of promoting health and hygiene and supporting rural communities', in 2001, HLL announced an initiative named Project Shakti, which would help create women entrepreneurs in villages. A pilot was launched in a village in Nalgonda district, Andhra Pradesh, wherein HLL hired local, unemployed women to sell its products door-to-door. This would earn the women a monthly income of ₹600–800 ($8–12) per woman.[4] The initiative was immediately praised by all and sundry, and the news of its 'success' travelled around the world. The exception was the *Washington Post*, which poked holes in the initiative in its despatch, 'Building Wealth by the Penny in Rural India, a Sales Force in Saris Delivers Soap, Social Change'.[5] But since these women were living below the poverty line, and had no other income, the meagre pay seemed better than nothing at all.

By 2019, HUL claimed it had involved 100,000 Shakti micro-entrepreneurs across eighteen states, selling its products to over forty lakh rural households in 160,000 Indian villages.[6] This number would change to 136,000 Shakti Ammas (powerful mothers) a year later. Fuelled by the success, this concept would then be replicated by Unilever in Bangladesh, Sri Lanka, Pakistan, Ethiopia, Egypt and Columbia and Vietnam.

Project Shakti had increased the company's rural penetration, making its products accessible in the remotest regions of the subcontinent, where smaller, unorganized companies had been operating until then. These were the farthest corners of the country where HLL could have never dreamt of reaching with its cost-heavy distribution system. A close duplicate of Project Shakti would be launched in 2013 with an objective to secure 'social licence' at places where the company ran manufacturing operations – Project Prabhat. This was driven primarily by instances of reprisals by local communities around factories on issues of effluent discharge, emissions, water exploitation and farmland acquisition and conversion, even leading to spontaneous movements by the affected local communities. Many factories were forced to shut down in different parts of the country, starting with Coca-Cola's infamous Plachimada bottling plant in Kerala, on issues related to water exploitation, groundwater contamination and indiscriminate disposal of waste. In anticipation of the building furore against them, corporates began running for cover.

One way to ensure peaceful co-existence was to address the pending woes of the local communities, from access to safe drinking water to livelihood. In the aftermath of the Plachimada fiasco, many companies started setting up 'foundations' and CSR programmes to work on these plans and avoid such challenges. Launched in December 2013, Project Prabhat focused on engaging with and contributing to the rural communities around HUL's key sites, including factories, branches and depots.[7] It was no different from the somewhat similarly named or unnamed projects of other companies. The idea was: spend a small sum on enhancing livelihoods, water conservation, waste management, and on health and well-being of communities around the factories and gain some peace in return.

And the strategy worked – to some extent. By 2020, the company would claim a total of 4.5 million beneficiaries in twenty-six locations across twelve states and two union territories through partnerships with over twenty NGOs, and was supported by more than 5,000 HUL employee volunteers.[8]

# 21

# SIZE 30

PROJECT MILLENNIUM HAD PROFFERED ANOTHER RECOMMENDATION – creating power brands. While taking stock of the company's assets at the end of the twentieth century, McKinsey calculated that there were 110 FMCG brands in HLL's portfolio, including those built organically and others, which had been acquired. Many were competing with each other on the same turf. Some were very small and contributed insignificantly to the revenue while consuming a lot of time and resources in production, marketing and sales. Moreover, the market was becoming fiercely competitive with the entry of large, global brands and with the resource-heavy marketing prowess of some of the global giants.

After its assessment, therefore, McKinsey advised to trim HLL's brand size from 110 to thirty or thirty-five, so that it was focusing on only three dozen power brands instead. As Vindi Banga would explain how they picked their 'power brands' later: 'We chose these for their strength, uniqueness and growth potential. In addition, they also spanned all the twenty categories and relevant benefits and price positions.'[1] Once the thirty-five brands had been identified, HLL pumped money and resources into promoting them – to rebuild its brand identity, grow market penetration and, thereby, increase margins. In several cases, the prices were artificially lowered to increase sales volume growth and, in others, different sizes with different packaging were launched under the same brand to make them affordable to the lower tiers of the society. Many products were re-launched, including the company's top-selling detergent brand, Surf Excel. The oldest kid in the classroom, Lifebuoy, was shaped up from a carbolic soap to a toilet soap, by giving it a new jacket and some fitment adjustments. As an extension of the now popular Lakmé brand, Lakmé beauty salons were launched all across the country. Among the retired veterans were the toilet soaps Hamam, Liril, Rexona and Breeze. It's a different story, however, that many of the retired or rested brands would be revived and re-inducted a decade later.

All this was done alongside modernizing the supply chain of hundred factories, 2,000 suppliers, 7,000 stockists and one million retail outlets with modern IT infrastructure so that there would not be any shortage of stocks in the marketplace. This process was called the Continuous Replenishment System.

Observing HLL's success on power brands, many other FMCG companies like Godrej, Britannia, Dabur and Marico would follow suit by 2005 and launch their own power brands strategies.[2] For HLL, the strategy yielded rich dividends. By 2016, six of the power brands would cross annual sales of ₹20 billion each, with Surf Excel exceeding the ₹30 billion mark.

Surf achieved the feat two years after Unilever literally proved the brand's famous tagline, '*Dirt is Good*', in Europe. The company ended up paying a penalty of €104 million to the European Union for violating the EU and EEA antitrust rules and forming a price-fixing cartel with Procter & Gamble and Henkel in 2002, causing it immense embarrassment.[3]

Among all its brand successes in India, a singular gigantic

disappointment was one that was launched with a lot of fanfare in 2001. In a relatively small Ayurvedic market largely driven by established local brands like Kottakkal from Kerala, HLL's Ayush had not made any headway. It would take almost two decades, and a ₹3.3-billion acquisition of another brand called Indulekha to re-launch Ayush, in order to take on yoga guru Baba Ramdev's Patanjali, which had started eating into HUL's traditional FMCG market with its range of Ayurvedic products.

While implementing the power brands strategy, it dawned upon the management that the company's presence in many non-core sectors was not bringing in any value. In fact, by the turn of the millennium, only twenty-five per cent of the company's total revenue was coming from the non-FMCG sector. And that too with a dismal margin. Margins lower than ten per cent are the threshold most large companies use as the cut-off for divesting a product or segment. The reasoning behind it is that any business offering margins below ten per cent becomes a drain on the enterprise, given its legacy, size and bureaucratic structure, and there is no scope for scaling it because of the presence of multiple players in the crowded segment.

Therefore, an initiative was launched to streamline the business and move the focus back to the FMCG sector. This would mean divesting fifteen of its non-FMCG or commodity businesses, ranging from animal feeds, speciality chemicals, nickel catalysts, adhesives, mushrooms and so on, spread across businesses altogether worth ₹17.5 billion.

As part of this strategy, the company also decided to divest from the production of thermometers, which were manufactured at its only factory in that category in Kodaikanal. The compelling reason for this divestment was that the factory in Kodaikanal had already been shut down on the orders of the Tamil Nadu Pollution Control

Board in March 2001. It had been an issue that had besmirched the company's reputation in India and globally during the decade that followed, along with another environmental issue in Kalimantan, Indonesia, where Unilever was found to be working with its palm oil suppliers in destroying sensitive Borneo rainforests to increase palm oil plantations.

Despite the Kodaikanal issue ruling HLL's boardroom and the media for many years, it witnessed many an 'action' by concerned citizens before Unilever sent its trusted global executive Douglas Baillie to India in 2006 to replace Banga. Baillie was commissioned to rebuild the company's sagging reputation: the tagline of the company changed to 'One Hindustan Unilever' and its name went from Hindustan Lever Ltd (HLL) to Hindustan Unilever Ltd (HUL). He returned to Rotterdam in 2008 once the mission was complete, now to take charge of the western European side of the business.

Five years after Baillie's return, Unilever increased its stake in the Indian entity to sixty-seven per cent, shelling out almost $3.16 billion in cash through the purchase of 320 million shares at a rate of ₹600 per share.[4] The Unilever stake in Hindustan Unilever thereby went up from a 54.5 per cent to a little over sixty-seven per cent – almost eight per cent short of its intended seventy-five per cent level. This shareholding level would undergo further changes only in early 2020 when the ₹45 billion GlaxoSmithKline Consumer Healthcare, makers of Horlicks and Boost brands, merged with Hindustan Unilever. This time around, in the acquisition-cum-merger, HUL offered 4.39 of its shares for each GlaxoSmithKline share and, for the process, Unilever had to issue new shares which brought down Unilever's holding in HUL to 61.9 per cent.[5]

---

Upon taking over as Unilever's CEO, Paul Polman started off by issuing an annual progress report on Sustainable Living Plan with a grand launch in November 2010 from four global locations.[6] For India too, the company started issuing similar annual progress reports, capturing information under three heads: improving health and well-being, reducing environmental impact and enhancing livelihoods for millions.

The reporting in the first and the last sections would appear more like the implementation of its aggressive sales and marketing programmes. For instance, Lifebuoy, Pureit, Domex and the food products would contribute to health and well-being, and Shakti sales agents, Rin Shine Academy and Fair & Lovely Online Academy, to enhancing livelihood.

The 2019 India report claimed that the company's water purifier, Pureit, provided ninety-five million litres of safe drinking water, Lifebuoy had reached seventy-two million people through its hand-washing programme and the Domex toilet cleaner impacted one million people through its Domex Toilet Academy.[7]

There is a market for everything. And every sale contributing to a 'cause' became the driving philosophy, thus creating a bankable image that every product sold by the company was contributing to a larger noble goal. The credit for this vision belongs to Paul Polman.

# PART IV

# SCIENCE, EVIDENCE AND REASONING

# 22

# AN UNEXPECTED ALLY

AROUND THE TIME THE DAMES & MOORE TEAM WAS COMPLETING its sample collection for its detailed analysis in early 2002, two young Hyderabad-based scientists arrived in Kodaikanal by a bus from Kodai Road, the nearest railhead.

Carrying their modest luggage, they walked over to a small lodge near the bus station where they would be stationed for the next couple of days, working to challenge a multinational behemoth on its professed ethical standards of corporate responsibility and accountability.

The duo, M. V. Balarama Krishna and D. Karunasagar, scientists at the Department of Atomic Energy's National Centre for Compositional Characterisation of Materials (NCCCM) in Hyderabad, had arrived in Kodaikanal by mere chance. A few weeks earlier, their boss Dr J. Arunachalam was shopping at a departmental store in Hyderabad for groceries when his eyes caught something he hadn't noticed earlier on a spice shelf. What he saw were grey- and white-coloured soft and dry flowery tissues of plant origin. The store boy explained that it was called *raathi pootha* in Telugu and *paththar ke phool* in Hindi, which was used to flavour biryani. Paththar ke phool can be literally translated as 'stone flower', meaning a flower found on rocks and granites. A strict vegetarian, Dr Arunachalam asked whether it could be used in vegetable biryani as well, to which the boy responded yes. He picked up a couple of packets and added them to his shopping basket.

Back home, he used the ingredient to flavour vegetable biryani the same night. Though his family enjoyed it, he could taste a difference in the taste. A few days later, when Dr Arunachalam hosted a dinner for a visiting German scientist at his home, he decided to serve his guests, which included a few of his team members as well, vegetable biryani. It was, of course, flavoured with the new spice. And this is how raathi pootha became the subject of their dinner table conversation. When the German scientist asked to see the sample, someone brought a packet from the kitchen. When the man expressed curiosity about the material, he was told it was a spice of plant origin. Chemical scientists by profession, most of them had never encountered this spice earlier. One of them suggested testing it to understand its chemical composition.

Returning home from the dinner, Krishna and Karunasagar tried to find some reading material on the newfound spice. They could identify it as a lichen, which is not exactly a plant but covers almost seven per cent of our planet. Wondering why they had never studied such an important organism earlier, they decided to do more research on the species. As they scanned for information, they were shocked. A composite organism that is formed by a group of algae or cyanobacteria living with multiple fungi species in symbiosis, the lichens can survive extreme weather conditions and is one of the oldest living organisms on the earth. But as material chemists, they were most fascinated to discover that it absorbs metals and minerals from its surroundings and deposits them in its cells, while inhaling nutrients from the air for its survival. The lichen was being used in certain research projects as a bio-monitor for measuring atmospheric air quality. Both the scientists were now hooked.

Next morning, Dr Arunachalam carried one packet of raathi pootha from his kitchen shelf to the laboratory. At the lab, after cleaning, drying and powdering the sample, he tried it in the inductively coupled plasma quadrupole mass spectrometer (ICP–QMS) that had recently arrived with support from the International Atomic Energy Agency (IAEA) to find any evidence of chemical elements in it. To his surprise, the results showed an extremely high spike, indicating a large quantity of metal deposits. Curious to find out which metal it was, his team tested it further for all possible heavy metals. After several trials, they arrived at one probable suspect – mercury.

It was a eureka moment for the team. But now there was no time to rest for they were confronted by a daunting question: If it was indeed mercury, where was it coming from?

It was a no-brainer that the location was somewhere with a large amount of mercury in the air. Could it be from near a mercury mine? They couldn't find evidence of any known mercury mine in India. Then they wondered if it could be from a location where mercury was being dumped as waste from a factory or another source. Intrigued, they decided to investigate more.

One of them went back to the store in the city and asked the staff about the suppliers of the raathi pootha. All they shared was that it came from the 'central store'. A few calls to the central store revealed that the supplier was a distributor in Chennai. After some long-distance calls to the distributor and with a bit of cajoling, he told them it was sourced from a seller in Madurai. Next, a little sweet-talking with the Madurai seller unearthed that he was getting it from traders in Batlagundu in the downhills of Kodaikanal. He said that raathi pootha was generally found in forests, from where it was gathered along with honey and other medicinal plants by tribal people. In Kodaikanal and surrounding areas, this was mainly done by members of a few dwindling tribes, including the Paliyan tribesmen.

The team had somewhat reached the bottom of the crucible with nowhere else to go. But Karunagasar's search led him to an old news clipping in the *Hindu* about a factory that produced mercury thermometers being shut down in Kodaikanal a year ago on allegations of indiscriminate mercury waste disposal. When he shared the news clip with the team, the scientists breathed a sigh of relief, for they knew this was the key piece of information they had been desperately looking for. A vague picture started emerging in their mind as to how and from where the mercury could have landed in the lichen.

The following day, they discussed at length whether to visit the surroundings of the closed-down factory. Initially hesitant about going on a 'treasure hunt' for academic research, Dr Arunachalam soon admitted if the factory had indiscriminately dispersed mercury in the surroundings, it could wreak havoc on its vicinity, which in turn could be proven scientifically. He reasoned this could be a worthy addition to the IAEA's coordinated research project (CRP) and funded as a sub-project on using 'plants as bio-monitors of trace elements in atmospheric pollution' with the help of nuclear and related techniques. Especially because mercury is usually present in its highly toxic ionic form in radioactive waste.[1] He recalled a CRP on the 'health impacts of mercury cycling in contaminated environments studied by nuclear techniques'[2] and after some quick calculation and planning, okayed the team's proposal to travel to the location to corroborate the source of the mercury in the spice and to collect samples, if confirmed.

Two years later, Dr Arunachalam would publicly confirm the

team's findings from the lichen samples. As he would tell the media, on laboratory analysis, the lichens picked up from the Hyderabad market had shown high amounts of mercury, which his team had traced to a place near the HLL thermometer factory.[3] He also shared this in detail with me in a long conversation after retiring from the NCCCM.

Back in 2002, Krishna and Karunasagar settled in their spare lodge room at Kodaikanal, within the limits of the budget set by the NCCCM. Dressed in casual clothes, they ventured onto the streets, where their primary intention was to talk to the locals about the thermometer factory. By then, they had read whatever they could lay their hands on online and in newspapers – from the issues of mercury waste disposal and protests to the TNPCB order to shut down the factory in March 2001.

After several conversations with people at tea shops, around the lake and near the factory on St Mary's Road, they gathered some key information: first, the local people were not aware of the dangers of mercury contamination in the air around them; second, the factory had been using liquid mercury for over seventeen years till 2001, which meant it could have been dispersed in the atmosphere for eighteen hours a day while the factory was operational; and finally, besides the atmospheric emissions, it was a fact that the company had disposed of mercury-laden waste to scrap dealers in Kodaikanal and beyond.

On returning to their room, the scientists chalked out a plan for the next day. The commonly found lichen in the area was *Parmelia sulcata* in addition to *Funaria hygrometrica,* a non-vascular plant known as moss, the samples for both of which had to be collected from at least three different locations – near the factory, from St Mary's Road and from Berijam Lake, a pristine lake located roughly twenty kilometres from the factory. The samples had to be picked from tree trunks of arm-span height. Only the top part of the moss samples had to be collected, discarding the roots. At each location, samples had to be gathered from at least three spots, and had to be mixed to have uniform quality and then stored in clean plastic bags.

With the assistance of some locals, after collecting the lichen and moss samples, they collected air samples by a novel method of charcoal trapping. This was essential because the most plausible form of contamination around the factory in the air could be elemental mercury, which could be measured directly from the samples. Hence the air around the factory was sampled on activated charcoal filters using a special kit.

The two scientists knew that charcoal, a good gas absorbent, would soak up the air with all the present impurities that could be extracted and then analysed to find out the concentration of the contaminants. About 200 milligrams of activated charcoal packed in plastic tubes with nozzles at both ends was used for the sampling. Both ends of the tube were plugged with glass wool so that air could pass through the activated charcoal bed to trap elemental mercury. Air was sucked in through charcoal at a flow rate of two litres per minute for fifteen minutes.[4] Finished with their task for now, they packed the samples securely and boarded the evening bus to reach Kodai Road railway station, from where they would return to Hyderabad.

Back in their laboratory in Hyderabad, they stored the lichen and moss samples in a refrigerator. The samples were cleaned to remove any adhering particles by submerging in water and by agitating them in an ultrasonic bath. Once cleaned satisfactorily, they were dried in an oven for twenty-four hours at a temperature of 40°C before being crushed to a powder in a specialized machine. Thereafter, experiments to measure mercury were carried out using

ICP–QMS and a cold vapour atomic absorption spectrometer (CVAAS).[5]

The trapped elemental mercury was extracted from the charcoal samples by shaking them with highly pure water's sound energy. The results proved to be jaw-dropping. The mercury levels observed in the lichen and moss samples outside the factory were almost forty times above the normal levels prescribed by the IAEA, which was of 0.2 microgram/kilogram (μgm/kg). The mercury profile of moss and lichen from twelve different locations indicated that the IAEA-fixed levels were only found in samples collected from a location twenty kilometres away from the factory, at the Berijam Lake. Lichen samples from near the factory had a mercury concentration of 8 μgm/kg of lichen – at least forty times the normal level. [6]

More alarming were the results from charcoal trapping. It showed that the air outside the factory had up to 2,640 times more mercury than the normal levels prescribed by global agencies.

Despite this dumbfounding discovery, Krishna was only modestly critical in his observations in his report, stating, '…Hg concentration in air near the thermometer factory was around 1.32 $\mu gm/m^3$ (microgram/cubic meter) which is very much higher than the nominal Hg concentration range (0.5–10 nanogram/cubic meter) reported as typical of non-contaminated areas.'[7] If the lower band of the prescribed ambient level of 0.5 $ng/m^3$ was taken for comparison, the mercury outside the factory would exceed by a factor of over 2,640 times, he would restate in a conversation with me. To understand the magnitude of what this means, it is worth noting that 1,000 nanograms form one microgram. That meant that people in the surroundings of the factory had been breathing 2,640 times more mercury than normal.

This fact would be picked up and amplified by a Supreme Court Monitoring Committee that visited the location and published a report about its findings in September 2004. The report stated that 'a Department of Atomic Energy study found mercury levels at 1.32 microgram per cubic meter against the normal level of 0.5–10 nanogram per cubic meter; effectively an aberration of between 132 to 2,640 times'.[8]

According to numerous works of scientific literature, total mercury concentrations in the air in non-contaminated areas vary between the ranges of 0.5 to 10 ng/m$^3$, while in contaminated areas, values up to 20 ng/m$^3$ have been reported. Interestingly, a study of the concentrations of the heavy metal in the mercury mining area in Idrija, Slovenia, has shown that the levels depend on the distance from the main source and the weather conditions.[9]

By the end of July 2002, the team sent its paper to *Environmental Pollution*, a peer-reviewed European journal publishing high-quality research papers and review articles on various aspects of environmental pollution and its effects on ecosystems and human health.[10] The paper was accepted by January 2003, after which it took another eight months for it to see the light of day. Finally, it was published in the third volume of the August 2003 issue of the journal, spread across four pages with an innocuous title, 'Study of mercury pollution near a thermometer factory using lichens and mosses'.

It turned out to be the most damning piece of scientific evidence, proving that the surroundings of the factory and the hill station of Kodaikanal had been polluted with mercury by over 2,600 times the normal limit, even after a year of shutting down the factory and its operations.

# 23

# LICHENS FULL OF CLUES

SINCE THE TURN OF THE NEW MILLENNIUM, I HAD BEEN contemplating taking a break from the hustle and bustle of journalism in New Delhi and the hectic travel it entailed. In the winter of 2002, owing to some unforeseen personal events, I decided to take a hiatus and boarded a train to my hometown, Bangalore, roughly 3,000 kilometres south of the capital. During the forty-eight-hour journey, a plan was forming in my mind to work for a non-profit until I returned to my regular job. Having been to Kodaikanal, where I witnessed the grave situation in the hill station first-hand a few months ago, I decided to join an organization that was working on the issue at ground level there. And so, I circled in on Greenpeace.

I spent a couple of months at home before I reached out to Greenpeace to find out if there were any opportunities available for a journalist keen to work on the growing crisis in Kodaikanal. Around this time, Greenpeace was moving its India office from New Delhi to Bangalore to focus on the major issues in the southern half of the country, and also because most of its staff was from that region. A south Indian myself, the shift of the Greenpeace office had found favour with me too. After an impromptu meeting at its makeshift office on Cunningham Road in Bangalore on a Wednesday afternoon, Greenpeace India's Executive Director G. Ananthapadmanabhan offered me a position. By early 2003, I was working full-time on the Kodaikanal mercury pollution issue, as part of Greenpeace's global anti-toxic campaign agenda.

Based on a few visits to Kodaikanal from my new base in Bangalore and multiple meetings with the local community and campaign leaders, including Mody, Selvi Meenakshi and leaders of the ex-workers' front, Raja Mohamed, K. Gopala Krishnan and Mahendra Babu, it became clear HLL had been handed an undue advantage because of the lack of scientific evidence. The community required scientific evidence demonstrating that the atmosphere had been contaminated with high levels of mercury, as well as medical evidence indicating that workers' health had been harmed as a result of continuous exposure to mercury.

Some work had started, documenting and studying the epidemiology of the workers through the Community Health Cell (CHC) initiative by Dr Mohan Isaac. But there hadn't been any serious efforts on two counts: there were no scientific studies to understand the extent of environmental pollution; and no progress had been made to retire the mercury waste lying at the factory. I focused my energies on these two areas alongside Mody, Meenakshi and the ex-workers, in addition to the pursuit to strengthen the medical evidence.

After studying more about how Greenpeace used science to verify the claims made by corporations, my first touchpoint was the Greenpeace Research Laboratory at the University of Exeter in southwestern England. I exchanged a few emails with David Santillo, the head of the laboratory, and with Kevin Bridgen, who was studying the environmental impact of toxic heavy metals. It was apparent a strong case could be built on science in this case.

David Santillo had already assigned senior scientist Ruth Stringer, who had previously surveyed waste stockpiles at the Union Carbide site in Bhopal and designed the clean-up strategies. Having worked on the Basel Convention and the Barcelona Convention, and ably supplemented by her biochemistry and chemistry education from the University of London, Stringer was on top of issues related to heavy metal contamination. By the time I joined Greenpeace, Stringer had visited Kodaikanal and collected a dozen samples of *Lobaria discolor* and *Parmotrema reticulatum,* two different lichen species commonly found in and around the location.

Our efforts were finally on track, though they were taking place at a snail's pace. While carrying out literature review for her analysis and study towards the end of 2003, Stringer stumbled upon an interesting paper that had just been published in *Environmental Pollution*. It was noteworthy because it had conducted a similar lichen sampling as her study, in addition to collecting samples of another possible biomonitor candidate, a 'moss' from around the Kodaikanal factory. Even more interestingly, the study involved charcoal trapping, which had been used to find out the mercury levels in the surrounding air.[1]

Stringer alerted Bridgen and Santillo at once. On a winter evening in 2003, I received an email from Santillo, with an attachment of a study on the pollution in Kodaikanal. Going through the article, aware that it had been published in a respected science journal, I was thunderstruck upon learning the extent of environmental devastation from its quantitative results. What simultaneously intrigued me was that this crucial evidence had caught the attention of a reputed Indian governmental agency like the Department of Atomic Energy. Having seen the draft results of the study conducted by Greenpeace and discussed it in detail, the DAE study intrigued me.

While the Greenpeace samples were limited to two species of lichen, the DAE had used both lichen and moss samples – two different bio-monitors. While our sampling area was limited to a distance of one and a half kilometres around the factory site, the DAE sampling had covered up to twenty kilometres away from the factory. In yet another stark difference, the Greenpeace study was restricted to bio-monitoring, while the DAE study had additionally carried out air monitoring by using a charcoal trapping method. And, finally, their study report had just been published in the most respected European environmental journal.[2] It checked every single box required to refute the claims and defences of HLL, and outpaced Greenpeace's study in every respect.

It was more than we could have hoped for. The first step was to establish a relationship with the DAE team, confirm the veracity of the study and explore all information beyond what had been reported in the journal. This was done within forty-eight hours through a few phone calls. My next move was to leverage this information for the next step. It was an easy task from here on, following the Greenpeace media strategy to instrumentalize the evidence.

We knew that the effectiveness of exposing a corrupt corporation or its dangerous activities depends on the amount of media coverage and the public interest it generates. If the information was not shared widely through the media, the small window of opportunity to influence the public opinion was lost. And so, the first call I placed was to Dr K. S. Jayaraman, the father of science journalism in India, under whose leadership I had graduated from a healthcare journalist to a technology writer, during my early days at the Press Trust of India (PTI), the country's premier news agency.

Dr Jayaraman was no ordinary journalist. He had completed a doctorate in nuclear physics from the University of Maryland in the

US after spending five years at the Bhabha Atomic Research Centre (BARC) under Dr Raja Ramanna and Dr P. K. Iyengar, architects of India's first nuclear bomb, named the 'Smiling Buddha', and had returned to India to set up the science journalism division at PTI in 1973.[3] He patiently listened to the details of the case and to the results of the study published in the *Environmental Pollution*. 'This is a story, boy!' he thundered on the phone from Hyderabad, where he had been living since retiring from PTI in 1998. 'I would file it for both PTI and *Nature*,' he assured. He was still contributing to the news agency and was working as the India editor of the international science journal *Nature*.

PTI's wire copies are subscribed to by all newspapers and the electronic media, so this meant we could get the story covered in India and globally in one go. And a report in *Nature*, however big or small, could draw global attention.

Dr Jayaraman worked quickly after that, in his characteristic style.[4] He reached out to the DAE team that had carried out the study and contacted the HLL officials for their response to it. It so turned out that HLL wasn't aware of the new evidence until Dr Jayaraman phoned them up. Dr Rajagopal, who headed the occupational safety division at HLL, made two arguments on the phone: the DAE study results were at variance with those that had been reported by HLL's consultants, Dames & Moore, and claims of the mercury levels being '1,000 times above normal' did not pose any health hazard. Taking a step further, he tried to claim that the local regulatory guidelines were considerably lax than the factory rules by suggesting that the levels 'are much lower than the fifty micrograms limit prescribed under the factory rules'.[5]

On the other hand, Dr Arunachalam, the leader of the DAE study, as we would discover, had shared a lot of disturbing information with Dr Jayaraman. The disused factory was still a source of mercury pollution, he said, because the factory scraps and the contaminated vegetation in the area had been re-emitting absorbed mercury into the atmosphere. 'Being land-locked and surrounded by hills, the trapped mercury vapour is still floating around,' he added. 'In our view, it will take years for the mercury to clear up.'[6]

Now that he had comments from both sides, Dr Jayaraman decided to go ahead. He filed the report for PTI on a quiet Saturday to get maximum traction through the Sunday newspapers. On Sunday, 17 January 2004, most newspapers carried the 600-word report with a headline, 'Closed Kodaikanal Factory Still Source of Mercury Pollution.'[7] This was enough to create jitters at Lever House in Backbay Reclamation, Mumbai, and the Unilever House in Blackfriars, London, besides shaking up the Unilever office in Rotterdam in the Netherlands.

A major milestone had been crossed in the case in the new year of 2004. There was now clear scientific evidence confirming the company's poisonous footprint in Kodaikanal.

# 24

# MERCURIAL FISH

THE FIRST IN A SERIES OF SCIENTIFIC ASSESSMENTS OF THE mercury poisoning in Kodaikanal was a study sponsored by HLL and conducted by its consultant Dames & Moore in 2001. In fact, after completing its preliminary study, the Dames & Moore team carried out another detailed study on the request of HLL. Of course, the unwritten objective was to establish scientific evidence to boost the company's claims, before anybody else could reveal something to the contrary.

The team collected a total of 476 samples for mercury analysis: 367 from the factory site and the remaining from its surroundings. The samples were collected from locations up to Kodai Lake on one side, south of Lavange Path on the other until where Kumbakkarai falls alongside the Pambar River. The samples included soil, sediments, water, tree bark, lichen and fish. The collection process was completed by the end of February 2002.

These samples were then sent for testing at the MGT Environmental Laboratories, Melbourne and Australian Laboratory Services in Sydney, TNO Laboratory in the Netherlands and HLL's own Research Centre Laboratory in Mumbai. The fish samples were sent to a couple of other laboratories with sophisticated testing facilities in Australia. Despite the conflict of interest, HLL's Research Centre Laboratory was chosen apparently because of its quick turnaround time for sample analysis. Their turnaround time was a few days as compared to that of several weeks by the international laboratories, which is important in a study of this nature, the Dames & Moore report indicated.[1]

The Dames & Moore report found mercury levels in the soil to be much higher than normal. The highest soil mercury levels were plausibly found within the factory area. The results left the Dames & Moore team stunned. This was followed by discussions between the teams and HLL, which the local community alleged was to decide whether to include and or leave out certain results in the final report. But this just concerned the readings of the samples. There were even more concerning observations about how certain samples had been omitted or how the test results of an entire parameter had been ignored. Dames & Moore classified the results between that from 'off site' and 'on site', and also between 'total mercury' and 'methylmercury'. From their report, it seemed their intention was to quantify the mercury levels and quantum within the factory site so that it could be used as a point of reference for any clean-up requirements. Especially because the demands of a clean-up of the factory and surroundings had already been raised by Greenpeace and the local communities. Beyond the factory site, the report attempted to prove there was no contamination and spread of the heavy metal – in the soil, in the lake and streams, in the flora and fauna and in the atmosphere – and therefore, nothing needed to be done beyond the four walls of the factory.

For instance, the mercury reading of soil within the complex showed highly elevated levels, but not in the majority of the samples collected from outside. The lichen too showed similar results. The twenty-two-acre lake, which was just 500 metres from the factory and located at the end of a downward slope of the factory site, with clear possibilities of water runoff, was found to be completely 'safe and secure'. Despite twenty years of mercury deposition in the lake, which could have bioaccumulated in the aquatic organisms, a fish that weighed half a kilo and a fully grown fish weighing almost four kilograms were shown to have the same levels of mercury (total mercury) in its tissues.

It is common knowledge in the scientific community that the longer a fish lives, the greater the quantum of bioaccumulation in its body tissues. Another curious aspect was that the four fish samples taken from the lake by Dames & Moore were not tested for methylmercury, though the consultants and scientists would be well aware that mercury bioaccumulates in fish and in other living beings as methylmercury. Also, this was in spite of them testing thirty-three soil, sediment and lichen samples for methylmercury. But this aspect found no mention in the Dames & Moore report.

Based on this study of the fish samples, sans for methylmercury, the report concluded that there had been no measurable impact on Kodai Lake from continuous mercury discharges at the thermometer factory, and there was no evidence of mercury having entered the food chain, namely by consumption of fish in this case.[2]

A cursory glance at the results would show that among the on-site samples, the bakery and scrap storage area had mercury levels up to thirty micrograms per kilogram of soil. In an area called South of Pond's Path, the mercury level was as high as 500 micrograms in a kilogram of soil. There was even one soil sample (labelled as AS22) taken from a depth of ten centimetres showing traces of mercury as high as 5,286 micrograms per kilogram of soil.[3] All these readings had to be seen against the ten micrograms per kilogram level recommended by the Dutch government for normal habitation and accepted globally as the non-dangerous level for human inhabitation. Anything above that is considered dangerous for any living organism, not just human beings.

The Dames & Moore report also concluded that outside of the three sets of areas within the factory, where the mercury levels varied from ten micrograms per kilogram to 500 micrograms per kilogram of soil, there could be up to a total of seventy-five kilograms of mercury dispersed in the soil.[4] Curiously, Dames & Moore chose not to estimate the total quantity of mercury dispersed in the three sets of areas with the highest concentration inside the factory campus – marked as A, B and C – generously conceding those areas had the highest concentration of mercury deposits. Tree bark samples collected from the factory site showed mercury levels ranging from 1.24 micrograms per kilogram to 20.4 micrograms per kilogram. The lichen samples had a much wider range – 18.3 to eighty-seven micrograms per kilogram.[5]

A number of lichen samples from other locations had also shown high mercury levels – 2.2 to 68 μg per kg. Proving a pattern of mercury levels decreasing, while travelling farther from the site of exposure, one lichen sample just outside the southern boundary of the factory showed 80 μg per kg, while another at a distance of 100 metres from there, showed 44 μg, and 2.3 μg per kg further south.[6] In order to explain the high mercury levels in lichen, Dames & Moore took refuge in an American case study.

A study on mercury in lichen conducted at the Theodore Roosevelt National Park had shown a thirty per cent decrease in mercury concentration over a sixteen-year period. So it was expected that mercury levels in lichen at the HLL site would show a similar progressive decline now that the factory had been closed down, thus terminating the sources of mercury emissions to the atmosphere.[7] In other words, it was also a damning admission of what had been going on there for the last twenty years and an indication of how dangerous the situation was.

Surface sediments gathered from the Lavange Path and the stream on its side showed mercury levels as high as 85 and 110 μg per kg in the tests run by the MGT Labs. Interestingly, the same samples returned only 41 and 26 μg per kg respectively in the analysis carried out by the HLL Research Lab.[8]

From all indications, HLL seemed more worried about results from the fish samples in the Kodai Lake. They tried to keep away from the fish – proper sampling and analysing – from the beginning. Perhaps they had taken a leaf out of the books about the Minamata disease and similar cases of methylmercury poisoning from around the world since the 1950s.

On the results reported from the fish samples, the experts had several observations: First, only four fish samples had been collected, against twenty-two samples of soil from outside the factory, twenty-nine samples of sediments, thirty-three samples of lichen and fifteen samples of water. Second, there were only three full-grown fish and one fingerling in the sample bucket. Last and most significantly, the collected fish samples were not analysed for methylmercury.[9] This left a huge, inexplicable gap about the levels of mercury present in the fish samples in methylated form.

Rather the report went overboard, spreading to almost three pages, explaining the fish sampling procedure, the general background concentration of mercury in fish, guidelines and standards for mercury in fish and so on. All the while failing to analyse the fish samples for methylmercury – the main cause of severe mercury poisoning, i.e., the Minamata disease.

# 25

# THE DAE RETURNS

DR ARUNACHALAM ENDED HIS CONVERSATION WITH DR JAYARAMAN about the DAE study – which proved that the quantity of mercury in the air of Kodaikanal was 2,600 times higher than the safe level – with this assertion: 'We will be coming back soon [for more detailed studies].' True to his word, the team would return to Kodaikanal not once or twice, but multiple times, scouring the area, collecting water samples, gathering sediments and fish samples from every possible vulnerable location.

But something curious had transpired after Dr Jayaraman's news reports on the 2002 DAE study. HLL had reached out to the team, claiming to engage it in a discussion to understand its sampling and study methods – similar to how the company had reacted to the CHC team's epidemiological study in Bangalore. One morning, an entire team from HLL turned up at the National Centre for Compositional Characterization of Materials (NCCCM) lab in Hyderabad, without prior notice, asking for a meeting with the DAE study team. Generously, although they weren't obliged to do so, some of the team members agreed. As the meeting ensued, it became clear that the company representatives were trying to find fault with the NCCCM study, with questions such as: 'Why are you trying to accuse the company of deliberately polluting the environment?' With Dr Arunachalam away, the other members tried to explain to the HLL representatives that the NCCCM, an organization focused on chemical research, didn't work for or against any corporation. The scientists there were simply dedicated to research in material characterization. The members of the DAE also pointed out that the published papers and the presentations at conferences had not referred to the company by name, and it was well established that the hill station of Kodaikanal had been polluted with mercury and the existence of the mercury thermometer factory was undeniable.

The hostile meeting with HLL had not gone down well with the DAE scientists, especially Dr Arunachalam. After HLL's efforts to 'engage with' the team, the NCCCM scientists had decided to carry out their upcoming assessment with even more rigour and focus to prove their independent judgement. Consequently, Krishna and Karunasagar made multiple trips to the hill station. They studied the topography, climatic conditions, possible transportation of mercury through wind and rain, possible impacts on flora and fauna, and also how it could be scientifically assessed. Taking time out from his busy schedule, Dr Arunachalam, too, made a trip to Kodaikanal accompanied by Krishna to understand the extent of the situation first-hand and strategize the options for the study.

The team members also made visits to another comparably located hill station: Oottacamund or Ooty to pick up a similar set of samples they would collect from Kodaikanal in order to compare the variations and ensure that the high mercury levels were not a natural background high-altitude phenomenon of the region. And, therefore, to use as 'control samples' to compare against the Kodaikanal samples in some of the studies.

After deliberations, they decided that the second study would aim to determine the levels of mercury in water, sediment and aquatic organisms of Kodai Lake and compare the results with those of two nearby lakes – Berijam, located at a distance of twenty kilometres, and Kukkal, which was double the distance away.

The samples were picked up from the three lakes by April 2004 with equidistant sampling points chosen to cover each lake's entire circumference. From each sampling location, a water sample and one sediment sample were collected. Water samples were collected at about two metres from the shore to avoid any suspended debris. In fact, the team hired a rowboat and used a homemade bailer to collect water samples from the desired depth of thirty centimetres below the surface, and also to avoid dead leaves and other floating debris. Sediment samples too were collected from the same locations of water samples in all three lakes.

The samples were stored in ice packs and transported to the laboratory, where they were stored at 20°C until further procedures. The sediment samples were separated from gravel and then air-dried at ambient temperature in a cleanroom. After drying, the samples were powdered, sieved and particles larger than the 100-mesh size were collected and stored in polythene bottles.[1] For the fish samples, the fresh fish were harvested from the lake, dissected and the edible muscle portions were homogenized in a mixer grinder. This body tissue mass was frozen and lyophilized and used for analysis.[2]

The study resulted in a landmark scientific paper in the *Environmental Pollution* in its September 2006 issue titled, 'Studies of mercury pollution in a lake due to a thermometer factory situated in a tourist resort: Kodaikkanal, India'. More significantly, the subtitle concluded the results of the study, stating, 'The lake was polluted by mercury from a thermometer factory'.[3]

The abstract of the paper made its conclusions clear:

> Kodaikkanal, India, suffered mercury contamination due to

> emissions and waste from a thermometer factory. Kodai Lake is situated to the north of the factory. The present study determined mercury in waters, sediment and fish samples and compared the values with those from two other lakes, Berijam and Kukkal.[4]

On analysing the results, the team had found that Kodai Lake waters had a mercury level of 356 to 465 nanograms per litre, with up to fifty nanograms per litre of methylmercury, compared to much lower levels in the samples from Berijam and Kukkal Lakes. The sediments collected from Kodai Lake returned 276 to 350 micrograms/kilogram of mercury with almost six per cent of methylmercury. Whereas the sediment samples from Berijam and Kukkal lakes showed ranges of 189 to 226 micrograms/kilogram and eighty-five to ninety-one micrograms/kilogram respectively. And the share of methylmercury in the total mercury was only three to four per cent in Berijam and two per cent in Kukkal.[5]

The study further found that though the factory site was at an elevation, the drainage would likely have carried the mercury deposited in the factory soil to the lake. It quoted the HLL commissioned URS Dames & Moore study to reassert this point. The results also suggested that since mercury vapour, once released into the air, was known to travel long distances, it could lead to widespread contamination. Referring to the results of fish samples with mercury levels ranging from 120 to 290 micrograms/kilogram, the NCCCM study unequivocally concluded that the lake was contaminated due to mercury emissions from the HLL factory.

By the time this study was accepted for publication by the journal, I had moved on from Greenpeace to Reuters. But because I was keenly following the case and sympathized with the clean-up cause, I immediately alerted key journalists who then reported the study prominently in their respective publications. In some time thereon, Krishna would present even more details at a conference in Chennai with Mody's and the Kodaikanal community's support. A year later, he would again present it as a detailed study paper at a well-regarded international conference in Lisbon, Portugal, on using mercury as a biomonitoring tool. It was there the study would gather the attention and praise of the global academic community.

At the Lisbon conference, Krishna stressed the key significance of the conclusion to his paper in *Environmental Pollution* – that the analysis of water, sediment and fish samples from Kodai Lake showed elevated levels of mercury even four years after the stoppage of operational emissions from the thermometer factory and despite the factory having shut down.[6]

# PART V

# A POISON NAMED MERCURY

# 26

# THE HUCKLEBY FAMILY TRAGEDY

IN DECEMBER 1969, AROUND THE TIME US PRESIDENT RICHARD Nixon was sending B-52 bombers with nuclear warheads to Vietnam, Ernest Lee Huckleby, a fifty-year-old school custodial worker and part-time farmer in Alamogordo, New Mexico, found himself struggling to make ends meet while trying to provide for his eight children and three-months-pregnant wife. In the shadow cast by the Cold War-triggered recession, Huckleby was not left with many options to feed ten hungry mouths. So when he and several of his friends heard that a granary in Texico, the Golden West Seed Company, was giving away floor sweepings for free, they jumped onto a flatbed truck to drive close to 400 kilometres to the warehouse.

Upon reaching, however, they were confused to see the grain bags. Some of the grains were dark brown; others looked rather pink. There was something wrong, clearly. One of Huckleby's friends shouted, 'Let's pick it up and give it to hog, anyway.'

'I don't know ... if I were you, I wouldn't,' said the man from the seed company.

'We aren't going to give it as it is. We'll mix these with the regular slops,' drawled another of Huckleby's friends.

After much debate, they decided to take the grains. They took a total of five and a half tonnes and drove back home to share it among everyone. Huckleby alone was able to get about 3,000 pounds of millet seed.

Back at the pen, his seventeen odd hogs, including a boar, didn't hesitate to eat the grains, unusually coloured ones included. Three weeks later, Huckleby noticed that some of the pigs were showing signs of illness and appeared to be suffering from what farmers called 'blind staggers' – a light food poisoning wherein the affected animals would walk with an unsteady, staggering gait as if they had gone blind. A few days later, the Huckleby family would enjoy a great dinner consisting of boar meat. In fact, they would say afterwards the meat was really flavourful and the fatback cuts juicy.

For almost a week or so, the family ate pork dishes for all three meals. On 4 December, one of his children, eight-year-old Ernestine, fell from a monkey bar at school and complained of back pain. She started showing signs of ataxia, agitation, visual impairment and impaired consciousness. When she didn't get better after a few days, her mother took Ernestine to a local physician who gave her some medicine. But this did not improve the girl's condition.

After Ernestine had been admitted to hospital, by now in a semi-coma and going blind, Amos and Dorothy Jean – two other Huckleby children, aged thirteen and eighteen – began showing identical symptoms. Both were admitted to the Alamogordo hospital about ten days after Ernestine, and thereafter all three were transferred to Providence General Hospital at El Paso, Texas, more than a hundred kilometres away with more extensive diagnostic facilities.[1]

Soon all the three children were in either a coma or semi-coma and had to be fed through gastric tubes, in addition to being monitored closely. Their doctors were worried that three people from a family were suffering from a disease that did not appear to be viral, and incidentally, some pigs on their farm were also suffering from blind staggers. An SOS went to the state health service from the district authorities by January 1970. Upon being alerted, Dr Bruce D. Storrs, the director of the State Medical Services and Chief State Health Officer, instantly observed that blind staggers in hogs could sometimes be caused by heavy metal poisoning – from arsenic or mercury – and its symptoms in humans resembled central nervous system disorders.

Without losing any time, the State Medical Services collected urine and blood samples from the Huckleby family members and sent them to the Center for Disease Control (CDC) lab in Atlanta and the Food and Drug Administration (FDA) laboratory in Dallas even as the Hucklebys consulted more doctors.

After talking to several doctors, the family finally learned the truth: They had all ingested large quantities of methylmercury, a substance widely used to treat animal food.[2] The health authorities were called in to investigate the source of the methylmercury. While they were being treated at the hospital, state health officers descended upon the family's house. After learning about the granary, they found that the grains fed to the hogs were possibly treated with a pesticide called panoger, a mercury compound. The CDC and the FDA analysed the data from the tests of the Huckleby family members and the hogs and found mercury accumulated in the animal tissues and body fluids of everyone in the family. They also confirmed that compounds containing organic mercury were the root cause.[3] The family represented a clear case of inadvertent misuse of seed grain treated with methylmercury.[4]

Forty-one-year-old Mrs Huckleby was also seven months pregnant. Out of fear for the safety of her life and that of the unborn, she was moved to the University of New Mexico's Medical

School at Albuquerque, where she remained under observation until she delivered the baby, who was declared clinically 'normal'. The joy, however, was short-lived. By the time the family named the baby Michael a few months later, they would realize that he was born blind, and mentally and physically impaired.

While Mrs Huckleby was still at the Albuquerque hospital for the delivery, all the three children were discharged from the El Paso hospital. Still in a coma, Amos and Ernestine were shifted to Gerald Champion Memorial Hospital in Alamogordo. Dorothy Jean was taken to the Roswell Nursing and Rehabilitation Center, where paraplegics and patients who have suffered strokes could recuperate.

When she came out of her coma months later, Ernestine was blind, had severe physical disability, and was unable to comprehend what was happening around her.

A year later, Ernestine would become the face of methylmercury poisoning in America after the *National Geographic* magazine published a photograph of the starry-eyed little girl holding a teddy bear close to her chest. The report was titled 'As We Live and Breathe: The Challenge of Our Environment'.[5] The photographer of the shot would later comment that 'of all assignments spanning thirty-five years, this one was the saddest'.[6]

A six-year follow-up study of the four poisoned patients by the School of Medicine of the University of New Mexico would reveal neurological deterioration in all the four patients, with the younger children showing greater damage and the newborn with maximum bruising because of transplacental poisoning. A study published in 1976 was even more conclusive on the severity of neurological damage caused by the mercury poisoning: 'The two of our patients on whom detailed sensory examination was possible demonstrated a peculiar dissociated sensory loss on five-year follow-up. Touch, pain, temperature, and vibration sense were preserved with marked loss of position sense, two-point discrimination, and stereognosis.'[7] More than fifty years later, the Huckleby family tragedy has remained in public memory as the first grave incident of methylmercury poisoning in the US – the same poison detected in the fish, sediments and water of Kodai Lake.

# 27

# BARTON BOOTH AND THE BLACK PILLS

ONE OF THE MAJOR SOURCES OF POISONING IN KODAIKANAL, especially among the workers of the factory, was direct exposure to elemental mercury. The HLL case also draws a significant parallel with mercury exposure incidents from history, when products containing mercury were believed to heal a host of ailments and its use was ubiquitous as a household cure and clinical remedy.

Until people started to develop strange symptoms.

In the late fifteenth century, an unusual disease that transmitted through sexual contact began raging across Europe. The visible symptoms of the mysterious disease included genital sores that appeared after engaging in intercourse with any infected person. It would progress to skin rashes all over the body, accompanied by fever and chills. The rashes would turn into foul-smelling, suppurating abscesses that would then erupt. A dirty illness with no cure, it became known as the 'French disease' because people believed the French troops had brought it to their shores. Thus began the search for a cure to the disease, which later came to be called the Great Pox. Much later, in 1530, it would be named 'syphilis' by an Italian physician.[1]

Finally, a remedy was discovered in the sixteenth century: mercury. Water-soluble mercuric chloride was found to be effective in treating syphilis. It was 'absorbed' by the body, wherever applied. It burned the skin at the site of application and was therefore presumed to be curing the rashes.[2] Mercury began getting noticed, accepted and being praised for its 'magical' properties.

By the first half of the eighteenth century, mercury had taken on the avatar of a miracle remedy in Europe. Concoctions and ointments made of mercury – in vapour form, liquid form and as solid compounds – as treatment for skin eruptions and dermatological issues to attack the syphilis virus 'trapped' in the skin.

It remained the drug of choice until the middle of the twentieth century, being used as an ointment, in vapour baths and taken orally. People and clinicians believed that quicksilver, as mercury was then known, would penetrate any layer of the body and purge the germs through sweat, salivation and excretion.

Small quantities of finely powdered mercury were recommended by reputed clinicians of the eighteenth and nineteenth centuries such as Augustin Belloste and John Abernethy to treat what they described as body-system failure. Abernethy's small mercury pills, known as 'blue pill' or 'blue mass', were so popular in America even Abraham Lincoln used to treat his melancholy with the 'blue pill' of pure liquid mercury, licorice root, rosewater and honey. According to records, however, he stopped it soon after moving to the White House.[3]

During the great age of monarchy, people in Europe too tended to believe that mercury and its forms could cure melancholy, cholic, syphilis, influenza and even parasite-related diseases. Mercurous chloride, or calomel, came into currency around this time in the shape of small pea-shaped pills packed with honey and sugar. It was said to be used by some of the most illustrious American and European personalities of the time, including Napoleon Bonaparte, Andrew Jackson, Louisa May Alcott and Edgar Allan Poe.

One reason for its remedial popularities was that constipation was an associated symptom of many of the diseases, and calomel would magically clear out bowels – thus giving the impression that the poison and germs in the body had also been purged. The story of the renowned theatre actor Barton Booth is the earliest recorded case of mercury use, or rather misuse.

Booth, living in Great Britain, was found to be suffering from a violent fever in 1727 that had lasted forty-six days. He was treated by the best doctors of the time, including the famous physician Thomas Dover. He would temporarily recover until the fever recurred four years later, this time as a form of an inveterate jaundice. He tried many a treatment, but to little avail. He even went on a sea voyage after being advised that the seasickness and consequent vomiting might help cure him. But the fever returned with a vengeance. This time, riding with colic.

His illness notwithstanding, he would keep returning to the stage whenever he was physically fit. But violent colic would resurface in 1733 and kill him by May the same year.

During the final two days of his life, Booth was under the care of Sir Hans Sloane, who ordered him to be bled therapeutically in an attempt to reduce the febrile tumours racking his body. After Booth's death, his would become one of the first celebrity autopsies, creating a long tradition.[4]

The autopsy report noted that the whole digestive tract was lined with crude mercury globules, about the size of pin heads. The inside of the intestines was thick black.[5] After doctors debated the autopsy report and the reason for his death at the age of fifty-two, it was ascertained that his death had been caused by heavy doses of mercury over a prolonged period. The mercury accumulated in the intestine had begun to give him colic pains and later chronic jaundice. It was quite possible that Booth was killed by a massive dose of mercury prescribed by quicksilver, a name supplied and embraced by Dr Thomas Dover. Not just in Europe and America, the tradition of mercury as a medicine prevailed in other regions too during this period – in various forms, colours and names.

In his search for immortality in ancient China, the first Emperor of the Qing Dynasty, Qin Shi Huang (259 – 210 BCE), ended up with mercury concoctions prepared by his court alchemists as the elixir of life. The result: Qin Shi Huang died of mercury poisoning at a young age without realizing he was dying of the elixir supposed to grant him immortality. His love for quicksilver was so immense, he had instructed that his body be buried in a mausoleum flowing with mercury and have its ceiling decorated with mercury arrangements. Ostensibly, his tomb still remains unexcavated as people fear the release of toxic levels of mercury once it is opened.

In north India, Europe and America, Tibetan pharmacies, until recently, used to sell a packaged pill named Schu-Mar 2, also known as Jewel Pill 25, accompanied by a brochure in both Tibetan and English. It explained that the late seventeenth-century physician–monk Tenzin Phuntsok treated himself with the mercury pill he had developed for an unidentified deadly scourge, in order to save himself from the mysterious disease.

The Chinese and Indians had been using mercury as a 'miracle medicine' for a very long time. In fact, Tibetan pill-making evolved from Indian and Chinese traditions wherein monks used to make pills locally known as *rin-chen ril-nag* for treating issues ranging from nervous problems to bone fractures. Rin-chen ril-nag can also be translated as 'black pills'. Black pills were thought to be the confluence of mercury and Tibetan Buddhism. They were partaken as part of the medicinal and miracle traditions of Tibetan Buddhists, some of which are still in force today. Even in the present day, Men-Tsee-Khang, or the Tibetan Medical and Astro-Science Institute, based in Dharamshala, sell these black pills in a modified form as *rinchen tsajor chenmo* or the 'precious pill', purportedly containing fourteen herbal and non-herbal ingredients, including *tsothel*, which is described as the king of the essence. The institute in its promotional material claims tsothel is mercury detoxified through complex processes and brought to tolerable levels of potency. These forms of mercury continue to be recommended as preventive medicine against gout, arthritis, malignant tumor, ringworm, leprosy, tumor, ascites and localized edema, among others, and to clear blocked channels due to impure blood.[6] Unsurprisingly, of course, all these tourist brochures claim that the medicines are prepared 'based on practical instructions of the past eminent masters of Tibetan medicine and empowered with spiritual blessing'[7] – a blessing scientifically proven to be highly toxic.

# 28

# THE MYSTERY OF MINAMATA BAY

MINAMATA IS A QUIET TOWN ON THE SHORES OF THE SERENE Yatsushiro Sea in southern Japan, surrounded by the Kyushu mainland and many small islands known for their pristine locales.

On 21 April 1956, at the Shin Nihon Chisso Hiryo company's hospital in Minamata, a doctor was examining a five-year-old girl with walking difficulty, speaking impairment and convulsions. Jotting down her symptoms, what flashed in his mind was 'mad hatter disease.'

The epithet 'mad hatter' can be traced to the classic *Alice's Adventures in Wonderland* (1865) by Lewis Caroll. In the nineteenth century, mercuric nitrate was commonly used to make hats. During a process called carroting, wherein furs of small animals such as rabbits, hares or beavers were carved from their skins and matted together, the orange-coloured mercuric nitrate was used as a smoothing agent. The resultant 'felt' was then repeatedly shaped into large cones, shrunk in boiling water and dried to make hats.[1] A form of madness was noticed among the hat makers seemingly as a result of this process, thereby coming to be known as mad hatter disease.

Also known as mad hatter syndrome or erethism, it is classified as a neurological disorder that affects the central nervous system. People suffering from the disease typically showed behavioural changes such as irritability, low self-confidence, depression, apathy and timidity. In cases involving prolonged mercury vapour exposure, patients suffered from delirium, personality changes and memory loss – some of the symptoms also found amongst the workers exposed to mercury at the Kodaikanal factory.

Although the prevalence of the disease waned as traditional hat-making dwindled as a profession over the century, people continued to report similar symptoms from different parts of the world. In fact, when Johnny Depp portrayed the carrot orange-haired Mad Hatter in Tim Burton's *Alice in Wonderland* (2010), he reportedly decided to depict mercury poisoning through his phosphorescent green eyes and orange hair, also changing his skin tone and accent according to the character's mood.[2] Interestingly, a decade later, Depp would also play a part in *Minamata* (2020), a movie based on the ecological disaster.

Back in Minamata in 1956, within two days of the five-year-old patient's medical examination at the Chisso hospital, her sister reported the same set of symptoms as hers. Even their neighbour's daughter was showing similar manifestations, the children's mother informed the doctor.

After a quick door-to-door survey in the area, eight more children would be discovered with identical symptoms. By 1 May, the local health authorities would be notified of a mysterious epidemic that infected the central nervous system.

The culprit, ostensibly a new affliction, would come to be known as the Minamata disease.

Perplexed, the government of the Kumamoto Prefecture suspected a rapidly spreading contagion in the bay area. People with symptoms were quickly isolated and disinfected. A Strange Disease

Countermeasures Committee was set up in collaboration with local medical practitioners, who had begun noticing odd behaviours in domestic animals by then. Most striking was the behavioural pattern of afflicted cats – they would start having convulsions, progress to madness and, finally, death. The locals called it the '*neko odori byo*' (cat dancing disease).[3]

The strangeness extended to other flora and fauna, too: birds were found dropping down mid-flight, vegetation stopped growing in the river, dead fish began floating on the sea surface, and so on.

Dealing with an undocumented, unknown behemoth of a disease, in August, the local authorities drafted the nearby Kumamoto University's School of Medicine for support.[4] Over the next few months, the school admitted patients directly into its medical facilities and conducted thorough examinations.

The school's efforts and documentation soon revealed that the disease, though perilous, was not contagious. The twenty-six patients admitted and another fourteen reported dead by October had no prior warning or mild discomfort before their symptoms aggravated. The disease would manifest suddenly in the form of sensation loss and numbness of the limbs, making it difficult for the victim to hold an object in their hands or even fasten a shirt button. The early symptoms of muffling voice and stammering, inability to walk and run without falling and impairment of the senses would give way to episodes of convulsions and eventual coma before the victims would succumb to their death.

As the researchers at the School of Medicine began to dig deeper into the cause of the outbreak, they observed that most victims belonged to the fishing hamlets on the Minamata Bay shores and were in groups of father, mother and children. Living close on the shores and dependent on fishing, they were indubitably consuming large quantities of fish and shellfish. The research further showed that the dead cats had been consuming food waste, mostly fish, left by the families at the dinner table – making it clear the disease was caused from food poisoning.

The research team announced on 4 November that 'the Minamata disease is rather considered to be poisoning by a heavy metal; presumably it enters the human body mainly through fish and shellfish'.[5]

But the next question was: how was it then entering the marine creatures? Could it be from the Minamata Bay, from where the local residents have been fishing and consuming seafood? Investigations ensued.

The prime suspect was the Shin Nihon Chisso Hiryo company, which released wastewater and industrial effluent into the Minamata Bay. An earlier internal assessment had shown that the discharges contained lead, mercury, manganese, arsenic, thallium, copper and selenium, but there had been no recent studies. With very little cooperation from the company, tying down the disease to a specific chemical was a daunting task. Over the next couple of years, many theories were floated, associating the disease with each of these metals. But nothing could be concluded scientifically.

The real breakthrough came in March 1958, when acclaimed British neurologist Douglas McAlpine visited the town. After detailed discussions about the cases with the School of Medicine team, he suggested that the symptoms presented a strong case for mercury poisoning. Taking his advice seriously, the researchers studied the quicksilver distribution in and around the bay. They were shocked to discover mercury everywhere – in the fish, shellfish, vegetation, water and the sludge at the bottom of the bay. On tracing the pattern, they observed a heavy concentration of mercury near the Chisso factory up to the canal, to the extent of two kilograms per tonne of sludge (2010 parts per million), less near Hyakken Harbour and the least at the confluence of the sea and beyond. The point of origin was clearly the factory.

Once the cause had been identified, the focus of the research was to establish the mercury-related effects in humans. To prove their correlation, hair samples of patients as well as those from the non-affected populace were analysed – in order to assess how much mercury had accumulated over time.

The hair sample analysis of the inhabitants of the heavily impacted areas, who believed themselves to be unaffected by the disease, revealed high levels of mercury, with the highest level recorded at 191 ppm. These people subsequently developed chronic Minamata disease. In patients, even though they had stopped eating local seafood as early as 1956, the maximum mercury value measured was 705 ppm.[6]

With these results, the team carried out animal modelling, wherein cats and fish were fed methylmercury-laced feed. Between ten to twelve weeks, the cats began showing symptoms and experiencing convulsions.

Once they had conclusively correlated methylmercury with the disease, by November 1959, the Minamata Disease Research Group of Kumamoto University reported to the Japanese Ministry of Health Labour and Welfare that 'Minamata disease was poisoning by MeHg (methylmercury) contained in the wastewater from the Chisso plant.[7]

Soon, Chisso quietly set up a research team to repeat the animal modelling in its factory. Once the cats began experiencing convulsions by the seventy-eighth day of the experiment, the research team was unceremoniously disbanded and the entire research shelved without offering any reason to the team.[8] Decades later, in 2020, it was discovered that one of the doctors in charge of the experiment had kept samples of cat brains in his personal custody, a key piece of evidence that would lead to new scientific revelations.

But back then, caught in a defensive position, Chisso, along with similarly placed companies in the region, funded a research to debunk the now-proven and accepted methylmercury theory. Later after some long protests, Chisso agreed to recompense patients certified by the Ministry of Health, Labour and Welfare to the tune of JPY100,000 and JPY300,000 for each death caused by the disease.[9]

An unexpected impact was on newborns: In 1961, a number of cerebral palsy cases were reported from the area, despite the fact that the mothers did not show any symptoms whatsoever. Contrary to the hitherto scientific understanding of the placenta acting as a protective cover – true in the case of most chemicals – the uterine sheath was transferring the methylmercury from the mother's body to the foetus.

With the study to link Shin Nihon Chisso Hiryo to the disease reaching an end, notwithstanding the withdrawal of grants and support by the government, Kumamoto University announced in 1963 that the Minamata disease was caused solely by the methylmercury effluent of the Shin Nihon Chisso company. Two years later, the company would formally change its name to Chisso Corporation.

Nevertheless, Chisso continued the indiscriminate use of mercury as a catalyst in acetaldehyde production at its Minamata plant, and it would take another five years for them to stop the practice.

A couple of years later, in 1965, Niigata, a town approximately 1,400 kilometres away on the other end of Japan, made headlines owing to a disease that produces symptoms similar to those related to Minamata disease. The Niigata poisonings provided critical experimental data. These findings showed that a full-fledged case of Minamata disease resulted from eating fish 0.5 to 3.0 times per day. The average serving of fish in a meal was generally estimated at either 150 or 200 grams, and the type of fish consumed was found to be contaminated at levels between 5,000 ppb and 20,000 ppb wet weight.[10]

The Niigata cases have since confirmed methylmercury is teratogenic, meaning it can cause birth defects if ingested by pregnant women. Between Minamata and Niigata, as many as twenty-two children were born with congenital malformations to women who had unwittingly consumed contaminated fish during pregnancy, but did not show symptoms of Minamata disease themselves. This, of course, proved the foetus is more susceptible than an adult human to damage from methylmercury. Autopsies conducted on children afflicted by foetal Minamata disease showed characteristic damage to brain cells. Methylmercury appeared to dissolve brain cells, leaving in their place empty cavities filled with inert fluid. In addition, methylmercury burns out the farthest links of the nervous system, in the fingers and toes, causing the characteristic numbness usually experienced by patients.[11]

Since then, the Minamata mercury poisoning catastrophe has been treated as a textbook case of inorganic mercury getting converted into organic mercury, and the toxic combination moving up the food chain to reach humans, manifesting in the worst ways possible.

Years later, advanced research indicated the possibility that Chisso Corporation had released methylmercury into the river. With the advent of sophisticated research infrastructure, the research continued to progress in this direction for over a decade until a shocking revelation came in 2020.

A team from the University of Saskatchewan (USask) reinvestigating the historic animal brain tissue samples of Minamata found that the tragedy was caused by an entirely different type of organic mercury and a deadly chemical called alpha-mercuri-acetaldehyde, which is a by-product of the acetaldehyde production.[12] Curiously, it also brought the cat dancing disease to full circle, using samples preserved from the original study conducted by the Chisso company doctor in 1959, in order to determine the causes of the sickness.

Despite the new findings, sporadic incidents of Minamata-like poisoning have since been reported from different parts of the world, with similar symptoms, and have come to be known as incidents of Minamata disease. For instance, there have been reports twice from Iraq as well as from Guatemala and Pakistan.

By the time a UN-sponsored global treaty to regulate the use of mercury called the Minamata Convention came into force in August 2017, Chisso Corporation had recompensed about 14,000 victims.

Like the unravelling of the origins and causes of the eponymous disease, the Minamata Convention too took a long time to fructify. The road to the mercury treaty had started at the 1972 Stockholm Conference on the human environment, when Japanese student Shinobu Sakamoto, crippled by Minamata disease, showed up at the conference and shook the conscience of the attendees.

The United Nations Environment Programme (UNEP, now UN Environment), which came into existence the same year, took on toxic pollution as an agenda from that point. With its Governing Council kicking off discussions in 2001 for a global assessment of all aspects of mercury and its compounds – health effects, sources, trade, transport, prevention and control – work on the treaty was formally begun. By 2009, the council decided to create a globally binding instrument for mercury, the first such treaty for a chemical element.

The Convention was adopted in five long meetings between 2009 and 2013 and opened up for signatures. With fifty member nations ratifying it, the Minamata Convention to protect human health and the environment from the adverse effects of mercury was enforced in August 2017.[13] Minamata mostly uncovered the repercussions of irresponsibly and ignorantly handling mercury in both organic and inorganic forms, and the treaty stood testimony to it.

In Kodaikanal too, mercury-laden waste was dumped in the water bodies, including the stream and Kodai Lake, while the local populace continued to consume fish from these toxic waters in immeasurable quantities. In addition, the Kodaikanal case also presented a strong case of metallic mercury pollution by way of inorganic mercury exposure by the factory workers who were handling the element for long periods daily.

It must be noted that evaporated organic mercury also poisons the local atmosphere as gaseous mercury by increasing its quantity far beyond safe or permissible levels. Transported by air, it gets deposited in nearby water bodies and bioaccumulates in aquatic organisms there before starting to move up in the food chain. Over the decades, from Minamata to Kodaikanal, what has regrettably remained a constant since the unravelling of the mystery of Minamata Bay is corporations around the world failing to acknowledge their mistakes and negligence when confronted with an ethical dilemma regarding human lives.

# 29

# ALOIS ALZHEIMER

ALOIS ALZHEIMER BEGAN HIS MEDICAL CAREER AT THE FRANKFURT mental asylum in Germany in 1888. The chief reason he joined the facility was its head doctor Emil Sioli, an ingenious psychiatrist, who was known for allowing his juniors complete freedom when it came to research.

At the hospital, alongside another renowned neurologist, Franz Nissi, Alzheimer spent sleepless nights trying to understand how the human mind and brain functioned. Together they conducted unparalleled research on the pathology of the brain and the nervous system. The work they did during this period would be published in six volumes as *Histologic and Histopathologic Studies of the Cerebral Cortex* between 1906 and 1918. Around 1901, at another Frankfurt mental facility, Alzheimer came across a middle-aged patient named Auguste Deter, who was showing unusual behaviours – such as difficulty in visual identification to short-term memory loss – which, over time, progressed to dementia. Thus, when her husband Carl Deter, unable to afford her treatment, requested to move Auguste to a lower-cost asylum, Alzheimer offered to take care of all her medical expenses in exchange for her medical records and brain upon her death.[1]

By the time Auguste Deter died in 1906, Alzheimer was working in Munich at the lab of Emil Kraepelin, father of modern psychiatry who first postulated that biological changes and genetic mutations were the primary causes of psychiatric conditions. On conducting an autopsy of Deter's brain, he identified a number of pathologic manifestations, including 'shrinking' of the cerebral cortex, tangled bundles of fibres (now called neurofibrillary tau or tangles) and abnormal clumps (now called amyloid plaques). The changes in the brain were pointing to senile dementia, an illness that had not been properly documented until then.

A few months after the autopsy and further studies, Alzheimer gave a lecture at the annual meeting of southwest German psychiatrists in Tubingen on an 'unusual disease of the cerebral cortex' with symptoms of memory loss, disorientation and hallucinations, narrating the case of Auguste Deter who died at the age of fifty-five. Immediately, the newly identified disease caught the imagination of the audience and received national attention. With Auguste Deter's brain, Alzheimer had access to a new disease and identified nerve tangles and amyloid plaques which had never previously been described. It was Kraepelin who named the disease after Alzheimer, and this was how Alzheimer's disease (AD) came to be identified.[2]

The presence of the tangles and plaques in the brain are still considered the main features of AD, along with the loss of connections between neurons that result in failure to transmit messages between different parts of the brain and from there to the other muscles and organs in the body.

But does mercury play a role in Alzheimer's disease?

In the last ten years or so, a number of studies have pointed to the role of mercury as a cause for AD, as contributory and environmental factors. More so because mercury is at least ten times more toxic to nerve cells than its closest cousin, lead. Only mercury, at low levels, was able to induce the hallmark changes seen in AD, compared to cadmium, manganese, aluminium, iron and lead. A substantial number of neurons, interneurons and CNS-endothelial cells of people who had died from a neurodegenerative disease like AD were found to be full of intracellular mercury deposits, demonstrating that mercury was easily able to penetrate the blood–brain barrier and enter the neurons, resulting in neuronal loss.[3]

A comprehensive review of previous research conducted in this area till date was done in 2019 to understand the role of mercury in Alzheimer's disease by looking at all the known factors associated with the disease; it revealed seventy factors attributable to mercury in various proportions. It was found that the presence of plaques, beta amyloid protein, neurofibrillary tangles and phosphorylated tau protein in the brain can be caused by mercury. Similarly, the functioning of the brain chemicals responsible for communication between nerve cells (neurotransmission) such as acetylcholine, serotonin, dopamine, glutamate and norepinephrine was slowed down by the presence of mercury. Many of the enzymes responsible for various brain functions were severely impacted by mercury, which was also found to trigger over-activation of the immune system and inflammation in the brain – two key features found in Alzheimer's patients. In addition, mercury inhibits the synthesis of DNA in the hippocampus, the part of the brain responsible for information consolidation, and short, long and spatial memory. It is also responsible for genetic mutations of some key proteins, which are the chief reason for the early onset of the disease in some people. Significantly, the abnormal response of minerals and vitamins like aluminium, calcium, copper, iron, magnesium, selenium, zinc and vitamins B1, B12, E and C found in normal mercury toxicity was observed in patients with Alzheimer's disease as well.

Other factors seen in Alzheimer's disease, such as increased platelet activation, poor odour identification, hypertension, depression, increased incidences of herpes virus and chlamydia infections, also occur due to mercury exposure. In addition, patients diagnosed with Alzheimer's disease exhibit higher levels of brain mercury, blood mercury and tissue mercury, according to peer-reviewed studies.[4]

Mercury poisoning has long been known by the term mercurialism, also known as hydrargyria or hydrargyrism. With direct evidence to link it to neurological effects, the new condition is known as neurologic mercury poisoning, neurologic mercurialism or nervous system mercurialism. Other variations with impact on the nervous system evolved over time, including mercury-induced nervous system disease and mercurial neuroanesthenia.

Research in humans and animals suggests that mercury is characterized as a neurotoxic heavy metal that increasingly bioaccumulates in the brain cells with increasing age. While being transported through blood, mercury trespasses into the brain by breaking the semipermeable membrane separating the blood from the cerebrospinal fluid, which prevents most chemicals from reaching the nervous system. Studies have reinforced that mercury impairs the blood–brain barrier.[5] Vascular disorders have also been associated with AD, and it is well known that mercury affects the cardiovascular system. Further, methylmercury has been shown to damage the central nervous system and is associated with vascular dysfunction, haemorrhage and oedema of the brain.[6]

Recent voluminous studies have also suggested that exposure to mercury, even in low concentrations, can cause cardiovascular and reproductive disorders, and that it contributes to developmental toxicity, nephrotoxicity, immunotoxicity and carcinogenicity. Researchers across the world are studying its role in various cardiovascular diseases such as hypertension, coronary heart disease and myocardial infarction. Mercury toxicity is strongly correlated with hypertension, coronary heart disease, myocardial infarction, cardiac arrhythmias, carotid artery obstruction, cerebrovascular accident and generalized atherosclerosis.[7]

There are also hypotheses that exposure to mercury and some other toxic metals could be the primary cause for Parkinson's disease, a motor neuron disease and neurodegenerative disorder causing brain inflammation and changes in the brain's oxygen levels. There has been considerable research to link mercury to Parkinson's, wherein the angiogenin protein found in the spinal cord and the brain to protect neurons from cell death degenerates and, therefore, malfunctions or halts communication (neurotransmission) between the brain and muscles and the skeletal system.

Along with these linkages to the incidence of Parkinson's, several correlations between mercury exposure and Parkinson's have also been documented. The etiology of a close cousin of Parkinson's, known as amyotrophic lateral sclerosis (ALS or Lou Gehrig's disease), has known to be a result of chronic exposure to mercury. Detectable blood mercury levels were six times more frequent in individuals with PD than in healthy controls. And the onset of the disease has been associated with exposure to elevated levels of mercury.[8]

Symptoms of Alzheimer's and Parkinson's were reportedly found among the ex-workers of the factory in Kodaikanal as well as among the local residents there. Unfortunately, the cases of workers who reported symptoms of the two diseases were not examined with the kind of seriousness shown by the Japanese in the Minamata case. The delayed investigations conducted by various teams were unable to draw conclusions to link the workers' illnesses to mercury exposure, may be because of their poor design and sophistication. Some of the afflicted workers and local people continue to exhibit symptoms associated with Alzheimer's and Parkinson's, but are sadly unaware of their own afflictions.

# 30

# FISH EATS MERCURY, MAN EATS FISH

THE LAW OF INDESTRUCTIBILITY OF MATTER IS THE GREATEST contribution of the eighteenth-century French chemist Antoine Lavoisier. But he is also known for being the man who proved the existence of oxygen through a famous mercury experiment jointly carried out with English chemist Joseph Priestley.

From its elemental form of silvery-white liquid, mercury changes into solid at minus 38.83°C. It evaporates at temperatures as low as 25°C, and starts boiling at 356.73°C. As proved by Lavoisier's law, it can change forms in chemical reactions, but never be destroyed.

In 1911, the Dutch physicist Heike Kamerlingh Onnes from Leiden University managed to cool mercury to the temperature of liquid helium, 4°Kelvin, and discovered that its resistance disappeared.[1] This established mercury as the first superconducting substance, and Kamerlingh Onnes would be awarded the Nobel Prize in physics for this research two years later.

Most of the mercury found in the atmosphere is elemental mercury vapour ($Hg^0$). It is also found in two oxidized states (combined with oxygen): mercurous ($Hg_2^{2+}$) and mercuric ($Hg^{2+}$), with properties changing according to its state.

By natural processes, mercuric compounds get removed from

the atmosphere faster than elemental mercury. They get bound to airborne particles and are removed by precipitation or in some cases even without it. Elemental mercury vapour, on the other hand, has a strong tendency to remain in the atmosphere for long and is not vulnerable to precipitation or getting deposited in the earth's crust.

Most of the mercury found in water, soil and sediments are in the form of inorganic mercury salts; in living organisms, plants and animals, it is in organic forms like methylmercury, a mercury–carbon compound. Methylmercury, a compound of organic methyl group (three hydrogen and one carbon atoms) bonded to an atom of mercury, is formed from inorganic mercury by microbial action in water bodies – lakes, rivers, wetlands and the ocean.

Mercury moves in the air in many ways. Primarily, it gets transported from atmosphere to water and land as wet deposits. In aquatic ecosystems, it can dissolve or exist in particulate form, besides undergoing chemical changes, depending on the other particles it comes into contact with. Bottom sediments in water bodies serve as reservoirs for mercury where it can bind with contaminants. There, it can get retained for a very long time, before slowly releasing into the water and the atmosphere.

Once any living being, plant or animal, is exposed to mercury, it enters the organism and gets accumulated in the body tissues. This can occur by inhaling gaseous mercury, or by ingesting food or water contaminated by it. In aquatic environments, mercury accumulates in the sediments or binds with the sediments, where it is consumed by small algae known as phytoplankton, which in turn is eaten by larger organisms known as zooplankton. Zooplanktons are consumed by small fish which are in turn eaten by larger fish. From there, mercury moves to fish-eating birds, reptiles and human beings. In scientific parlance, this process becomes known as bioaccumulation.

Once mercury enters the body cells of living beings, it sets off a dangerous chemical process termed methylation. This happens in the water or the sediments too, wherein mercury transforms from its inorganic form to methylated organic form by combining with carbon molecules, assisted by microorganisms like bacteria. Through a series of chemical reactions, mercury can be converted by bacteria in the sediments to methylmercury, a form that is incredibly toxic to humans and wildlife. The body cells of fish absorb the methylmercury from the water as it passes over their gills and upon feeding on other organisms. So its concentrations increase in the bigger fish. Consequently, the larger predator fish usually have higher concentrations of methylmercury from eating contaminated prey.[2]

The production and accumulation of methylmercury in the freshwater ecosystems is an efficient process for accumulating mercury which can then be ingested by piscivores – fish-eating birds, animals and people.[3] Only after being methylated can mercury start moving up from organism to organism through the food chain. The emissions from coal-based power plants are one of the sources of methylated mercury, as proven by a plethora of research on the impacts of mercury emissions from coal-based power plants over the last half century. Simple studies of the mercury levels in the hair and blood of people living near coal-based power plants to researches on its manifestations as illnesses and long-term health effects have all proven beyond doubt the seriousness of the issue.

Of course, this is in addition to living organisms directly inhaling mercury vapour. With global energy consumption going up due to economic growth, coal remains the mainstay in meeting energy needs. Because it is burned in unsafe ways, however, coal will continue to emit dangerous gases like mercury at shockingly high levels for the foreseeable future as the coal corporations are backed by the political leadership in their respective countries. The 2018 Global Mercury Assessment by UN Environment reported that thirty-eight per cent of all mercury emissions came from the coal sector. It sources the largest quantity of mercury, and virtually all the mercury used in its processes is eventually released into the environment.[4]

Besides methylmercury, inorganic mercury too is absorbed by living organisms and bioaccumulates, albeit in a lower quantity and at a slower pace. The removal of methylmercury does take place inside the organisms but is a gradual process that can take years because of its long 'half-life', the time taken for the disintegration of radioactive materials to half its original quantity. All isotopes of mercury are either radioactive or observationally active, meaning they can be predicted to be radioactive. Recently, pharmacokinetics studies have proved that methylmercury has a half-life of fifty days in the human body, meaning it takes fifty days for a single gram of mercury in the body cells to denude to half a gram.

# 31

# ALMADEN TO NEW ALMADEN

UNTIL 1850, MOST OF THE WORLD'S MERCURY SUPPLY CAME FROM three mines – Almaden in Spain, Idrija in Slovenia and Santa Barbara in Peru.

The Almaden mercury mine, dating back to the Roman Empire, is the world's oldest and the largest source of mercury. It also has the highest concentration of quicksilver anywhere in the world. The name 'Almaden' is believed to have originated from the Arabic word 'al-mahden', meaning metal (also mine), after the Almaden mines came under the control of the Arabs, following their invasion of Iberia in the early eighth century.

An estimated 250,000 metric tonnes of mercury have been extracted from the Almaden mines to the present day, which would translate into one-third of the total liquid metal consumed by mankind to date. Almaden deposits have been, and still are, extremely rich with mercury content of around eight per cent, much higher than any other mercury mine. Just to compare, the mines of Abbadia San Salvatore in Monte Amiata, Italy, had a cinnabar concentration of between 0.6 and two per cent[1].

But after servicing the world for 2,000 long years, mining at the Almaden mines stopped completely by 2001 and all metallurgical activities at the mine were halted by 2004.

Trade at Almaden first began flourishing after Bartolome de Medina had invented a new metallurgical process, known as yard benefit, to extract gold and silver by amalgamation with mercury in 1554 CE. The process was especially useful because of its cost benefits, its effectiveness in extracting silver from low-content ores and the lower fuel requirement. This heralded a new age for mercury, paving the way for large-scale commercial and industrial purposes.

Amalgamation indeed dates back to a century before the birth of Christ. Gaining popularity quickly, it was put into use for metal extractions, leading to increased use and demand for mercury. By around 1000 CE, quicksilver was being widely used in amalgamation to extract gold. Over the next 1,000 years, mercury gradually came to occupy a prominent place in livelihood, moving from artisan's workshops to hospitals, factories and, finally, to households.

Even today, amalgamation is practised as part of small-scale artisanal gold mining (ASGM) operations, exposing over ten million workers to the toxic element and releasing between 650–1,000 tonnes of mercury per year into the environment.[2] The UN Environment puts the number of people dependent on the sector for employment at an estimated ten to fifteen million, including four to five million women and children. The mercury released every day into the air, water and land from the mining operations in over seventy countries consolidates to an alarming amount, which threatens the lives of the people and the environment.

By the middle of the twentieth century, the search for mercury deposits began in North and South America and many other parts of the world by new-age explorers. Back in the sixteenth century, the Spanish expeditions had led to large gold and silver deposits being found in Mexico, Peru and Bolivia and also generated large-scale mercury demand for use in amalgamation.[3] These new-age explorations would eventually lead to the discovery of mines in the state of California, which were named the New Almaden mines in mid-nineteenth century, a key historical point from when the US began challenging the supremacy of Spain in the global mercury market. Today, countries such as China, Kyrgyzstan, Mexico, Peru, Russia, Slovenia, Spain and Ukraine possess most of the world's estimated 600,000 tonnes of mercury resources. Mexico continues to reclaim mercury from the Spanish colonial silver-mining waste.

In the US, there are still untapped mercury deposits in Alaska, Arkansas, California, Nevada and Texas, though mercury has not been mined since 1992. Of all the known reserves, California continues to have the largest potential. The US stopped mining mercury in 1992 with the closure of its last production facility, the McDermitt mine in northern Nevada. Thereafter, mercury was only recovered from various end-use products and processes. Since 1998, no data has been made available on mercury production.

The only source of mercury in the US now is dental amalgam, electronic waste, end-of-service automobile switches, fluorescent lamps and compact fluorescent lamps (CFLs), laboratory and medical measuring devices, mercury-contaminated waste and thermostats. As per a recent estimate, the US still consumes approximately 40 tonnes of mercury a year for various purposes. The leading domestic end-users of mercury are manufacturing industries of chlorine-caustic soda (chloralkali), dental products, electronics and fluorescent-lighting. Presently, only two mercury cell chloralkali plants are in operation in the US.

While most countries have put an end to mercury mining in the last two decades or so, China continues to produce the poisonous metal in large quantities – to the tune of 3,500 metric tonnes in 2019. It is followed by Mexico, Tajikistan, Peru, Norway and

Kyrgyzstan.[4]

The 2017 UN Environment report on global mercury supply, trade and demand, taking into account the magnitude of China's domestic mercury business, estimated a range of 800 to 1,000 tonnes as its annual production from mining. Another report, however, quoting the World Bank, says China's trading partners have documented mercury coming from the country, and there are periodic reports of undocumented Chinese mercury appearing in Africa. Both China and Mexico – the two largest current-day producers of mercury – have interestingly ratified the Minamata Convention, which forbids countries from starting new primary mercury mines and orders to decommission all existing ones.

# 32

# FEVER THERMOMETERS, LIGHTS AND BULBS

IT IS MEANINGLESS TO DISCUSS MERCURY WITHOUT FIRST comprehending the ubiquitous nature of the liquid metal in everyday life. Unseen by the naked eye in most devices, it has also managed to elude any attention to the dangers surrounding its uses and disposal methods. Mercury in the electrical and electronics sectors ranges from batteries, lighting, pumps, switches, relays, measuring devices, cooking ranges, computers and TV screens. A variety of button-cell batteries contain mercury, including zinc air, silver oxide and alkaline manganese oxide batteries. Button-cell batteries are small, thin energy cells that are not rechargeable and are commonly used in watches, toys, hearing aids and other small and portable electronic devices. They last as long as ten years or more and, owing to lack of awareness among users, its disposal guidelines remain precarious.

In an attempt to phase out mercury use in the last decade, some of the largest battery manufacturers, including Sony Corporation, New Leader and Energizer, began to manufacture non-mercury button-cell batteries like lithium button-cell batteries and non-miniature, cyclical alkaline batteries that do not contain mercury.

Sadly, many of these replacements turned out to be more expensive than the mercury-containing ones.[1] The only liquid metal at room temperature, mercury expands and contracts evenly with changes in temperature and pressure. As such, it is extensively used in various devices meant for measuring temperature and pressure. In the medical field, this includes a vast array of equipment used in medical diagnostics involving temperature and pressure, such as barometers for calculating pressure, sphygmomanometers for blood pressure, fever thermometers and strain gauges that measure forearm blood flow or arterial inflow.

Mercury-containing devices are in use for numerous applications in the industrial field, for pure scientific research and for observing the climate. All of these use quicksilver ranging from one gram to 5,000 grams per device, depending on its type and use.[2] In addition, thermostats use mercury switches to sense and control room temperature, through communication with heating, ventilation and air conditioning (HVAC) equipment. The use of mercury in thermostats has drastically come down in the developed world during the current decade. For instance, in the US it has come down to zero usage in 2016 from fifteen tonnes a year in 2001.[3] But it remains in use in many parts of the world.

Many mercury-dependent measuring devices are no longer manufactured or sold in the US and Europe. However, because non-mercury alternatives are still very expensive, China and some other Asian countries still manufacture these devices using mercury. The global estimate for mercury consumption in these applications is based heavily on Chinese production of sphygmomanometers and thermometers. Over 270 tonnes of mercury were estimated to have been used in the production of only these two devices in 2004, which represent around eighty per cent of the total mercury consumption in the sector.[4]

Another mercury-dependent sector is lighting. Mercury-filled lamps fall into broad categories of fluorescent, metal halide, ceramic metal halide, high-pressure sodium, mercury vapour, mercury short-arc and mercury capillary lamps. Yet another is of display devices. Most home and office equipment, including computers, televisions, global positioning system (GPS) units, hand-held communications and entertainment systems and digital cameras use LCD displays which contain mercury.[5]

Automobiles and recreational vehicles too have mercury-added lamps, in addition to high-intensity discharge (HID) headlamps, navigation systems, instrument panels using LCD screens and backlighting with mercury. In China alone, mercury used in the production of (mostly) fluorescent tubes and CFLs, was estimated at fifty-five tonnes in 2004, which may be an underestimate. Many of these lamps are exported.[6] In the US, at least fifty major light makers have phased out the use of mercury in the last two decades. A similar trend has emerged in Australia, Japan and some European countries. But, the market is still heavily supplied by Asian, and particularly Southeast Asian, countries, making it apparent the threat is far from over.

The mercury inside bulbs, displays, electrical and electronic devices poses no health risk as long as the device is functioning and intact. However, the challenge is to manage the flow of mercury from products through breakage, scrap smelting, recollection for safe storage, and waste disposal through incineration, landfill and recycling. In any case, even if all these challenges were resolved, the question of safe and effective mercury disposal remains unanswered.

# PART VI

# MERCURY RISING IN KODAI

# 33

# 'DUMP FOR A DUMP'

RIGHT BEFORE THE SCIENTIFIC EVIDENCE ARRIVED IN KODAIKANAL, Unilever was once again left red-faced with embarrassment. Soon after I joined Greenpeace, I was presented with a proposal to retire the 300-odd tonnes of mercury-laced waste lying at the factory in a landfill in a northern Indian state. The discussions brought forward by the TNPCB was that the company would acquire land in a desolate location and secure the place for disposing of the mercury waste in landfills.

Greenpeace and the local community condemned the outrageous proposal, and we called out that it tantamount to attempting to pass on the problem to other parts of the country, without considering the risk it posed to the lives of the people in and around that location. The campaign team stayed firm that the waste had to be shipped back to its place of origin, the United States. A strong message had to be sent to corporations trying to dump their waste in 'third world' countries. Moreover, as the regulator was advised, there were mercury-recycling facilities in the US where the waste could be recycled and disposed of permanently.

Next, the campaign team elucidated at length to the company officials the dangers of mercury landfills and the practices for mercury waste disposal followed elsewhere in Europe and the US. As a matter of fact, Navroz Mody had foreseen the possibility of the waste lying at the factory becoming a long-term source of mercury emission as soon as it was moved from the scrapyard to the factory. And there were already multiple sources of mercury emission at the factory site. Therefore, in early 2002, Mody and the Local Area Monitoring Committee tried to force the company to send the waste for recycling and permanent disposal via the state regulator. After multiple meetings with desk-level officers at the TNPCB, where the campaign team provided documents and clarifications on the global best practices and case studies, the regulator was on board with the demand. Sheela Rani Chunkath played a crucial role due to her deep understanding of the issue and, therefore, her stern stand on the matter.

On 12 March 2003, the regulator issued an order asking the company to ship out the 290 tonnes of mercury waste with due safety and care and by following proper protocols.[1] It wasn't an easy proposition, but not impossible, for a company of the size of Unilever. Since the US was not a party to the Basel Convention regulating movement of hazardous waste at the time, the company had to work on a bilateral agreement by the Indian government with its US counterpart to enable the shipment. After crossing this major hurdle, preparations began to ship the waste to a mercury recycler in the US, namely Bethlehem Apparatus in Hellertown, Pennsylvania.[2]

HLL's environmental consultants, Dames & Moore, developed a protocol for its repacking, labelling and safe transportation to the designated port in the US, besides the protocols to ensure the safety of the personnel handling the waste onboard. Once the protocol was approved by the regulator, the waste was moved from the factory site in special trucks to a warehouse downhill near Madurai, where it was packed into 1,416 specially made leak-proof drums. From there, it was transported to the Tuticorin Port for transshipment to New York.

Until the shipment left Indian shores, it was crucial for us to follow its movement, but the company remained tight-lipped about the details. With no social media back then, it was the traditional media, newspapers and TV channels that had to be solely depended on to be the watchdogs.

Here too it was Dr Jayaraman who proved his exceptional journalistic skills yet again. Born in Mayiladuthurai, east of Kodaikanal, he had been deeply concerned about the devastation being wrought in the hill station. He'd also enjoyed a long association with astrophysicists at the Kodaikanal Solar Observatory, a facility set up in 1899. On 16 April 2003, PTI published Dr Jayaraman's first report on the waste movement, after the packing was completed and the shipping was set for 23 April aboard a carrier named *Indmax Dalian*: 'HLL has at last arranged to ship the hazardous mercury and related wastes from its now defunct thermometer factory in Kodaikanal back to US.' Quoting me as a 'Greenpeace official', the article appeared in newspapers across the country the next day under the headline, 'India Sends Hazardous Waste Back to US'.[3]

For the first time in history, a developing/underdeveloped country was sending back a consignment of waste material to a developed country. Developing countries were often used as dumping grounds by their richer counterparts for electronic goods like printers, copying machines and computers as a way of saving money on waste disposal. Even today the electronic waste dumping by developed countries continues unabated with countries in Asia and West Africa being the chief destinations.

This action conveyed a powerful message to the developed

world. In a stroke of Promethean creativity, Dr Jayaraman would describe this phenomenon as 'reverse dumping', explaining how '1416 drums filled with 290 tons of hazardous mercury waste from a thermometer factory, at Kodaikanal in Tamil Nadu' were being sent back to the US.[4]

The next day, a majority of Indian newspapers carried the report with more creative headlines. For instance, the headline in the leading newspaper of the time in New Delhi, the *Statesman*, read, 'Dump for a dump, from India to US'.[5] But the catchphrase of 'reverse dumping' caught on. International news agencies like Reuters, AFP and AP flashed it to the world, after which it was used to describe any waste shipment returned to its place of origin.

Then came some startling information from a reliable insider at the Tuticorin seaport which was being closely watched by us. The shipment had not left the seaport on 23 April, as scheduled. The consignment had to leave Tuticorin on 23–24 April in three or four different carriers, because the carrier *Indmax Dalian* had limited space. However, the US authorities had objected to the toxic waste shipment being split into separate consignments. They insisted it on a single carrier.[6] Because there wasn't any carrier available to accommodate 290 tonnes in one lot, the shipment had been delayed and the company was left scrambling to arrange a viable carrier.

One more problem awaited the company: storing a shipment of hazardous waste material at a busy transhipment location. The US Code of Federal Regulations for Transfer Facility Requirements requires that any cargo carrying mercury can be stored at a transfer facility for only up to ten days during the course of transportation, as Greenpeace USA pointed out to me.[7] Casey Harrell from Greenpeace USA, who was monitoring the cargo arrival at the American side, shared copies of the relevant portions of the Federal Register with me while his team took up the issue with their authorities. This reflected the poor planning and callous attitude of the company in handling such a dangerous consignment. It was obvious that the arrangements for a single carrier shipment had not been made in advance. Rather, the responsibility had been left to the shipping agents to handle as they wished.

On behalf of Greenpeace India, I filed an objection with the Indian regulator on this severe lapse. This act of negligence called for close monitoring at the port location until the cargo had left the port. But the question was: who could be entrusted with this responsibility?

My next stop was the office of the *Hindu* on Mount Road in Chennai. Over a cup of coffee, senior editor M. R. Subramani revealed that the *Hindu BusinessLine* had a resourceful shipping correspondent, T. E. Raja Simhan, who could help us out. He called to explain the situation to Raja Simhan, who got to work immediately.

On 4 May, Sunday, the *Hindu BusinessLine* published a detailed report on the status of the cargo lying at the port, which referenced the concern voiced by Greenpeace about the shipment remaining at the port for a prolonged period. It said: '17 FEU (forty-foot equivalent units) loaded with the mercury waste to leave on May 7 by the container vessel, *Indamex-Chesapeake*, belonging to the CMA-CGM line'.[8]

In addition to article in the *Hindu*, the largest TV network of Tamil Nadu, Sun TV, was alerted to the developments. Its Tuticorin correspondent and cameraman agreed to monitor the movements from within the port. Then on 6 May, in a daring act, our team, along with the Sun TV team, sneaked into the port and reported the visuals of the consignments being loaded onto the vessel. The following day, I formally visited the port office with a representative of the local community, where we confirmed that the *Indamex-*

*Chesapeake* had indeed left the port that morning, carrying on its board the dangerous cargo.

All this while, I had been inundated with calls from the media, from international press such as the *New York Times* and Associated Press to the local Tamil newspapers and TV channels. In fact, the calls had begun on 16 April, since Dr Jayaraman's report had been published. The international news outlets were waiting for the cargo's departure to file their reports. The information was first shared with Saritha Rai, the India correspondent of the *New York Times* and George Iype, the correspondent of the Associated Press, who remained in constant touch with me. Subsequently, we informed all interested media over calls.

The *New York Times* would report on Greenpeace's triumph thus: 'In what environmental activists in India are hailing as a major victory, tons of hazardous waste from an abandoned thermometer factory owned by India's largest consumer products company, Hindustan Lever Ltd, is heading to a recycling plant in the United States for safe disposal.'[9] The report quoted me as 'the corporate campaign coordinator for Greenpeace India', terming the shipment 'reverse dumping'.[10] In fact, this was one of the first questions put to me: 'Do you think this is reverse dumping?' Dr Jayaraman's coinage had managed to rouse an international debate, I realized.

The detailed reports of the *New York Times* and AP, including the consignment arrival at the New York port on 29 May served one more purpose: to make the US authorities and civil society aware of what was coming for them. We handed over the responsibility to Greenpeace USA, which followed up on the shipment's safe arrival in New York, and from there until its final destination at Bethlehem Apparatus in Hellertown, Pennsylvania. For almost two months until the first week of June 2003, every single one of us were on our toes as the news thrust the country into global headlines for all the wrong reasons.

# 34

# DIRECT ACTIONS

THE 'ACTION TEAM' OF GREENPEACE, TRUE TO ITS TITLE, KEEPS busy. The campaign team explores ways to work with victim communities, regulators and the civil society, using scientific research, and hold the wrongdoers accountable for their actions. The policy team engages with the government to advocate for greener policies, while the communications team coordinates with the media and handles the digital and traditional messaging of the campaigns to ensure maximum visibility for the work of other teams.

The action team might unfurl a gigantic banner atop a factory or a monument like the Taj Mahal, confronting a CEO directly, or chaining themselves in front of a company's office and so on. The core principle is that the means of creating awareness about an issue have to be peaceful, and without causing any damage to an individual or property. It should also have a clear message. The 'direct actions', as Greenpeace calls it, originated from one of its founder's advisory to the organization to follow the Quakers' tradition of 'bearing witness' – registering protest by being at the scene of an objectionable activity. Following the advice, its campaigners soon started taking meaningful actions to stop unacceptable and dangerous practices by governments, corporations, mafia and lobbies, in the process, even risking their lives at times.

By positioning themselves in front of a dangerous situation, campaigners try to bring attention to previously hidden environmental abuses, inspire public outrage and get destructive practices and policies withdrawn or amended.[1] It is the responsibility of the action team to come up with innovative ideas for various campaign areas and to keep staging new actions, so that the issues remain fresh in the minds of the general public and administrators, besides forcing the perpetrators to resolve them.

In the summer of 2003, the team came up with the idea of 'lake action'. As part of it, the campaigners would hold a large banner on a boat in the middle of Kodai Lake with slogans like 'Clean up Mercury in Kodai' and 'Healthcare for Workers'. So far the only other major 'action' against HLL was the protest in November 2002 when the volunteers had chained themselves in front of the HLL office in Chennai. The protest was also part of a vehicle tour called 'jatha', which began from Bengaluru on 10 November, covering various hotspots of industrial pollution in southern cities such as Mangalore and Doddaballapura in Karnataka, Chennai and Cuddalore in Tamil Nadu and Kochi and Kasaragod in Kerala.[2] When the jatha, carrying the message of 'No More Bhopal', reached Chennai, some of the twenty-odd activists travelling on the bus chained themselves to a bar in front of the HLL office.

I had several reservations about the proposed 'lake action', more so with 'actions' that wouldn't help the organization gain any significant visibility or traction in general.

First, this 'action' would not get any attention from the company. A banner hoisted in the middle of the lake might make for a good photo opportunity but would not generate great media interest. Also, because of the poor presence of electronic media in the hill town, the only traction it could get would be from the tourists. I suggested trying a more 'powerful action'; but my objections were overruled by the Executive Director of Greenpeace India.

On a sunny day in December, Samir Nazareth and Adarsh Varshney, two core members of the action team, stood on a boat, with Mody sitting in the middle, holding up an oversized yellow banner stretching across the thirty-foot-long rowing boat for an hour, while the rower helped keep the boat afloat against the heavy wind. All the crew members on the boat were wearing white surgical suits. As expected, the event provided us a good photo opportunity.

A more significant action would take place at the Annual General Body (AGM) meeting of HLL, in which almost 2,000 ardent shareholders of the company would assemble at the Birla Matushri Hall at Marine Lines, Mumbai. HLL had a reputation of being one of the most trustworthy companies among capital market investors. Patient shareholders never lost their investment in the company's shares. Rather its share value had only gone higher and higher since its formation as Hindustan Lever Ltd in 1956. Unlike many other fly-by-night operators and dubious companies, Lever had treated its investors very well, who in turn implicitly trusted the company. The investors were paid dividends every year and at the annual shareholders' meeting, some tokens of appreciation would be distributed to the attending shareholders. It was how the company had generated a cult-like following among its shareholders over a long period of time.

People would travel from faraway places like Pune and Thane to attend the meeting. Many of them read the company's annual report diligently, like school children preparing for their final examinations. They would appear, notes in hand, to ask questions at the meeting. Every year they all returned satisfied with the company's performance that year and the rosy projection of its performance subsequently.

I had proposed that our next 'action' take place at the AGM which the action team concurred with. The objective was not to embarrass the company and its management so much, but to inform its trusting shareholders about the company's wrongdoing.

The first challenge was to gain access to the venue. The entry to AGMs is generally controlled by issuing attendance slips and proxy forms along with annual reports that are dispatched directly to the shareholders' addresses by post. The action team was ready with an alternative strategy to enter the venue. But there was a problem. The professional security services manning the gates would throw them out immediately, should they be identified. They might even hand the intruders over to the police.

We wanted to ensure we were entering the venue in a legitimate fashion. This meant that all those planning to be present needed to be shareholders of the company. We would have to buy at least one share of the company in order to be invited to the meeting. Unfortunately, the company had already closed the books and sent out the AGM invites and proxy forms, along with that year's annual report. This left us with one last option: Shareholders can engage proxies to attend the meeting on their behalf with the help of duly signed proxy forms. We tried to seek the help of a few sympathizers, who would be willing to sign proxy forms for us. Our endeavour hit another roadblock at this point, because we only had four or five signed proxy forms when we needed at least a dozen. Then with two days to go for the 13 June 2003 meeting, we were aided by a bearded saviour: Ganesh Nochur.

A long-time resident of Mumbai, Nochur was a dynamic civil rights activist. Having been associated with Medha Patkar on the Narmada Bachao Andolan and the consequent tribal habitat displacement in western India, Nochur was now working with the Bhopal Gas Tragedy victims to get them justice. Nochur recollected the annual reports of companies piling up in the stockbrokers' offices those days – annual reports sent by companies to investors who used to engage stockbrokers to trade on their behalf. The brokers, in turn, provided their office addresses as the investors' addresses. He reached out to a couple of them in Mumbai and briefed them on the requirement. With Nochur acting on our behalf, the remaining proxy forms came in without much trouble.

Two days before the AGM, to bring the Mumbai media up to speed on the developments, Greenpeace organized an event to release the report of the Indian People's Tribunal headed by Justice S. N. Bhargava, which had found that ex-workers of HLL thermometer factory suffer from occupational health problems. With that to set the ball rolling, everything was in place for the AGM. All the dozen-plus people supposed to enter the AGM were briefed on the drill after people from other locations arrived in Mumbai the day before. The action team carried out the last recce of the venue and made note of the ongoing preparations there.

The next morning, by 10.30 a.m., everyone assembled in front of the Birla Matushri Hall in Marine Lines. After briefing everyone one final time, we checked to ensure if there were any last-minute concerns from the protesters. By 10.55 a.m., all the dozen-plus proxies were inside the hall and seated at different corners. Soon, all the dignitaries were invited to be seated on the dais. Senior executives led by the chairman and CEO, Vindi Banga, occupied seats, and the programme began.

As the seating and introductory announcements were made, the Greenpeace volunteers began circulating a small, postcard-size card with a message to the audience which read: 'A business that makes nothing but money, is a poor kind of business'.[3] This quote had been borrowed from the year's HLL annual report, which had previously borrowed it from the American businessman Henry Ford, founder of the Ford Motor Company.

No one suspected that anything was amiss. Everyone assumed that the card was being distributed by the company staff. Especially because the message was highlighted in the annual report, which was in the hands of some of the shareholders. At least until the first volunteer got up to ask a question after the addresses had been delivered by the executives and the stage was available for questions from shareholders.[4] Someone tried to prevent him since he hadn't registered to ask a question, but eventually he was allowed to get up on stage. He started with posing, 'Are you aware that hundreds of our ex-workers and the local community are suffering because of the irresponsible act committed by our company in the hill station of Kodaikanal? As a shareholder, I am ashamed that our company is acting against what we preach.' As he stood flashing Henry Ford's message, shock waves went through both the panel on the podium and the audience. There had been instances previously where shareholders pointed out the lapses in selling a loss-making business, acquiring a company for a high value, or for lack of expected returns on share prices in the past year. But never in the history of its AGMs had a shareholder accused the company of wrongdoing in this manner.

Once he'd recovered from the shock, Vindi Banga tried to respond, somewhat ineffectively, assuring the audience that the company was looking into the matter. He went on to say the company had 'acted responsibly' and as soon as the issue was brought to the management's notice, the factory had been shut down. He did not, however, elucidate their plans as to how they were going to deal with the burning issue of workers' health and the clean-up of the factory site and its surroundings.[5]

Another questioner pointed out that Justice (retd.) Bhargava's report too had found fault with HLL for its environmental impact analysis in Kodaikanal, concluding that the ex-workers of the factory were suffering from the effects of occupational health hazards. Banga responded to this by claiming the IPT panel was 'shying away' from the claims in its own report and had included a disclaimer in it saying, 'it has no responsibility for the contents'. By picking up a stray line from the victims' affidavits section of the report, for which the panel had provided the disclaimer, it became clear the company did not have a clear defence.

Meanwhile, in the Backbay Reclamation office of HLL, the senior executives were furious as to how this had occurred. How had the activists sneaked into the meeting? Who had allowed them entry? Did someone from the company help them, perhaps some trade union leaders?

The chairman asked the company secretary to find out the gaps in their security at the AGM. In the meanwhile, the corporate communications division was asked to prepare a response to the points raised at the meeting and in the IPT report.

A serious search was conducted by the company secretary's office. Their dedicated team went through the entry forms, proxies and registers and gathered information from the security company and the company officials as to who had been manning the entry. After it had considered all possibilities, including a gate-crash, they reported to the senior management the next day that the volunteers had, in fact, entered the meeting hall as proxies. But they could not rule out the possibility of a couple of people sneaking in without proxy authorization. The senior management left with a warning to all divisions involved in organizing the meeting – from the company secretary to the communications department – to take all precautions to avoid such embarrassments in the future.

The news that the reality of the Kodaikanal issue had reached their shareholders was not received well by the top company executives or Lever's London and Rotterdam offices.

The following day, when the incident was reported by newspapers, it would also reach the ears of the larger shareholders of the company. By that time, the corporate communications division had prepared a point-by-point counter on all the levelled allegations. This was done after a lot of back and forth between various teams – from health and safety, environment, legal, company secretary and the factory manager – and clearances from the vice chairman, chairman and the global headquarters. HLL decided to issue its response as a press release, countering the issues raised by Greenpeace and its volunteers at the AGM.[6] But what the company didn't realize at the time was that it had been tricked into formally engaging in a debate in public on the topic.

On 15 June, Greenpeace released their response to HLL's counter, refuting the hollowness of the rejoinder and castigating the company for its callous attitude towards the people of Kodaikanal. To refute the 'IPT's no responsibility disclaimer', as referenced by HLL, it quoted the IPT disclaimer itself which read, 'It should be noted that the statements presented below are entirely the version of the person or group that has submitted it before the Indian People's Tribunal Panel. Therefore, the IPT has no responsibility on whatever is said in the statements.' Greenpeace argued it would become clear to any reader that the phrase HLL had picked up, related only to the statements submitted/deposed before the panel by the victims and not to the report's conclusions.[7] The Greenpeace statement reminded the company that the panel had conclusively pointed out its findings on the company's lack of accountability, and it had not hesitated to stand by its report.

It further advised the CEO to read Part III of the IPT Report where the recommendations of the panel criticized the company for 'the manner in which information has been presented, the contradictions in the statements and subsequent re-workings of the mercury balance' and chastised the company for its 'concerted attempt to misrepresent with incorrect declarations and the true facts in this matter'.[8] Besides being another milestone in the struggle, in more ways than one, the 2003 'AGM action' would serve as an example and mock exercise for more powerful actions and messaging in subsequent years.

# 35

# RAINBOW WARRIOR IN MUMBAI

RUTH STRINGER HAD FELT DISAPPOINTED ON LEARNING THAT THE Greenpeace lichen study had been outsmarted by the DAE study. But as a true scientist, she was pleased to see scientific discoveries revealing the glaring omissions of HLL. She was particularly satisfied with the results of the air sampling carried out by DAE. So, when the Greenpeace Research Laboratory picked up the DAE study, Stringer was preparing to travel to India sometime in the first quarter of 2004. She advanced her travel plans to release the Greenpeace report early, to keep the heat up along with the DAE study and confront HLL with more scientific evidence.

She reached India in December 2003 to coincide with the arrival of Greenpeace's iconic campaign vessel *Rainbow Warrior* in Mumbai. The plan was to release the report formally from the campaign ship and hand over a copy directly to the company officials at its Lever House office in Backbay Reclamation in Mumbai. The action would surprise them in serendipity with *Rainbow Warrior*'s Mumbai other planned actions in Mumbai.

The vessel had many other agenda items, like most of its archetypal campaigns. Since its launch attempt to disrupt the Icelandic whaling fleet in 1978, it had become the backbone of

Greenpeace campaigns around the world – like most of its actions on climate change, such as initiatives to save the ocean, anti-GMO efforts (Genetically Modified Organisms), and anti-toxic, anti-whaling, anti-seal hunting, anti-nuclear testing and anti-nuclear waste dumping campaigns.

The first green campaign vessel of its sort, *Rainbow Warrior* had attracted global attention since it was bombed by the Direction Generale de la Securite Exterieure (DGSE), the French government's intelligence agency, in July 1985 at the Port of Auckland in New Zealand. The incident sank the ship, killing Dutch freelance photographer Fernando Pereira. At the end of two years of embarrassment and shame, French Prime Minister Laurent Fabius, admitted the state's involvement and the country ended up paying a compensation of $8.1 million to Greenpeace following an international arbitration.

Since then, it had locked horns with many powerful nations, corporations, lobbies and mafia. Even the news of the *Rainbow Warrior*'s arrival would send shock waves among the alleged offenders and authorities.

The Indian authorities were no different.

The 2003 India tour of *Rainbow Warrior* was held on the twenty-fifth anniversary of Greenpeace launching the first and original *Rainbow Warrior* campaign vessel, a 40-metre refitted fishing trawler named after *Warriors of the Rainbow* from an old native American prophecy that went along these lines: 'When the earth is ravaged and the animals are dying, a new tribe of people shall come unto earth from many colours, classes, creeds who by their actions and deeds shall make the earth green again. They will be known as the warriors of the rainbow.' Picking up this prophecy, the veracity of which has been claimed and counterclaimed, a 1962 book titled *Warriors of the Rainbow* by William Willoya and Vinson

Brown, quotes, 'Just before it was too late, the Indian would regain his spirit and teach the white man reverence for the earth, banding together with him to become Warriors of Rainbow.'[1]

*Rainbow Warrior* was sailing from the Gujarat coast where it went to campaign against dangerous ship-breaking practices and the consequent marine pollution at Alang, the site of the world's largest ship-breaking yard, where old and retired vessels come for its death. They are rather broken down into pieces to retrieve all valuable remnants, while dumping the waste including deadly asbestos, into the sea and along the shores.

On 12 November, when the vessel landed at the Alang port, another trawler named the *Genova Bridge*, laden with toxic substances like asbestos, waste oil, sludge, the carcinogenic polychlorinated biphenyl and tributyltin was beached at the port for breaking up. Without wasting any time, the *Rainbow Warrior* asked the port authorities and the Government of India to send the vessel back to its port of origin, the UK. After continuous protests and demands for it to be sent back, the Indian Ministry of Environment and Forests directed the Gujarat Pollution Control Board to inspect the vessel. Upon searching, the board found the allegations of toxic load to be true.

Then came the blow. The Gujarat Maritime Board, which oversees the port operations, asked the Indian Navy and rhe Coast Guard to seizc *Ruinbow Warrior* and arrest its crew. The board was angered by its actions of forcing to send back old vessels meant for breaking down, impacting the shipbreaking industry in the state. But to the surprise of most Greenpeace volunteers, the request was turned down by the Navy and Coast Guard.

Acting on the behest of the state authorities, the customs office at Alang confiscated all the original papers of travel permissions of the vessel, refusing to return them despite repeated requests. Adding to that, under mounting pressure from the ship-breaking industry, no local shipping agent was willing to represent Greenpeace and the *Rainbow Warrior* to talk to the customs. A few days later, the vessel made a quiet retreat from Alang and sailed to Mumbai without any travel documents. When it anchored at the Mumbai Port on 30 November, it was not allowed to dock in for almost eight days. As many as twenty-six crew members, belonging to fourteen different countries, were stranded at sea, with dwindling food and water supplies for over a week.[2]

After a lot of negotiations and interventions, when it was finally allowed to dock, the members of the crew were not allowed to disembark. Some of the crew members were to be relieved so they could take flights to their home countries. Others on the shore had to replace the relieving crew. In effect, the *Rainbow Warrior* was left with the challenge of accommodating nine days of scheduled activities in the next two days before the ship left for Cochin on 9 December,[3] causing everything to be done in a rush.

The media was invited for an onboard briefing on 8 December and the Greenpeace Research Laboratory study of mercury pollution in Kodaikanal was formally released, followed by a question-and-answer session. But we had also planned a small 'action' to coincide with the event.

Ruth Stringer and I emerged in front of Lever House at Backbay Reclamation without any notice. As we sought an appointment with the senior company executives inside the lobby, a large banner was unfolded outside Lever House, from the balcony of the next building with this message: 'HLL, own up responsibility for Kodai Pollution.'

Since the events of the AGM were still fresh in their memory, the company officials were reluctant to meet up with us, even in the company's own lobby. Also, because by that time, they had been informed that a huge banner had just been put up outside their office with messages against the company. On the intercom, they tried to convince us to leave the report at the reception desk. Upon our insistence and on sending a message that we would not leave the lobby without meeting a responsible senior executive, two senior officials came down – one from occupational health and safety and another a senior attorney of the company. In a conversation after handing over the report, Stringer explained its contents, the graveness of the issue and its ramifications.[4] I asked questions about the resolution of the issue and demanded a timeline for the clean-up. In total, the meeting must have lasted about ten minutes.

As we were leaving the Lever House building, several print and electronic journalists flocked to us outside. Copies of the report and of the prepared press release were shared with the media. Also, we agreed to provide some soundbites to the waiting TV channels. Albeit brief, our actions on that day had significant impact because we had struck the iron at the right time. And it helped us put our hands to the plough for the next steps.

# 36

# SHAREHOLDER ACTIVISM

AT GREENPEACE, THE TEAMS HAD BEGUN PREPARING FOR THE NEXT shareholders' meeting much in advance. Going by the previous years' experience, it was clear the company management would take all measures to ensure that our volunteers could not gain entry into the venue.

Since there were months to go before the AGM, I suggested that it would be easier if all the volunteers going into the meeting venue owned an HLL share each. The volunteers were identified and requested to buy one company share each through brokers. This would make one a legitimate shareholder and give them the power and authority to attend the meeting and ask questions to the company. In addition to the Greenpeace staff and some volunteers from Mumbai, ex-workers from Kodaikanal needed to be brought to the city, after each of them had also bought a share. This was to allow the victims to confront the company executives on their wrongdoings as individual shareholders.

Mody was contacted forthwith, and he began working with the ex-workers to ensure their presence in Mumbai for the meeting. Meenakshi pitched in with her support by personally meeting some of the ex-workers and enlisting them.

Contrary to the last year's action, the plan was that multiple actions should unfold at the event so that even if one attempt was foiled, another could succeed. The action team came up with a lot of ideas. The worst-case scenario was, of course, the possibility of police action and our volunteers getting arrested. Therefore, to prepare ourselves, we briefed an efficient local lawyer in advance who was kept on standby in case we needed legal support. Otherwise, it was the routine drill of 'Greenpeace actions' – recce, briefing, communication preparations, action materials and so on. With carefully designed strategies and airtight preparations, it was time for the second AGM action, on 29 June 2004, at the Birla Matushri Hall in Marine Lines, Mumbai.[1]

Early in the morning, I received a call from a journalist who asked me, 'Will you be spoofing the HLL AGM today?' This was a cause for concern. The journalist's question seemed to be born out of our actions at the previous meeting and his desire to witness whatever we had planned this time. But then again, I couldn't rule out the possibility of his leaking the entire plan to HLL or the company using him to find out our intentions.

Alarm bells began ringing in everybody's minds. More surprises were waiting for us when our volunteers arrived outside the venue at 10 a.m., almost an hour before the scheduled time. Heavy police cordons had been set up outside the hall. There were police barricades on the road outside, and at least fifty policemen in uniform were on duty. We could not tell if there were more of them in plainclothes. The venue looked like a volatile military post. Then I received a call from a volunteer who said, 'It doesn't look like we will be able to go inside as planned.'

'We will go ahead,' I replied. 'There will be no changes to the plan.'

Surprisingly, we faced no resistance at the entry point. The shareholder form had granted us entry smoothly. The same volunteer called back, saying, 'I am in. No problem at the entrance.'

The message was relayed to all other volunteers through a text message since moving in groups could raise suspicion. The exception was the ex-workers from Kodaikanal, each of whom had been accompanied by a Greenpeace volunteer from the hotel because of their poor knowledge of the city. Then came another challenge. There were metal detectors and body searches at the entry points. At least two of the action team members were carrying large banners to hold up inside the hall. Would it be seized upon discovery? It could also spoil the entire action plan. But there was no time to change our minds or discard the banners. The only option was the calculated risk of carrying the banners inside.

The action team leaders, Adarsh Varshney and Samir Nazareth, came up with the idea of tucking the banners inside their boxer shorts. It worked because the security guards did not dare search their undergarments. Both of them, along with the two banners, were inside the venue by 10.50 a.m.

Learning from our experience the previous time, as a wily strategy, this time we had also decided to register at least ten Greenpeace campaigners and volunteers who would ask questions at the meeting and each of them had been told to prepare the questions ahead of time. The ones who would ask questions walked to the podium and entered their names in the register once everyone was inside the venue. The person guarding the register, likely a company official, was scrutinizing the people writing down their names as if attempting to figure out who they were. Ten Greenpeace volunteers had registered their names. In fact, not only that, they were also the first ten names on the list.

As the meeting opened with an address by the chairman and managing director of the company Vindi Banga, two wide yellow banners came up in the audience. They were carrying messages that read, 'HLL, take responsibility for Kodai Mercury,' and 'HLL, apologize for Kodai Mercury Pollution.'[2] Immediately, the press photographers and videographers seated facing the podium jumped to stand on their chairs for a better view, aiming their cameras towards us. This caused some chaos and confusion for a couple of minutes. During this commotion, all Greenpeace volunteers inside the venue pulled over a white T-shirt emblazoned with 'HLL, clean up Kodai' over their shirts. Within a few minutes, the security guards and company officials moved to the volunteers holding the banners and asked them to bring them down. When they refused, the volunteers were moved out of the hall with mild force.

After the speeches by the company executives, it was time for the question-and-answer session with shareholders. The first name was called out: Miriam Joseph. A woman wearing a white kurta and blue shawl walked up to the podium. As she began speaking, praising the shareholder value of the company and touching upon certain aspects of the social responsibility projects mentioned by earlier speakers, the company executives heaved a sigh of relief. At least, she wasn't criticizing the company. What they didn't know was that Miriam had moved to India a year ago after spending time with the BBC and Channel 4.[3]

She quickly moved on to the atrocities committed by the company at the closed mercury thermometer factory in Kodaikanal and demanded to know which steps were being taken to remediate the contaminated site. She then raised the issue of rehabilitation of the ex-workers and demanded, as a shareholder, a public apology from the company. In response, Vindi Banga got up to say that the company was doing the best it could and working with an external consultant and the Pollution Control Board to resolve the issue to the satisfaction of all concerned.

Then came the second questioner, S. A. Mahindran, the president of the ex-workers' union. He recalled the case of an ex-worker, Vijayalakshmi, who had worked as a contract worker in the factory for five years since she was twenty-one. A young and healthy person, her health had started deteriorating after working for a few years at the factory. Ignoring the advice of doctors, she continued to work there through her illness, hard-pressed for a livelihood. She suffered multiple miscarriages, developed a tumour in her uterus and had been living with irregular periods for a while since then. As many as twenty-three of his colleagues had died young, Mahindran said, and further inquiry into all the deaths had revealed complications resulting from mercury exposure such as lung- and heart-related problems and kidney failure.

The third questioner was Nochur. One by one, all of them were posing questions about Kodaikanal – the impact of mercury, health conditions of ex-workers, damage to a pristine ecosystem and so on. Vindi Banga fielded all the questions to defend his firm; it may very well have been the toughest day of his career at HLL.

The last of the ten names was mine. As the campaigner leading the activities, I had moved closer to the podium at the beginning of the session to ensure all the Greenpeace questioners got their chance and to boost their confidence. Once my turn came, I pointed out that the company had been deliberately delaying the clean-up and remediation by not submitting the required protocols to the Tamil Nadu Pollution Control Board, believing the delay would result in reduction of the mercury levels in soil and air on its own. I emphasized that the DAE study had showed mercury levels outside the factory at dangerous levels too.[4]

A company official, who had been standing near the podium until now with his eyes fixed on me, booed me while I was walking out. Another person came closer to me and whispered some words in my ears in Marathi, which I did not understand. Having completed the mission successfully, we all moved out of the venue with glee. As the team stepped outside the venue, the media thronged around us and hurled a barrage of questions in our direction: 'What are you going to do next?' 'Do you think HLL will resolve the issue?'

The communication team distributed the press releases that had been kept ready. After a quick debrief, standing on the wayside and cheering one another, it was time for us to call it a day.

# 37

# FROM BOARDROOMS TO TV STUDIOS

THOUGH THE AGM ACTION WAS OVER BY NOON, THE DAY WAS just beginning – for me and for HLL officials. High drama began unfolding at Lever House by afternoon, with TV channels flashing the questions raised by shareholders at the meeting. Many channels were showing visuals of shareholders posing direct questions to the chairman regarding the company's accountability with respect to Kodaikanal. Banga was furious, especially because he had given strict instructions to all concerned to take every possible security measure in order to ensure that the previous year's debacle wouldn't be repeated. But it had. And in certain respects, it had received even more attention and media frenzy this time.

All divisions involved in the AGM were asked to check for gaps in their part of the event, and report their findings to the vice chairman, M. K. Sharma, who was handling the Kodaikanal issue by then. The health and safety, and environment and operations divisions categorically said they had provided all the required inputs to the communications and legal divisions and were not directly involved in organizing the meeting. The office of the company secretary responded that it too had no direct role in managing the event, beyond providing the list of the shareholders. The legal division too claimed no direct involvement in the meeting. The corporate communications division responded that since the event was an AGM, the media had been expected to turn up without invitation, and it would have been unfair to turn them away. But they had ensured no unidentified reporter was allowed inside the hall and none of the activists could use the media route for entry.

The buck stopped at the marketing division. They had taken the support of an external event management firm, so when it came to taking responsibility, the division blamed it on the event manager. With media queries flooding in, the corporate communications division began preparing a response justifying the company's position and carrying details of all the actions being taken by it on the Kodaikanal issue. But halfway through, a message arrived from their global counterparts advising not to release a media statement this time.

Learning from the previous years' experience, the higher-ups at the company had chosen not to engage the opponent while on the defensive side. A famous African proverb was quoted by someone, 'Even if you dance for your enemy on the rock, he will accuse you of splashing water on him.' But despite the company's hands-off approach, the issue was raised at the next board meeting by one of the independent directors.

I was flooded with the media queries within hours of the 'action': Reporters wanted to clarify doubts; editors wanted some additional details. Meanwhile, we had to arrange a modest lunch for some volunteers, send home the ex-workers by train and so on. By that afternoon, a couple of national TV channels reached out with a request to feature us on their prime-time evening programme. This was on a day when the other major news was the conviction of eleven accused in the 1993 Mumbai serial blasts case. One of the requests was from NDTV, and we agreed to join its evening show.

Inside the studio with anchor Sreenivasan Jain, defending the company rather reluctantly on the other side was Gurcharan Das, the former CEO of Procter & Gamble Worldwide. It seemed obvious that he had acquiesced to join the show after the company executives had refused to share the platform with members of Greenpeace on such a high-decibel issue.

On the show, in order to create a lasting impact on the viewers, I had worn the same T-shirt from the morning action. Das astutely chose not to defend the company's actions directly but attempted to present a ringside view in his arguments and create a round fence for HLL. At the same time, expressing concern about the growing tendency of activists to take on corporates.[1] In response, I quoted from the 2003 Annual Report of HLL and reminded the company of its own statement that 'to succeed requires the highest standards of corporate behaviour towards [our] employees, consumers and the societies and [the] world in which we live'.[2]

The half-hour programme was a scoop of its own kind. In those thirty minutes, the Kodaikanal issue became a topic of interest across the country, cutting across different sections of people. It also heralded the arrival of shareholder activism in India. Since then, protests at Unilever AGMs have become routine – both at the India as well as the global AGMs.

---

The campaigners for justice for Kodaikanal – activists and local community volunteers – had been raiding the Hindustan Unilever AGM in Mumbai every year until 2015, a year before the final settlement with the ex-workers took place, barring some years in between when the 'actions' were paused because of logistical issues and poor interest among lead campaigners.

Every year the company redesigned its strategy to deal with the raiders, avoid confrontation inside the AGM venue or mitigate the damage. The campaigners kept innovating and came out with new tactics every year to enter the venue, interrupt, pose uncomfortable questions and attract the shareholders' attention to the unresolved issue. In the 2015 AGM, some fifty-odd volunteers, including twelve ex-workers from Kodaikanal, reached the venue. A concerned shareholder named Deepika D'Souza brought up the long-pending issue, to which CEO Harish Manwani responded that 'the matter would be attended to immediately'. While the AGM was in progress, protesters faced a hostile police force, preventing them from distributing pamphlets, outside the venue. The attending shareholders were asked to surrender these pamphlets when they entered the venue. As the meeting went on, volunteers from the city joined the protesters in raising slogans of the company's improper conduct and human rights violations. The police eventually informed them they were barred from protesting anywhere near HUL's offices by a court order.[3]

The Kodaikanal mercury issue was raised at Unilever's global AGM multiple times over the last two decades, by shareholders affiliated to like-minded organizations. On a few occasions, the matter was accompanied with some drama. For instance, in 2015, Unilever's annual shareholders meeting in Leatherhead, UK, was interrupted by a group of people from 'Campaign for Justice in Kodaikanal', led by an outspoken former teacher Saleh Mamon, holding placards with messages like '#HULCleanUpUrMess' and asking unpleasant questions to Paul Polman on his company's failure to address its liabilities.

A week earlier, a report in *Sunday Times* had described the gravity of the situation in the Indian hill station with a screaming headline, 'Poison case puts Polman's green boasts on the line'.[4] Quoting the report, Mamon, who attended the meeting as a proxy shareholder, posed a slew of questions to Polman. His questions were on the need for an independent assessment of the extent of mercury contamination at the site given that the 2001 company-sponsored study was out of date and deeply contested; the need to have a monitoring mechanism set up to protect the environment from further spread of contamination; when the decontamination would resume; why the standard for clean-up was not according to the UK guidelines, i.e. 1 mg/kg, or 10 mg/kg as per the Dutch rules; the reason for the lack of an independent epidemiological study carried out to assess the mercury poisoning of ex-workers even after fourteen years of closing the factory; and why the company had not instituted an interim framework for the medical care of its ex-workers.

Polman in his response expressed appreciation for the questioner's concern about the issue but described the newspaper report as 'biased', claiming the company had held as many as sixteen meetings with the people involved to resolve the issues. In the subsequent AGM in 2016, Polman, who two years later formed an organization called 'Imagine' to help corporates eradicate poverty and inequality and stem runaway climate change, would be shouted down by shareholders with calls of 'Unilever is not as pure as it claims!'.[5] During this time, there were also protests by affected communities and their supporters in front of Unilever's global offices in London and Rotterdam.

Over the last two decades, numerous protests from environmental groups, activists and local communities have taken place at Unilever's AGMs and in front of its offices and facilities, since the first Mumbai AGM raid by Greenpeace in 2003 – probably more than any other corporation in the world. Every time it attracted wide media attention and generated heavy interest on social media. Eventually, these would go on to probably become one of the chief reasons why Unilever desperately wanted to settle with the ex-workers and move past the issue.

# PART VII

# GREENPEACE COMES TO INDIA

# 38

# 'MAKE IT A GREEN PEACE'

IN THE MIDST OF THE ALASKAN RAT ISLANDS IN THE BERLING SEA lies Amchitka, a 300-square-kilometre earthquake-prone, volcanic landmass. Equidistant from the western shores of the US and Canada, up in the North Pacific Ocean, the island is home to some 3,000 endangered sea otters, bald eagles, peregrine falcons and other forms of ocean life and wildlife. It came to be known as Rat Islands after a mischief of mice jumped off a sinking Japanese ship and settled there in 1780, and formed part of the US after President Andrew Johnson purchased Alaska for a sum of $7.2 million from the Russian empire in 1867. It was also where the US chose to carry out its nuclear tests in the sixties, namely, the Long Shot in 1965, Milrow in 1969 and Cannikin in 1971.

Not long after the Americans dropped nuclear bombs over the Japanese cities of Hiroshima and Nagasaki towards the end of the Second World War and wreaked carnage with Agent Orange in the Vietnam War, the Canadians began getting nervous upon witnessing two high-impact nuclear tests by their neighbour that created sky-high waves on the island shores.

The first of the three had left the citizens shocked. The second had breached the limits of their tolerance. Thus, when they heard about the possibility of a third test, many Canadians such as the conservationists Jim Bohlen, Irving Stowe and Paul Cote started to grow restive. They were getting exasperated that the local Sierra Club in Vancouver, the Canadian wing of the influential US environmental organization, of which they were members, was not doing enough to stop the nuclear tests. Then, recalling that in 1958 the Quakers had tried to sail a ship near the Bikini Atoll in South Pacific protesting against the atmospheric testing of hydrogen bombs, they began to quietly discuss this idea.

The bottled-up emotions exploded out of Bohlen when he received a call from a reporter. He blurted, 'We thought it would be a hell of a good idea to take a ship up to the Aleutian Islands and protest bombing.' The next day, on 9 February 1970, the headline in a local newspaper read: 'Sierra Club Plans N-Blast Blockade'.[1]

It wasn't a well-thought-out plan. Neither was it well received by officials at the Sierra Club headquarters in the US. The Canadian affiliate was advised to play a more neutral role as conservationists. But having gone to the press already, Bohlen, Stowe and Cote decided to stay the course. They formed a 'Don't Make A Wave Committee' with the sole aim of protesting against the upcoming nuclear test and made plans to procure a small craft for sailing to the place of action. Soon they realized, though, that the name 'Don't Make A Wave Committee', too long and verbose, wouldn't stick. 'People don't really relate to it, didn't know what it meant,' Bohlen would complain in one of the preparatory meetings in a Unitarian church at the 49th Avenue of Vancouver. Just then a hippy fieldworker from the federal government's Company of Young Canadians, Bill Darnell, jumped in with a phrase, '[It] had bound together the concerns of the planet and opposition to nuclear arms in a forceful new vision that would inspire some of the most effective environmental protests of all time'.[2]

'Make it a green peace!' Darnell shouted.[3]

And thus Greenpeace was born. In its brief history of fifty years and counting, the organization would pioneer a new kind of activism that would challenge many conventions and practices in the fields of conservation, environment, conflicts and the use of science.

# 39

# PHYLLIS CORMACK, EDGEWATER FORTUNE, CANNIKIN

THE NEWLY FORMED GREENPEACE QUICKLY PROCURED A 1941-made wooden fishing vessel that could carry a maximum crew of twelve people and displace about a hundred tonnes. Its name was *Phyllis Cormack.*

The *Phyllis Cormack*, aged and filthy as it might have been, was the conduit for transforming fantasy into reality. The problem was, now that the reality was staring at them, they could no longer avoid seeing it clearly: the kelp beds, tides, riptides, williwaws, red tape, legalities, gales and nothing between the members on it and the icy seas but the mossy, antique wooden tub. And then the Bomb.[1] At around 4 p.m. local time on 15 September 1971, the boat chugged into the North Pacific Ocean, wave by wave. It had ignored the last-minute calls from many, including Prime Minister Pierre Trudeau, who gave assurances that he had asked the US to stop the test.

The sailing *Phyllis Cormack* thus formally became *Greenpeace.* On board *Greenpeace* were three journalists and a photographer, including Ben Metcalfe of the Canadian Broadcasting Corporation (CBC), besides Bohlen, Stowe, Cote, Darnell and four other conservationists, along with the ship's sixty-five-year-old captain. And a historic journey soon got underway.

On 16 September, for a morning commentary on CBC radio, Metcalfe reported from the boat:

> We Canadians started the Greenpeacing of America last night, represented by 12 men in an 80-foot halibut boat on our way to the United States nuclear test island of Amchitka in the far Aleutians. Our goal is very simple, clear, and direct one – to bring about a confrontation between the people of death and the people of life. We do not consider ourselves to be radicals. We are conservatives, who insist upon conserving the environment for our children and future generation of man.[2]

Bob Hunter, a countercultural journalist on board, had carried with him a book of native American prophecies and myths called *Warriors of the Rainbow*. It became popular among the passengers, who kept reading it before passing it on to the next.

Sailing in the North Pacific was difficult, more so in a thirty-year-old wooden fishing boat. Additionally, the test had been delayed from its original schedule to sometime in early November.

Upon being refused entry into the Dutch harbour to replenish their dwindling supplies of food, water and fuel by the US Coast Guard, the boat stayed on the waters, off the island of Akutan. On 30 September, it was intercepted by the US Coast Guard and put under arrest by the commander of the *USS Confidence* for failing to notify the customs on its arrival at Akutan. With diminishing supplies and fuel, the arrest destroyed the morale of everyone onboard.

Then they received a surprising piece of telegram which rooted to the spot. Behind the commander's back, the crew of the *Confidence* sent the protesters a cablegram. Signed by seventeen sailors, it read:

> DUE TO THE SITUATION WE ARE IN, THE CREW OF THE *CONFIDENCE* FEEL THAT WHAT YOU ARE DOING IS FOR THE GOOD OF ALL MANKIND. IF OUR HANDS WEREN'T TIED BY THESE MILITARY BONDS, WE WOULD BE IN THE SAME POSITION YOU ARE IN IF IT WAS ALL POSSIBLE. GOOD LUCK. WE ARE BEHIND YOU ONE HUNDRED PER CENT.[3]

The message had come at a point when the *Greenpeace* crew was desperate for something to give a leg up to their morale.

The arrest became a turning point in their journey. Besides diverting the *Cormack* from her course, it came at a crucial time in terms of the sprits of everyone on the boat. No one could find out when Cannikin was going to explode, and the tension of waiting was becoming unbearable.[4] So they decided to retreat. But then more interesting developments unfolded with the nuclear test being delayed till the first week of November.

With three high-profile journalists on board, who shared daily updates through *CBC*, *Vancouver Sun* and the *Georgia Straight*, Greenpeace was able to quickly raise funds to buy a 154-foot converted minesweeper, *Edgewater Fortune*.

After being readied overnight, *Edgewater Fortune* headed to Amchitka with a twenty-eight-member crew as *Cormack* was retreating. Of course, four of the *Cormack* crew changed boats at the crossing. *Edgewater Fortune*, now rechristened as *Greenpeace*, was pulling off when the US President Richard Nixon announced the deadline of 4 November for the test. Beating back a storm and regaining the time lost in stops for repairs and fuelling, it sailed 1,100 km towards Amchitka. The vessel was closing in further when the nuclear device exploded on 6 November 1971. The 5-megatonne blast generated a reading of 7.0 on the Richter scale. Cannikin was intended to test the design of the Spartan anti-ballistic missile (ABM) interceptor – a high-yield warhead that produced copious amounts of X-rays and minimized fission output and debris to prevent blackout of ABM radar systems.[5]

Outrage started to pour in – from the Canadians to peace-loving citizens around the world. As these voices against the nuclear tests grew louder, nearly four months later, the United States government would announce an end to the tests in Amchitka, stating 'political and other reasons.'[6] Greenpeace had emerged victorious.

A year after the Amchitka tests, the French were planning to conduct nuclear tests at Moruroa Atoll in its Polynesian islands, some 5,000 kilometres off New Zealand in the South Pacific Ocean. Sensing the urgency and opportunity, Metcalfe gave snippet advertisements in some newspapers looking for a volunteer to sail to Moruroa and spoil the French show. By now, Darnell was heading the Greenpeace Foundation after receiving Bohlen and Stowe's backing for the top job. A Canadian-born former ski lodge operator would pick up the advertisement somewhere in the South Pacific and respond to it: David McTaggart, a stout, bald man, had quit his business over the trauma that followed in rescuing two of his employees, one without a leg, from an explosion caused by a gas leak down under in New Zealand.

He phoned up Darnell in Vancouver and asked him if Greenpeace could arrange for him a new, inflatable life raft and a long-range radio trans-receiver for him to sail to the Moruroa Atoll in his small boat, *Vega*. Darnell readily agreed, and McTaggart set out on a voyage. Indeed, it would turn out to be a long voyage with Greenpeace, where he would steer the organization clear off many turbulences and tornadoes in the consequent years and decades.

His days of tribulations started soon after the successful campaigns on board *Vega* in 1972 and 1973 to Moruroa Atoll. Beginning with a suit against the French government after French commandos boarded his vessel and allegedly beat him up, then by opening the first Greenpeace office and a bank account in Vancouver and later setting up Greenpeace offices in Paris and London by 1977. Settled in Europe thereon, he would return to Vancouver to negotiate a raging dispute between the Canada office and the US Office towards the end of the seventies.

In 1979, Greenpeace Vancouver sued the office in San Francisco for violation of trademark agreements; San Francisco retaliated by suing for slander. McTaggart rushed from Europe to clear things up, managing to persuade Greenpeace's European offices to pay off Vancouver's debts and uniting the North American and European groups under one umbrella – Greenpeace International, headquartered in the Netherlands.[7]

Over the next decade, McTaggart would lead the organization from an obscure small-town community group into a global organization of consequence. His association with Greenpeace would continue until McTaggart's untimely death in a car accident on 23 March 2001, the same day Hindustan Lever's Kodaikanal thermometer factory was shut down by the regulator for charges of environmental destruction after an exposé and protests led by Greenpeace.

# 40

# LOVE CANAL

AROUND THE WORLD, 'LOVE CANAL' IS A BUTTONED-DOWN SLANG used to describe the vagina. The exception is perhaps the people living in the state of New York, for whom it is an aborted canal project off the Niagara River around six kilometres south of Niagara Falls. It also marked the site of an environmental disaster that struck them half a century ago and where the global anti-toxic campaign found its origin in the 1970s.

Love Canal was dug to link the Niagara River to Lake Ontario, into which the Blackwater River from Watertown flowed down and emptied. It was excavated in 1894 to develop the area with water and electricity, under the leadership of engineer William Love, thus giving birth to its quirky name. But complications ensued and the project was abandoned halfway through.

Then, during the half-decade period till 1953, an entity named Hooker Chemical Company used the partially dug canal to dump almost 20,000 tonnes of chemical waste, including some well-established carcinogens, such as halogenated organics, chlorobenzenes and dioxin. After capping the sixteen-acre waste-fill with clay, Hooker sealed it and, after a while, quietly sold it off to the Board of Education of the City of Niagara Falls for a proceed of $1, by a deed which contained an indemnity clause absolving Hooker of any future damages and claims. Nevertheless, the board built the 99th Street Elementary School on a part of the land and sold off the remaining land with constructed houses.[1]

Over the years, the area turned into a bustling suburbia with close to 1,000 families, shops and other facilities. Most of the children from the colony attended the school, while people lived in houses built over the sealed hazardous waste. And then by the middle of 1970s, things began to turn dour. Through conversations, the mothers of the schoolchildren discovered that several of them had experienced miscarriages or given birth to babies with congenital defects, and the children of the locality were contracting cancer and dying of such illnesses at higher rates than normal.[2] Then in 1976, when groundwater levels began rising after an abnormal season of heavy snow and rainfall, part of Hooker landfill began to breach and leach, exposing the toxic waste and thereby contaminating the nearby water sources.

This set off some alarm bells.

In a series of investigative news reports in April 1978, *Niagara Gazette*, a prominent newspaper of the city, began to unravel the mystery behind the illnesses and deaths in the locality. The newspaper dug out details about the waste dumping by Hooker and the sale of the sealed landfill all the way back to twenty-five years and beyond. These reports would lead to one of the affected mothers, Lois Marie Gibbs, filing a suit in the local court in August 1978.

As things started going national and receiving media attention, President Jimmy Carter stepped in and declared a federal State of Emergency for the entire Love Canal area, offering rehabilitation. For the 239 families who lived in the first two rows near the landfill site, the government provided funding for a permanent relocation.[3]

The rest of them were encouraged to stay back, with assurances that they were safe.

By 1980, however, the Environmental Protection Agency (EPA) revealed that the blood tests of the remaining residents had indicated chromosome damage, making them more prone to genetic disorders and cancer. Outraged, the residents took two EPA employees hostage on a sudden move and demanded relocation of all the families. On 1 October 1980 President Carter signed a bill for the permanent relocation of all the families in the Love Canal area.[4]

Gibbs led the frontal attack from the locality. Through a 'Not in My Back Yard (NIMBY) campaign', she organized the local residents, first by forming a community association and later by taking on the state and the felonious corporation. Protracted battles followed, both in courtrooms and in front courts. By the end of 1983, the residents led by Gibbs and the Occidental Chemical Corporation, which had acquired Hooker Chemical Company by then, reached a legal settlement, wherein the latter agreed to pay nearly $20 million reparation to the residents.

Gibbs' work would contribute to the creation of EPA's Superfund programme, otherwise known as the Comprehensive Environmental Response, Compensation and Liability Act, the aim of which was to clean up toxic waste sites across the country. She would go on to win the 1990 Goldman Environmental Prize and the 1999 Heinz Award, besides getting nominated for the Nobel Peace Prize in 2003. Much later, in 1995, Occidental Chemical Corporation would have to pay another $129 million, to cover the federal government's clean-up costs at the site, in an action pursued by the government under the Superfund law.

Similar to Gibbs' organization, many other anti-toxic campaign organizations sprung up across the US during the late 1970s and early 1980s. Most of them merged by the mid-1980s to form the National Toxics Campaign and worked in collaboration with personalities such as actress Meryl Streep, whose organization, Mothers and Others for Pesticide Limits, was leading a campaign against the use of daminozide, the carcinogen also known as alar sprayed in apple orchards to ripen all the fruits simultaneously.

While this was unfolding in the mainland US, Greenpeace was busy working on a more perilous global issue offshore. Having started its activities in North America in the beginning of the seventies, Greenpeace's focus was now on a much larger issue impacting the existence of the planet itself – a campaign against incinerating toxic materials in the ocean through what it called the International (anti-)Ocean Incineration Campaign.

This was at a time when the US Defence Department was planning to procure ocean incineration vessels to burn stockpiled chemical munition waste, and the EPA was preparing to burn intractable industrial effluent off the East, West and Gulf coasts. In 1983, it mounted a fierce broadside against the US government for considering new waste disposal methods without first mandating toxic waste reduction and elimination.[5]

This was also the time when movements to build grassroots organizations with egalitarian doctrines and combating environmental destruction with a sense of community identity and ownership were taking shape. Owing to the mindless actions of the states and the indiscriminate profit-seeking ways of corporations, these movements were clustered mostly in the developed world where cases of gross infringement and damage to the environment and the larger biodiversity had been increasing year after year.

The campaign to eliminate toxic pollution generated by multinationals gained international significance because of its global proportions and the dangers it posed to the entire planet.

The momentum for anti-toxics campaigns became fierce, including issues such as the use of Agent Orange, and the risks posed by radiation informed the stance of anti-toxics campaigners, who framed their protests around health risks and corporate indifference towards host communities.[6]

Among all the developed countries, the US turned out to be the momentous, political rallying point for communities around the world, displaying concern about the growing environmental catastrophe, its dangerous health impacts and, therefore, for the anti-toxics movements. The reason being the US was far ahead of other nations in spreading consumerism and the consequent increased manufacturing – from housing to packaged water.

The new Left American activists who believed technology and science to be the vehicles for the capitalist state's imposition of modernity on local communities, started to protest against toxic dumps and plants, leading to a rise in eco-populism. With the federal government in Washington passing increasingly stringent anti-pollution laws, US multinationals began to look elsewhere for potential sites to relocate their plants.[7] This would eventually lead to the spread of the hazardous waste from the US to Europe and from there to Asia and then to Africa, as manufacturing facilities that produced heavy toxic waste were moved to vulnerable locations in developing countries that had jumped at the opportunity for the sake of generating employment and economic growth.

But the spread of eco-populism and development of resistance among local communities in the developing world would take much longer and many environmental disasters. One of them was the Bhopal Gas Tragedy.

# 41

# 'THE POISON GAS IS SPREADING!'

'*BACHAIYE HUZOOR, IS SHAHAR KO BACHAIYE* ... (LORD, PLEASE save this city)', cried a headline on 17 September 1982 in a small, obscure Hindi weekly from Bhopal named *Rapat*, with a circulation of about 2,000 copies an issue. The report was written by its printer, publisher and editor, Raj Kumar Keswani. It referred to the imminent catastrophe about to strike the city of Bhopal due to the pesticide-producing Union Carbide factory located in the middle of the city. The report was followed by two more dispatches with definitive evidence of the impending catastrophe quoting company documents on 1 and 8 October with the headlines '*Jwalamukhi ke muhane baitha Bhopal* (Bhopal on the mouth of a volcano)' and *Na samjhoge to aakhir mit hi jaoge* (If you don't understand, you will be wiped out)'.

While the third report was at the printing press for the 8 October edition, Keswani's prophetic warning turned true for the first time. A mixture of chloroform, methyl isocyanate (MIC) and hydrochloric acid escaped through a leaking valve from the factory, forcing people of the nearby slums to flee with their belongings. They would return to their homes only after eight to ten hours, once the gas in the air had subsided.

Convinced of a catastrophe in waiting, Keswani was hot on the heels of the story. He wrote another long piece along the same lines in the Hindi daily newspaper *Jansatta* on 16 June 1984, and a letter to the chief minister of Madhya Pradesh about the possible danger. His warnings were largely derived from the problems cited by Union Carbide's own safety report of May 1982.[1] But the government failed to pay heed to the cries of help and Keswani's repeated warnings of the disaster looming on their horizon.

Then came the fury of the poison, followed by death and destruction. On the intervening, chilly winter night of 2 and 3 December, a foreman cleaning the inside of the piping near the methyl isocyanate (MIC) reactor in the factory missed inserting a slip blind – a metal shield – to stop water from reaching the reactor, causing disaster to strike.[2] Almost 30 metric tonnes of the dangerous gas MIC, belonging to the organic family of cyanides and cyanates, began to leak, spewing venom through the night. Most people ran helter-skelter to save their lives and families. Those who were sleeping died in their beds and others choked to their deaths.

As the poison gas filled the air, the factory staff, the city administration and even the fire brigade and the police left in chaos. The police, unaware of which gas had leaked and what to tell the public, blared around on loudspeakers, 'Run! Run! The poison gas is spreading!' Consequently, people ran outside and inhaled more poison than they would have otherwise.[3] Death and devastation continued unabated for days and months, and even for years.

The exact human toll is still unknown; but an estimated 5,000 people died within two days, and eventually, this number swelled over 20,000. A total of 200,000 in a city of 800,000 – the population of Bhopal in 1984 – were exposed to the gas. More than 60,000 of them required long-term treatment.[4] The Bhopal Gas Tragedy was a catastrophe of unthinkable proportions. But unlike natural disasters it was caused by the callousness and negligence of a corporation and accentuated by misdemeanours one after another, finally leading to an apocalypse.

Around the time, Greenpeace, with no presence in India as yet, began to closely watch the developments in the country from its global headquarters.

# 42

# BIRTH OF THE *RAINBOW WARRIOR*

'IT IS SAID THERE WILL BE A TIME WHEN THE TREES ARE DYING, blah, blah, blah. There will be a tribe of people who come and save the Earth and they will be called the Rainbows,' so goes the altered version of the Native American or First Nations Prophecy from the book *Warriors of the Rainbow* published in 1962.[1]

Since its publication, some of the book's verses have been widely misquoted to suggest that a time of crisis will dawn upon the earth, when people of diverse races will join together to save the planet. In fact the misinterpretation of the original verses have inspired millions to think about the fragility of the planet and attempt to live in sustainable ways. It has also motivated many to take to the path of conservationism and environmentalism for the larger interests of the planet. So when Greenpeace bought a used ship from the British government in 1977 for an amount of £44,000, the first words that struck the organization while trying to come up with a name for the ship was the rhetoric passage from William Willoya and Vinson Brown's book: '*The world is sick and dying, the people will rise up like Warriors of the Rainbow.*' And they named it *Rainbow Warrior.*

It was the 1955-built, 418-tonne, 145-foot-long *Sir William*

*Hardy*, which was being used by the Ministry of Agriculture, Fisheries and Food as a research vessel. Whatever the boat's outward appearance, an expert ship-making engineer confirmed that it would, eventually, make a good campaign vessel. Greenpeace, however, was yet to cobble together £44,000 to pay for the boat. It took them eight months to raise enough money to make a ten per cent down payment, and the balance then had to be paid within sixty days.[2] While the team was struggling to find resources to pay for the boat, McTaggart managed to convince the Dutch World Wildlife Fund to provide a £40,000 grant for a campaign against Icelandic whaling. It came at the most opportune time and brought things back on track. Soon *Sir William Hardy* was transformed into *Rainbow Warrior*.

Painted dark green, with the word 'Greenpeace' emblazoned across its side and the image of dove carrying an olive branch on the bow, the boat was rechristened *Rainbow Warrior*, a name inspired by the same collection of Indian legends that had influenced the first Greenpeace crew.[3] On 29 April 1977 *Rainbow Warrior* sailed out from its London repair dock, flying the flags of Greenpeace and the United Nations, the latter reflecting a global crew belonging to twenty-four nationalities. First it journeyed to the East Lothian coast, to support a protest of more than 3,000 people against the construction of a nuclear reactor. Next to its first Icelandic mission to stop whaling. Thereafter, it reached wherever there was a large attack on the earth, with abundant support, protesting against issues like nuclear testing, whaling, ocean incineration, toxic dumping and so on. Up until 1985, it moved from location to location to support the causes to save the planet, including the grey seal hunt in Orkney archipelago off the coast of Scotland and nuclear tests in the Pacific. By March 1985, it was heading to the Rongelap in the Marshall Islands on a different life-saving mission.

Rongelap is a coral atoll of sixty-one islands in the Pacific Ocean, covering a land mass of twenty square kilometres and 145 kilometres east of Bikini in Marshall Islands. The US had carried out sixty-six nuclear tests at the nearby Bikini and Eniwetok islands between 1946 and 1958, many of its explosions causing a radiation fallout on Rongelap. Two decades later, the islanders were feeling the heat of it: there were high rates of thyroid cancer and leukaemia; children born with deformities or suffering from retarded growth. The most significant blast was of a Hydrogen-bomb, code named 'Bravo', on 1 March 1954. At fifteen megatonnes, it was more than 1,000 times the strength of the bomb dropped on Hiroshima.[4]

The local people approached *Rainbow Warrior* when it reached the Marshal Islands with a unique request – to allow using the boat to evacuate the entire population along with their belongings to a safer island 200 kilometres away.

Between 17 to 30 May, the *Rainbow Warrior* worked to relocate about 300 indigenous people of the island along with 100 tonnes of materials, over multiple trips, by dismantling and moving everything they had to the new place.

The next stop was Moruroa, where the French were preparing for a nuclear test. As is the practice, Greenpeace cabled the French president Francois Mitterrand informing him of the planned protest. Later, while the ship was at Honolulu, a French secret service agent, Christine Cabon, infiltrated the vessel posing as a committed ecologist. Unaware of her intentions, the team drafted her with some clerical jobs on board. She was on a mission to gather information so that her handlers, the French Secret Service, could sink the *Rainbow Warrior.* It was called *Operation Satanique*, the mission to sink the *Rainbow Warrior*, as later confirmed by Admiral Pierre Lacoste, who headed the French Secret Service,

DGSE, from 1982 until he was fired in the aftermath of the 1985 debacle.[5]

As the various French agents made their final preparations, the *Warrior* headed for meetings and rallies in New Zealand prior to setting out for Moruroa. In the afternoon of 7 July, a cool Sunday, the ship was met by a welcoming flotilla of thirty boats as it made its way to the Marsden Wharf in Auckland.[6] The flotilla was to join *Rainbow Warrior* in its protest all the way up to Moruroa.

At 11.38 p.m. on 10 July, while *Rainbow Warrior* was docked at the Marsden Wharf for the night, the first bomb previously planted by a French Secret Service agent went off. The explosion blasted off the crew members and some photographers sitting in the mess who were enjoying late-night drinks. Someone dashed into the engine room to notice a hole the size of a car, through which water was gushing inside. As the ship began keeling over, everyone who could gather themselves jumped off the vessel.

Then came the second explosion.

Someone who jumped off the boat telephoned the vessel leadership staying at a hotel nearby and the local Greenpeace office. A short while later, a TELEX message went to all the Greenpeace offices around the world:

> URGENT, URGENT, URGENT: APPROXIMATELY TWO HOURS AGO, RAINBOW WARRIOR SUNK BY TWO EXPLOSIONS IN AUCKLAND HARBOUR, NEW ZEALAND. SABOTAGE SUSPECTED. VERY LITTLE NEWS FORTHCOMING AT PRESENT. ONE CREW MEMBER MISSING. PLEASE DO NOT, REPEAT NOT, CALL AUCKLAND OFFICE AS TELEPHONES ARE JAMMED. WILL HAVE MORE INFO IN AN HOUR OR SO.[7]

It would turn out to be the darkest day in the life of a great activist, who had travelled around the world motivating people to protect the planet. Everybody in the organization was left shattered. An incident of this magnitude was not out of the realm of possibility. The organization was becoming more influential and taking on larger missions, but none had really expected this to happen.[8]

There was one casualty – the Dutch freelance photographer Fernando Pereira. The crew sat around, mourning the death of their friend and the loss of the beloved *Warrior*. The loss of life could have been far greater, but, fortunately, many of the people who might have been asleep at the time of the blast were either awake or off the boat.[9] The attack would turn out to be a blunder on part of the French government, as the Auckland police and the New Zealand government would expose afterwards. Two years later, the French government would pay New Zealand NZ$13 million in compensation and formally apologize for the bombing incident. The Mitterrand government would also pay ₣2.3 million to Pereira's family. A new *Rainbow Warrior* would replace the one bombed by the French by 1989, often referred to as *Rainbow Warrior II.*

The *Rainbow Warrior II* would visit India soon, after Greenpeace set up a formal office in India in 2003 to the west coast of the country, while on a campaign covering three stopovers. The first was in Alang, Gujarat, where it would protest the first world countries' practice of dumping toxic waste of the shipbreaking industry, second, in Mumbai to demonstrate against Unilever for its criminal liability in the Kodaikanal mercury issue and the final, in Kochi where it would expose a government-owned company that was still manufacturing DDT, a globally banned pesticide. It would also use its presence in India to unmask the Dow Chemical Corporation for its liability in the Bhopal Gas Tragedy.

But most importantly, it would release a scathing, revealing report onboard, indicting Unilever for its role in the Kodaikanal mercury poisoning.

# 43

# ANNIE LEONARD AND THE TAJ MAHAL

BY THE TURN OF THE MILLENNIUM, GREENPEACE WOULD ALSO become closely involved in the Bhopal Gas Tragedy campaign in India, having supported the survivors and their outspoken fronts for over a decade. It started with a class action suit filed in a New York federal court against Union Carbide and its former CEO, Warren Anderson, for violating international human rights law, environmental law and criminal law. Soon afterwards, the organization began working through an Indian affiliate of Greenpeace International in 1995.

First, two senior officials from the Amsterdam office visited India, after reaching out to Medha Patkar, who was working on the Narmata Bachao Andolan (NBA) along with other agrarian and environmental issues at the grassroots level, mostly in the western Indian states. Patkar directed them to her colleagues Ganesh Nochur and Pradeep Sharma in Mumbai and apprised the Greenpeace team of the political and environmental developments in the country.

A few months later, a young campaigner from Greenpeace International, Annie Leonard, came to India with a scouting mandate. Leonard, presently the co-executive director of Greenpeace

US, met a young woman named Nirmala Karunan in New Delhi. The duo travelled around the country to meet various non-profits involved in environmental conservation initiatives. Leonard forged collaborations with some civil society voices and non-profits focused on the environment and biodiversity issues while Karunan studied the feasibility of setting up an Indian Greenpeace entity.

Consequently, an informal office was set up in New Delhi the same year. Karunan joined as the first staff and stayed on at Greenpeace for the next two decades, witnessing and supporting several of its trials and tribulations in the country.

In about a year, Greenpeace India launched its first campaign – the anti-toxics campaign to raise awareness against all types of toxic waste generation and disposal, ranging from mercury to MIC and beyond. The efforts were led by Malini Morzaria, an anti-toxics campaigner from Greenpeace International, who arrived in New Delhi in the hot summer of 1996 and remained there for a year.

Morzaria coordinated with global leaders Leonard, Bob Edwards and Rachel Kellett on the one hand, while working closely with Karunan, Sathyu Sarangi, Praful Bidwai and other Indian stakeholders across New Delhi, Bhopal, Mumbai, Ankleshwar, Kandla and Alang. Nityanand Jayaraman was inducted, who later brought Navroz Mody inside the fold as the Kodaikanal campaign kicked off in the new millennium.

Because of the growing practice of waste being shipped into India by western countries – covertly, as usable equipment with life left and also as waste consignments – in order to get rid of their dumps, the India team focused on the toxic waste trade. The Basel Convention to control trans-boundary movement and disposal of hazardous waste sponsored by the UN Environment (UNEP) came into force in 1992. The Greenpeace campaign asked the Indian government to sign and ratify the Convention.

In 1995, the first Non-Violent Direct Action, as it was known in Greenpeace parlance, was staged in front of the Ministry of Environment and Forests office in New Delhi. The simple action involved a woman draped in a white saree depicting Planet Earth to remain standing as dirt and rubbish were thrown at her by volunteers who represented human beings. It was not an attack as such on any entity but rather a way to demonstrate the burdens humans were heaping on the earth.

A year later, the famous action at Taj Mahal took place, under the campaign leadership of Leonard. On a cool, sunny morning, a hot air balloon went above the sixteenth-century ivory-white marble mausoleum on the bank of river Yamuna in Agra, some 230 kilometres south of New Delhi. The balloon carried a message saying 'Nuclear Disarmament Now.' The action was not well received by the new Government of India under Prime Minister Atal Bihari Vajpayee, who had been quietly working on a second set of nuclear tests long after the 1974 nuclear tests in the Pokhran desert. India would subsequently test two sets of thermonuclear devices on 11 and 13 May in 1998.

With this incident, Greenpeace had landed on the government's radar. Its application for registering as a non-governmental entity was turned down, even as Leonard's visa was revoked. The counsel from its Amsterdam office to the Indian team was to lie low for some time until the din and dust of the Taj Mahal action settled.

Greenpeace India Society would take another four years to register as an Indian entity in Chennai. By quietly slipping to the southern state of Tamil Nadu, the registration was carried out with the help of a city-based environmental law firm, Mohan and Devika Associates. Once the paperwork was complete under the Tamil Nadu Society Registration Act, Greenpeace resumed its work with renewed vigour. It started with the Kodaikanal mercury campaign in March 2001, later banding forces with the survivors of the Bhopal Gas Tragedy.

By May 2002, Greenpeace would accompany the Bhopal survivors under the banner of the International Campaign for Justice in Bhopal (ICJB) to the annual general meeting of the Dow Chemical Company in Midland, Michigan, where they confronted the Chief Executive Officer, Michael Parker. The same month, the organization released the ten Bhopal Principles on Corporate Accountability at the World Summit on Sustainable Development (WSSD) in Bali.

In August, a computer centre was set up by Greenpeace outside the Dow factory in Bhopal to help survivors send emails to the company, demanding justice from Union Carbide and subsequently crashing the company's mail servers with flooding mails. The high point came later in the month when it traced the hiding Warren Anderson, the chair and CEO of the Union Carbide Corporation (UCC), to his luxury home in New York, where he was issued an 'arrest warrant'. Soon after the December midnight tragedy, he was arrested in Bhopal and then granted bail, after which he escaped to the US. He never returned to India to face the trial and was declared an 'absconder' by the Indian courts, though the US government never entertained his extradition requests.

The Bhopal campaign further escalated in November when tens of Greenpeace activists trained in handling hazardous materials landed in the city from different parts of the world to lend expertise to ICJB and the local community, and to safely contain the unsecured hazardous pesticide stockpiles lying in the middle of the city. A police-led baton charge ensued, and seventy protesters were arrested for criminal trespassing. Two days later, Dow Chemical issued an internal memo, which read, 'But what we cannot and will not do – no matter where Greenpeace takes their protests and how much they seek to undermine Dow's reputation with the general public – is accept responsibility for the Bhopal accident.'

Leonard could support these campaigns only from the US. Her visa requests were never approved by the Indian government thereafter.

Greenpeace would soon find a parallel between mercury and other poisonous waste being leached from the Bhopal factory to the groundwater and the Kodaikanal mercury poisoning issue. They had now discovered two errant global corporations – Dow and Unilever.

# PART VIII

# COURTROOMS, FROM CHENNAI TO LONDON

# 44

# THE INDIAN ERIN BROCKOVICH

THE VAIGAI RIVER HAS BEEN THE LIFELINE OF MADURAI CITY SINCE pre-historical times. Originating from the green and black gorges and the fissures of cliffs and crags, it flows gently, stroking pebbles and shingles on the way, streaming, bubbling and pouring mountain nectar. Many small streams join this once-marvellous brook during its 300-kilometre course from its origin, deep inside the Western Ghats, until it empties into the lakes of Ramanathapuram, alongside the Bay of Bengal. On its course is a dam by the same name, built by the British towards the end of the nineteenth century, some thirty kilometres west of Kodaikanal.

When the great Tamil communist leader of the last century, P. Ramamurthy, fondly called PR by the people, was considering names for his daughter, he could come up with nothing as apt as Vaigai. PR was the tallest Left leader of the region and led the largest bloc in the first elected assembly of the undivided Madras state in 1952. The political machinations had seen the last governor-general of British India, C. Rajagopalachari, influencing the then-Madras governor to instal him as the state's first chief minister, despite PR's bloc having held the majority.

In a style similar to her father's, Vaigai Ramamurthy started taking on issues of the vulnerable and defenceless as a practising lawyer. Maybe because of her liberal backgrounds, her clients were mostly from oppressed groups. She soon became known as a well-respected human rights counsel for the unprivileged.

In 2005, Vaigai (as she is referred to) was apprised of an environmental disaster and its resultant human rights concerns in Kodaikanal by Chennai-based environmental law firm Mohan and Devika Associates, which was working closely with Greenpeace. The case was about Hindustan Lever's denial to tackle the health problems that had afflicted the ex-workers of its closed-down thermometer factory. After scrutinizing a plethora of documents and talking to some stakeholders, Vaigai realized the pitfalls of fighting the case within the contours of the Indian jurisprudence and legal system. The Indian judicial system had no provision for class action lawsuits, unlike in the West, where a group of people could sue a private corporation for allegedly causing them certain damage. The closest Indian option is the Consumer Protection Act, 1986, which at its best, could be used to seek reprieve against an unfair trade practice, 'defects in goods' or 'deficiencies in services'.

Vaigai pondered over the next few months to figure out how to handle the case. She knew the Indian judicial provisions were deficient in holding corporations criminally liable for their omissions and commissions. There was no way a corporation could be held criminally responsible by the affected party. The only course of action was to approach the state that could exercise its powers, invoking various statutes to make corporations liable. Should the state fail to do so, the parties could approach the judiciary with a prayer to direct the state to act by means of a writ petition. The writ of Mandamus is often used by the courts to direct the state or an authority to perform the duties that it has failed to perform or refused to perform. It is supplemented by other writ provisions like *Quo Warranto*, *Certiorari* and Prohibition. Articles 32 and 226 of the Constitution of India provide for approaching a high court or the Supreme Court with a writ prayer under these provisions against the state. But it had never been carried out solely against a private corporation for damages.

So Vaigai advised the members of the community led by Jayaraman and Mody to first write to the state and central government authorities, including the Inspector of Factories, Pollution Control Board, Government of Tamil Nadu and the Ministry of Labour of the Government of India, demanding action against the company and to compensate for the damages they had suffered at the hands of the company. This was the first step.

A more challenging task was identifying and locating the people whose lives had been affected by the company's actions. This was also to ensure the representation of a sufficiently large group, proving a sizeable number of people had been severely impacted. The leaders of the ex-workers' union were put in charge of this task, as they were best suited to do it. Under the guidance of Mody, the workers had formed the Pond's Hindustan Lever Ltd Ex-Mercury Employees Welfare Association and had been in regular touch with many of the affected ex-workers.

The leaders of the association – Mohamed, Krishnan and Mahindran – began scouring Kodai and the nearby areas in search of workers who had left the company and had suffered from exposure to mercury. All three were supported by Mody and Meenakshi.

Very similar to the door-to-door search carried out in the nineties by American activist Erin Brockovich, who led a landmark case against the California firm Pacific Gas and Electric Company (PG&E). In that case, the lawsuit ended in favour of the victims, with the company paying an astronomical $333 million in 1996. This landmark settlement was based on the alleged contamination of local drinking water sources with hexavalent chromium, which had been used by the company to prevent corrosion of the natural-gas pipeline connected to the San Francisco Bay Area.

Inspired by the Hollywood movie based on the case, the Steven Soderbergh-directed *Erin Brockovich* with Julia Roberts playing the titular role, the three of them started going from house to house with files and documents – talking to people, verifying their employment history with the company, hearing their medical problems and scanning through their medical documentation. As the word spread, many people came forward on their own to reveal their stories. But the three were faced with new problems now. Several victims had not kept any records to prove they had been employees of the company; others had not stored their medical records; and many had no interest in being part of a case that, in their opinion, would be a waste of time and resources. The association leaders waded through tricky waters – from retrieving records from statutory agencies like ESI and EPFO and the office of the Inspector of Factories, recovering medical records from government hospitals and insurance companies to convincing those wary of going on the record.

After spending many long hours over several months, the three of them were able to amass documents of over 500 ex-workers who had evidence of noticeable, documented symptoms caused by exposure to mercury. They went back to Vaigai with the list and documentation as they continued with efforts to add to it the names of more victims. And thus the first big hurdle was crossed.

# 45

# MODY, MOHAMED AND KRISHNAN

BY THE TIME MODY, MOHAMED AND KRISHNAN RETURNED TO Vaigai with the list towards the end of 2005, some of the government agencies had sent their responses. For a long time, Mody and the ex-workers association had been corresponding with the Pollution Control Board and the Director of Factories. Vaigai had devised her legal strategy, asking the state and central governments to prosecute and penalize the company and compensate the workers. This way, the responsibility could be laid at the government's feet, rather than pursuing the company directly. Taking recourse to legal options, she charted out a course of action, establishing *corpus delicti* – a move, she believed, would take a couple of years to conclude in the courtroom.

Once the strategy and action plan were in place, Vaigai and her assistants began scouring through voluminous sheaves of documents running into thousands of pages. The documents ranged from employment histories and medical records of workers, regulatory actions against the company by way of orders and directives, published scientific studies by reputed institutions, reports by government agencies and company-appointed consultants, licences and permissions granted to the company, annual reports and regulatory submissions, to news reports in Indian and international media and anything the team could lay its hands on. Simultaneously, they scrutinized the provisions of the Indian Constitution and the state and central laws to see if any rules could be used to their advantage. Additionally, they were relentlessly studying to connect and conjecture from judgments in similar cases across the country – from high courts and the Supreme Court.

It took months to comprehend, analyse and summarize the information under various heads in order to start drafting the suit. There were multiple meetings with Mody, Mohamed, Krishnan, Mahindran, Jayaraman and others involved in the issue, and telephone calls were made to them regularly for details and clarifications during the drafting process.

The efforts led by Vaigai and her team expended over many sleepless nights spent on their first-floor office on Armenian Street in Chennai's busy Parry's Corner culminated in an airtight petition in March 2006. It prayed for the issuance of a writ of Mandamus to the state and central governments to evolve a scheme for the economic rehabilitation and healthcare of the ex-workers of Hindustan Lever's clinical thermometer factory in Kodaikanal, who had suffered due to exposure to toxic mercury at the factory. It also demanded that the company should bear the costs of such reparations. Further, the petition asked the state and central governments to prosecute the erring company for violating various provisions of the Factories Act, 1948, under which the company had been issued permissions to operate.[1] The petition also sought the court's direction to the Government of India to revise the occupational health and safety standards with reference to mercury exposure in the Factories Act and the compensation amounts in the Workmen's Compensation Act, 1923.[2]

The petition was finally filed on 22 March 2006 in the Madras

High Court, right before the court's long annual summer break. Seven respondents had been named in it, with Hindustan Lever Ltd being the first. Others included the Labour Secretary, the Chief Inspector of Factories, the Deputy Inspector of Factories, the Certifying Surgeon of Inspector of Factories of the Government of Tamil Nadu, the Tamil Nadu Pollution Control Board and the Ministry of Labour of the Government of India.

Hindustan Lever made its best efforts to ensure that the petition was not admitted. It raised many procedural and technical objections against the admission of the petition, aware that once admitted it would be a thorn in its side.

The company brought in well-known Supreme Court lawyer Dushyant Dave from New Delhi, whose mere presence had filled the courtroom with local lawyers and the media. In a heated exchange of arguments on the merits of workers allegedly suffering from mercury exposure-related illnesses, Dave argued that the workers would have deliberately swallowed mercury while at work in order to claim damages from the company later. His argument was immediately called out by Counsel Vaigai for being preposterous and outrageous. In the end, the strategic move failed to produce results as the court rejected his argument, admonishing him instead for a remark that stood out as ludicrous.

Later, in an interaction with me, Vaigai recalled that the bench was extremely receptive to the petition during the processes of admission and listing. And the case moved swiftly during the initial phase, once the court *prima facie* felt satisfied with its merits.

On 29 June 2007, almost a year after the case had been admitted, the court issued an order setting up an expert committee to decide whether the workers' and their family members' alleged health conditions and disease symptoms were related to mercury exposure. The committee was directed to submit a conclusive report within three months after hearing from the ex-workers and the company, and studying the documents and evidence supplied by all concerned parties.[3] The order suggested the structure of the committee too – it would be under the chairmanship of an expert from the Industrial Toxicology Research Centre (ITRC), Lucknow, along with members from the National Institute of Occupational Health (NIOH), All India Institute of Medical Sciences (AIIMS), Christian Medical College, Vellore, and Maulana Azad Medical College, New Delhi.

The composition of the committee shocked everyone, even if it hadn't surprised the HLL management. The company had been working with many of these agencies since as far back as the Greenpeace action on 7 March 2001 in front of the factory. In fact, one of the most important – and the earliest – studies had been conducted by a retired director-grade scientist from ITRC, Dr P. N. Vishwanathan, who assessed the ecological or human risk at the factory site. Dr Vishwanathan, a former member of the WHO Task Group on Environmental Health Criteria for Mercury in 1989, where he worked with seven other experts from the US, Europe and Japan, was qualified for and competent to carry out the task. He visited the factory site between 16 to 19 March, within two weeks of the exposé, and submitted his eight-page report to the company. The conclusion to the report read, 'At present there appears no evidence to show any ecological or human risks due to Hg (mercury) release from the unit.' The scientist further claimed that the demands of the local community were based on 'unknown or imaginary future risks' and thanked HLL in the report for the opportunity to conduct the study.[4] Dr Vishwanathan, simply carrying out a paid consultancy project, had no qualms about thanking the accused company in the report. And HLL had referred to his report to bolster their argument ever since.[5]

In fact, while the ex-workers were considering their legal options, the company had began working with select experts from ITRC, NIOH and AIIMS to review its own epidemiological study.[6] Interestingly, many of the workers and the local community alleged that the experts apparently reviewed the HLL study without having 'access to complete sets of individual medical records' and 'without meeting any of the workers'.

And so, when Dr A. K. Srivastava – one of the experts from the ITRC had already submitted its opinion in support of Hindustan Unilever – was asked to head the committee by the court, it left many shocked.[7] Some of the other experts in the committee were also familiar faces for the company executives because of their previous association on various issues, including the Kodaikanal occupational and environmental studies that a few of them had conducted. For instance, Dr K. Anand was part of the five-member AIIMS team that gave endorsement to HLL's occupational health and safety measures in November 2001, in its attempt to establish that 'there is no evidence to suggest any adverse health effects that can be attributed [to] mercury exposure'. With at least three 'experts' in the newly set up committee in favour of the version of 'no health impact', the company was at an advantage even before the report had been prepared and submitted to the Madras High Court.

But there was one reliable voice on the five-member committee – Dr Jayaprakash Muliyil, a community health specialist representing the Christian Medical College, Vellore. As he told Sarah Hiddleston, a British journalist who reported on the case in a well-researched piece for *Frontline* magazine in 2010, the expert committee undertook a rapid assessment to conclude 'if there was evidence for a study'. They then decided not to carry out a study since they could find 'no evidence' which would require a detailed study. Although Dr Muliyil could not say with certainty whether any of the workers suffered specifically from mercury poisoning, he shared with Hiddleston that it was not possible for him to rule it out either. Indeed, he felt it was 'highly likely' that they would have suffered.[8] Dr Muliyil, along with Dr Anand had examined twelve victim workers aged between twenty-nine and fifty-nine years when the committee did a whirlwind tour of the factory and the vicinity on 10 October 2007.

The 234-page report of the five-member committee appeared to be trying to defend the company, its response to the mercury exposé and the workers' health issues, in every respect, going beyond the brief. For instance, an annexure report by one of the committee members, Dr S. K. Dave of the NIOH, said this on record: 'It is incorrect on the part of the petitioner to state that the company has not carried out environmental or biological monitoring.'[9]

One of the arguments forwarded by the committee in its effort to disprove the claim of fatal health effects on the ex-workers was the sixty-day half-life of mercury in the human body. By definition, a half-life is the time taken by a chemical to deplete from its original quantity to half. As such, 100 units of mercury entering a human body will come down to almost 0.1 unit of the metal after 600 days (one year, seven months and twenty-three days) but still not get eliminated. So, anything with a half-life is never eliminated *in toto*. A person working with mercury vapour who is forced to inhale the vapour for eight hours daily and for 320 days in a year, will experience a growing load of mercury in addition to the already high levels of the heavy metal in his body, as the process of accumulation happens as that of the process of elimination. In effect, the body burden, load of mercury in the body system, would keep increasing as long a worker works in the factory.

Would any of the committee members allow their family to be

exposed to mercury vapour for days and years because the half-life of mercury vapour in the human body is sixty days, asked Krishnan, with whom I had spent a lot of time on mercury balance calculations in 2004. He lamented the committee was not acknowledging the scientific logic that in the case of a person working in the factory for many years, mercury would damage the organs within a couple of years.

In the meantime, Dr T. Rajagopal, HLL's Medical Advisor, ensured a key piece of evidence was judged credible. He had published a study using the epidemiological reports of the 255 ex-workers kept confidential by the company's health team; the reliability of the study had been questioned by NIMHANS expert Dr Mohan Isaac and the CHC team in 2002. Snubbed by the CHC team in Bangalore, Dr Rajagopal had begun working overtly and covertly to garner support for his study. He believed it was a crucial weapon of offence and defence to defeat the ex-workers. He wanted to prove that the health data the workers had shared while working at the factory itself demonstrated they had no health issues from mercury exposure.

By 2005, Dr Rajagopal had presented the study at the 32nd International Congress on Occupational and Environmental Health in the Production and Use of Chemicals, otherwise known as MEDICHEM, in Paris. More significantly, the paper, written by him along with two of his colleagues, H. V. Ravimohan and P. Mascarenhas, was published in the *Indian Journal of Occupational and Environmental Medicine*. It appeared in the journal within a month of the writ petition being filed by the ex-workers on 22 March 2006.[10]

Part of the journal's editorial advisory board, he held the power to decide what and when a study was to be published. In the advisory board, at various times, he had enjoyed the company of

Dr C. S. Pandav, who wrote the report favouring the company on behalf of AIIMS and also of the head of the court-appointed committee, Dr A. K. Srivastava.[11] The company study had concluded that 'on the basis of the results of environmental monitoring, biological monitoring, clinical evaluation and review in comparison to published data on dose-response relationships, there is no evidence to suggest that any of the employees in the thermometer plant suffered from health effects that could be attributed to mercury exposure'.[12] It also pointed out that 'analysis of the mortality data of ten individuals who died either in service or after leaving employment has also not indicated any mortality that could be attributed to effects of mercury-related exposure'.[13] The mortality data sans any post-mortem reports.

But it was the concluding line that appeared odd for having been included in a credible journal for a peer-reviewed scientific study – it stated that the 'community concerns have mainly been fanned by interested groups without any scientific evidence to substantiate claims of ill health amongst employees at the thermometer plant'.[14]

# 46

# 'ELEMENTARY MERCURY'

AT THE TURN OF THE MILLENNIUM, WHILE THE KODAIKANAL mercury poisoning case was steadily unfolding, Tom van Teunenbroek, a highly ambitious young Dutch professional, was working for TNO, a governmental research organization conducting contract-based research and offering specialist consulting services in the Netherlands. After completing his master's degree in biochemistry and toxicology from Utrecht University in 1988 and a fellowship from the State University of Illinois, Chicago, until 1991, he struggled for nine long years to find a meaningful job. During this time, he set up and ran a company named Ameco Environmental Consultants, along with another Dutch citizen, providing odd services like financial management and consultancy from Utrecht.

His first career break came in 1999 upon receiving a job offer from TNO, which was established in 1932 to support companies and governments with innovative, practicable knowledge. In two years, he became a project manager and became involved with the remediation issues of polluted industrial sites. During this work, he came across Greenpeace, which was campaigning for the affected communities as well in some of the cases.

Thus in April 2001, when the Tamil Nadu Pollution Control Board (TNPCB) asked Greenpeace to recommend a consultant to advise on the health impacts of mercury pollution in Kodaikanal, Mody and Jayaraman sought the support of their colleagues in Amsterdam. The Greenpeace International office suggested van Teunenbroek without a second thought, having collaborated with him before. They would later regret this decision.

This case also became a turning point in van Teunenbroek's career, as he broke away from Greenpeace and began defending HLL instead. The Greenpeace officials had failed to realize that one of the company's two headquarters was in Rotterdam in the Netherlands. And that the Rotterdam executives of the company were able to network expertly with their Dutch compatriots.

Within a few weeks of being drafted for his opinion by HLL, on Greenpeace's recommendation and the TNPCB's agreement, van Teunenbroek gave his report. The one-page report, dated 28 May 2001, defending HLL's omissions in Kodaikanal, launched him as a global environmental and health expert. He was soon elevated to a Dutch negotiator position for the ministerial WHO Environment and Health declaration in 2010 and, eventually, to a full-time coordinator of the EU flagship project on the safety of nanomaterials, NANoReg, a collaboration of thirteen countries and sixty institutions, by the second decade of the new millennium. He accomplished all of this without any formal training in clinical medicine or medical research experience. Interestingly, after the stint as a negotiator, he would also claim to be a 'neuro-toxicologist on the effects of etiological factors [predominantly metals] affecting signal transduction and higher functions'.[1]

In his report, he cast several aspersions on the workers with elevated levels of mercury and advised a follow-up study to 'ensure if there are other sources of mercury exposure which could explain these deviations'. Considering the site in discussion was a remote hill station, the notion of examining the workers of the thermometer factory for other sources of mercury exposure since 1983 left us reeling with disbelief. Van Teunenbroek ended his report with this line: 'My conclusion on a thorough review of the clinical protocol, the clinical evaluation as well as the methodology and results is that there is no mercury related health risks to the employees.'[2]

Coincidently, TNO's laboratory would soon turn out to be one of the eight testing facilities used by the consultant Dames & Moore for examining the mercury levels in the soil, water, sediment, lichen and fish samples of Kodaikanal.

Having shared a good relationship with the TNO, Greenpeace Netherlands could not sit quietly on van Teunenbroek's 'chameleonic betrayal'. It protested to TNO vehemently about van Teunenbroek's terse report, which lacked supplementary analysis, evidence and interpretation on such a globally important issue.

Van Teunenbroek left TNO soon thereafter. When he wrote a second paper in October 2003 to validate the follow-up analysis he had suggested in 2001, he no longer had the backing of any organization and did so in his individual capacity. His 2003 report was even more assertive and forthright: 'My *professional expertise* coupled with an extensive literature survey on the epidemiological aspects and dose effect relationships vis-à-vis exposure to *elementary mercury* substantiates my scientific opinion that there are no data which support the claim that the employees, who were exposed to mercury, have acquired ill-health on account of such exposures.'[3]

Quoting this statement, Mody and the members of the local community pointed out that the final report displayed a lack of 'professional expertise' since he did not seem to even understand the elementary difference between 'elemental' and 'elementary'.

HLL was perhaps hoping van Teunenbroek's reports would

finally end Greenpeace's campaign. Nevertheless, the company continued in its efforts to bolster their position in as many ways as possible.

By this time, another epidemiological study of the workers by the Indian Association of Occupational Health (IAOH), headed by chief medical officers of Reliance Ltd and Siemens Ltd, had certified that 'any adverse consequences of workers health are highly unlikely'. The Centre for Community Medicine at AIIMS, signed by one of its additional professors, Dr Pandav, had found 'no evidence to suggest any adverse health effects that can be attributed to mercury exposure'. The AIIMS report came after a presentation on 9 November 2001 made by Dr Rajagopal to a select faculty group of five doctors, including Dr K. Anand who would later join the high court-appointed committee. By then, the ITRC and NIOH studies had also come out. So had the report of the Certifying Surgeon, who had been entrusted with the onerous responsibility of medically examining all workers in a factory, once a year, under the provisions of the Factories Act, wherein he had stated that 'the employees are healthy and sound'.

Environmentalists would allege that these dozen-odd reports have been carefully orchestrated by the company since after the 2001 mercury waste exposé and had sullied the case of the workers who had been inhaling highly poisonous mercury vapour on an average of eight hours a day for several years. For the workers, an even more troubling fact was that these reports came from some of the most reputed national medical institutions of the country, such as AIIMS and ITRC – institutes created to safeguard the interests of citizens.

# 47

# COUNSEL VAIGAI

AFTER THE REPORT OF THE EXPERT COMMITTEE WAS SUBMITTED to the Madras High Court in 2008, the fate of the case was almost sealed against the interest of the workers. The endorsements for the HLL epidemiological assessment covering a section of the workers, annexed in the report included the letterheads of organizations like ITRC, NIOH and AIIMS. In addition, HLL also had peer reviews of the assessment by three international experts and many national experts; publication in a journal of occupational and environmental medicine; and presentation at an international conference. All of these aspects had allowed this particular assessment as a key piece of evidence in HLL's favour.

Across the fence, the ex-workers' arguments seemed agonizingly meagre by comparison. Even the sole international consultant brought in by Greenpeace had switched sides. The defences advanced by the workers, including a review of the studies by Dr Rakhal Gaitonde, a public health expert, and two other clinical medicine experts, could not dent the large body of studies and endorsements presented by the company. The court-appointed committee's occupational health expert, Dr Dave, supplemented the main report with an additional report that disproved the claims and evidence presented by the ex-workers using scientific evidence, which the workers argued, had been 'selectively chosen'.[1]

Dr Dave's supplementary report referred to the lack of scientific evidence in individual cases, which a renowned clinical expert had assiduously linked to mercury exposure. For instance, referring to the well-documented case of Ruth Priya, he commented that 'such observations without proper history of exposure or in the absence of scientific literature cannot be accepted'. Workers, on the other hand, found the reference of 'without proper history of exposure' out of place as she had worked in the mercury packing division of the factory from 1991 till a year before the closure of the factory. They also suggested that Dr Dave was feigning ignorance on the large body of 'scientific literature' regarding the impact of mercury toxicity in pregnant woman, foetuses and newborns.[2]

Next was a case of developmental biology, where the mercury exposure had led a young lady working in the factory to give birth to children with deformities. Gynanasundari Jayaprakash had lived near and worked at the factory for many years. Her 'health problems started with body swelling and gastric burning, accompanied by headache and nausea'. She had suffered a miscarriage and, later, both her children, at the time of their birth, showed deformities in their legs in the form of cleft foot, a typical foetal developmental impact caused by mercury toxicity.[3] But Dr Dave explained that 'mercury cannot cause mutation and geno-toxicity', attributing it to a congenital disorder, even though he would have been aware it cannot be definitively linked to genetics, and in fact could equally be a case of developmental biology disorder.[4]

The committee, however, concluded that 'it failed to find sufficient evidence to link the current clinical conditions of the factory workers to the mercury exposure in the factory in the past'.

In order to appear balanced, statements like 'the ex-workers not only had an opportunity to get exposed to mercury but also had to go through a process of losing job and facing consequent socio-economic dislocations,' had been added, completely dismissing the health risks due to the mercury exposure.[5] Rather bizarrely, this observation was supplemented with a loaded claim: 'This could have induced lifestyle changes which could have had an effect on perceived health status.'[6]

In effect, while it agreed there was a serious problem with the 'health status' of ex-workers, it ascribed them to reasons beyond mercury exposure, thereby navigating the company out of the mercury-infested waters.

In their turn, Mody, Mohamed and Krishnan pointed out the bias of the committee members by making a few arguments: The committee spent exactly sixty minutes to examine a mere twelve workers out of more than 500 people gathered before them and concluded that none of the workers exhibited symptoms relating to mercury exposure; by doing so, it not only had chosen to not examine further but also unilaterally decided no further investigation by any other scientific body was warranted. Shamefully, the one child examined by the Committee and declared healthy would die a week later.[7]

With the case going in an unexpected direction, they decided to file a case in the High Court of Justice, Queen's Bench Division, UK, home to one of Unilever's two headquarters. This was the best they could do while fighting one of the top five consumer giants of the world.

As the litigation went on at a febrile pace, the ex-workers' association was struggling to meet the bare minimum expenses of its office-bearers to travel to Chennai for court hearings and other minimum legal and logistical requirements. The expenses began mounting even higher after they filed a suit in the High Court of Justice in the UK.

Once the contents of the report were made public by the summer of 2008, gloom and despondency spread among the ex-workers. Even the most vociferous fighters had nothing more to look forward to.

Mohamed filed an affidavit before the high court soon, raising objections to the Committee Report and informing the court that the conclusions of the report were based on an epidemiological study wherein the researchers had used the health records of over 300 workers, who had been denied access to their rightful health information by the company. This was significant also because Hindustan Unilever had relied on these data to prepare its legal defence.[8]

The individual data that some workers managed to get out of Hindustan Unilever showed one-off readings at extreme levels between 100 and 200 micrograms. Only a total of eighty-one of the 152 workers received their medical reports; ninety-eight workers had urine mercury readings exceeding fifty micrograms, Mohamed told the Madras High Court, in his affidavit.

For her *Frontline* report on the Kodaikanal case, Hiddleston had interviewed Dr Linda Jones, a renowned epidemiological expert from New Zealand who was aghast upon being apprised of the ongoing developments in the Kodaikanal issue. With her long experience working with people exposed to mercury, she was convinced that for identifying impacts of mercury exposure it would be crucial to study the symptoms and not just the subjects' urine or blood readings.

In a population study, generally, an indicator like urine is used to find traces of elemental mercury. About fifty micrograms of mercury per litre is the standard international cut-off value for mercury in urine and is considered acceptable in some sense. But realistically, a person with just five micrograms or less mercury in their body could still suffer from symptoms of poisoning because of this individual variation.[9]

This was the reason Jones didn't trust the urine and blood levels of mercury, a factor the company had depended on in its epidemiological study. She explained it was not possible to tell whether the mercury reading represented what is being stored in the body or the quantity passing out of it. When it comes to determining and treating mercury poisoning, what really needs to be done is an assessment of the symptoms, mood, tremor, gait, sometimes personality change and cultural withdrawal.[10]

There were many other 'interesting' observations in the committee's report, for instance, a quote from the response to an enquiry made to the local government medical practitioner, Dr R. Balaji. It was to find out whether he had treated any case of mercury poisoning, and it sounded like asking a telescope operator to prove how black holes die.

With such a loaded report before the court, it seemed as if the end of the road was near. Most ex-workers and their allies began to see their impending defeat as *fait accompli*. Except Vaigai, who wasn't prepared to concede just yet. She had understood the designs of the defendant over the last two years since the case was first filed. The events thereafter had confirmed her feelings that the company was squarely at fault.

With the report reaching the division bench, the long-awaited hearing began on 12 June 2008 before Chief Justice A. K. Ganguly and Justice F. M. Ibrahim Kalifulla. As it progressed with new submissions by the parties after going through the reports, arguments and counter-arguments, Justice Kalifulla was replaced by

Justice K. Chandru by December. The hearings went on at feverish pace through the year until Justice Ganguly's last day in the court, with as many as ten hearings in the past four months of the year. After that, the proceedings grew cold for close to two and a half years.

Then in 2011, the case took a U-turn unexpectedly. Hindustan Lever by now had become Hindustan Unilever.

# 48

# SLEEPING LION

THROUGHOUT THE DECADE, NO ONE HAD TROUBLED THE SLEEPING lion, the Directorate General Factory Advice Service and Labour Institutes (DGFASLI), an entity with the power and courage to take on the behemoth. Born three years prior to India's independence, after 1950 the DGFASLI had turned into a statutory body under the Government of India's Ministry of Labour, initially called the Chief Adviser of Factories. It provided advice to the central and state governments on administration of the Factories Act, 1948, and on coordinating the factory inspection services. Later, it would metamorphose into assisting the Ministry of Labour in formulating national policies on occupational safety and health in factories and docks. Besides these, it also had the arduous responsibility of advising factories on the safety, health, efficiency and well-being of workers.

When the hearing resumed before a new bench with Justice M. Venugopal and Justice Elipe Dharma Rao in 2011, the court looked to see whether all respondents had submitted their responses. While the first, Hindustan Unilever, and the second to sixth respondents – falling under the ambit of the Government of Tamil Nadu – had sent their versions, the seventh was missing. Well aware this gap would create an issue, Vaigai had sought directions to ask the Ministry of Labour of the Government of India, the seventh respondent, for its version. As expected, the court ordered the response of the ministry as well.

All through the trial, Unilever thought the Ministry of Labour had no say in the case, given the matters of labour and factories are state subjects governed by their respective governments and therefore, the Government of India or its agencies had no role to play. But that logic was fallacious.

As per the Seventh Schedule of the Indian Constitution that allocates powers and functions between the centre and states, the federal government holds exclusive powers to frame legislations on labour and safety, while both the centre and states can make laws about the welfare of employees and factories. This makes the Ministry of Labour and the labour departments of state governments equally responsible for ensuring the health and safety of workers.

Generally, the Ministry of Labour creates new legislations or amendments to existing laws on issues of workers' health and safety in consultation with state governments and workers' unions. The DGFASLI first prepares the draft before they are sent to the ministry. In addition, the agency has superintendence over the state factory inspectorates on the implementation of the Factories Act. The DGFASLI was also the due authority of the ministry on issues concerning occupational health and safety, so it was involved in the case in no time.

This was done with the help of a labour-lawyer-turned-labour-leader-turned-politician, Mallikarjun Kharge, and an economist-turned-politician-turned environmentalist, Jairam Ramesh.

By early March 2010, the local community approached Jairam Ramesh, who was the Minister for Environment and Forests in the UPA government of Manmohan Singh. After being apprised of the

TNPCB's role in diluting the remediation standards, he called for an explanation from the state government. On being told about the ongoing developments at the Madras High Court and how the Ministry of Labour could turn things around, he spoke to his good friend in the Congress party, Mallikarjun Kharge, the Labour Minister.

Kharge had started his career as a labour lawyer, graduating to a labour leader in northern Karnataka. Once he was informed about the situation, he gave instructions to his ministry to initiate an independent study. So, when the High Court of Madras nudged the DGFASLI at the instance of Counsel Vaigai, Hindustan Unilever was left scrambling for a defence. The company could also sense the pitfalls because it had never engaged the key statutory body on the Kodaikanal issue, having put all its eggs in the occupational health science basket.

Acting on the orders of the Madras High Court, under instructions from Kharge, the Under-secretary of the Ministry of Labour issued a notification on 9 September 2011, setting up a committee comprising representatives from the ITRC, NIOH, Central Pollution Control Board, Bureau of Indian Standards, Chief Inspector of Factories, Chennai and the Social Security Division of the Ministry of Labour. The committee was to be chaired by the DGFASLI.[1]

Curiously, the terms of reference of the committee was to look into the rehabilitation and the healthcare of the victims, the revision of occupational health and safety standards for mercury exposure in the Factories Act and the quantum of compensation provisioned in the Employees Compensation Act, 1923.[2] By prescribing the terms of reference for 'rehabilitation and healthcare of the victims', the Ministry of Labour had conceded the workers had suffered from occupational hazards. The only question was of how much. The other two terms focused on the more significant aspects of policy changes required in view of the Kodaikanal case – revising the health and safety standards for mercury exposure and the quantum of compensation required in similar cases in the future. By having representatives from ITRC and NIOH, the committee had taken into account the scientific aspects of the occupational health and toxicology of the manifestations of mercury exposure.

From the DGFASLI, the then-Deputy Director Dr M. Rajaram took charge of the committee, and the first investigative meeting was held on 22 September. The next day, a director-level medical expert from the DGFASLI, Director in-Charge of Regional Labour Institute, Chennai, and the Tamil Nadu Labour Commissioner were inducted as additional committee members. More importantly, the DGFASLI did not choose the ITRC and NIOH representatives, who served in the 2007 high court-appointed committee, and were accused by the local community of colluding with the company. Instead, it identified independent experts with impeccable records from both the institutes – Dr S. S. A. Zaidi and Dr R. C. Murthy respectively.

After a three-day visit to Kodaikanal and meetings with hundreds of people from all sides of the issue, including over 102 victims, and reviewing thousands of pages of documents and literature, the committee concluded its findings and recommendations in two months – on 9 November 2011.

Also following protocol more effectively than the previous committee, it held a public hearing for the survivors and family members of the deceased victims in the presence of company representatives. Case by case, clarifications were sought and recorded from both sides. Medical examination was carried out on the spot by a team led by the medical expert, and the victims' medical records were examined and scrutinized in detail. Finally, when the findings and recommendations were presented, the results were damning for Unilever.

It was found that some of the supposed victims, who had appeared before the committee for medical examination, had shown signs of mercury poisoning, but their symptoms had not been assessed by any competent authority.[3] The committee pointed out this was a necessary measure to decide the extent of compensation in such cases as per the statutory provisions. It also zeroed in on mercury exposure and the consequent illnesses among the workers using Unilever's own reports.

Debunking its epidemiological survey and endorsements by so-called experts, the committee looked at the raw mercury urine readings presented in the Dames & Moore Report submitted in May 2002. According to it, the mercury level in the urine samples of workers had been rising since 1988 and had continued to do so until 1991, declining thereafter, strangely coinciding with the integration of Pond's India with Hindustan Lever.

The committee concluded there had been high exposure to mercury among the workers in the mercury-filling room. Contrary to this raw data, the company's epidemiological survey, published by Dr Rajagopal in the *Indian Journal of Occupational Health* and used as a critical piece of evidence in its defence, had reported that 'urine mercury levels expressed in group mean to show that it did not exceed the permissible limits'. The committee critiqued this was contrary to the data provided in the Dames & Moore report.

It further expressed surprise over not finding any health effects of mercury in the epidemiological study, noting that the committee's medical examination of over 102 workers on 4–5 October 2011 had shown 'typical symptoms of mercury poisoning as evidenced by the witnesses presented during the investigation'. In fact, fifty-one surviving and fifteen deceased workers and local people, including a British citizen, had displayed visible signs and symptoms of mercury poisoning.

The workers who had died either in service or after leaving the company had no mention of mercury exposure on their death certificates, and those who had lost their children to premature death too had no certificate stating the parents had suffered from mercury exposure. The Committee recommended an examination of the survivors by a specially constituted medical board to ascertain the extent of mercury poisoning individually and in groups, before deciding the percentage of disability. This was an important requirement called for by the statutes to fix the quantum of compensation to be awarded to the affected individuals. The compensation was statutorily decided and awarded based on the percentage of disability, the age of the worker at the time of exposure or incident and the last drawn wages.

As per the prevailing laws, once the percentage of disability had been calculated and certified by the medical board, victims could approach the Employee Compensation Commissioner for necessary relief. As per the Employees Compensation Act, 1923, an occupational disease like mercury exposure in a factory environment could be treated as an injury arising out of work and had to be compensated by the employer. Even the outdated provisions had provided for compensation between ₹120,000 to ₹914,000 for death and ₹140,000 to ₹1,097,000 for permanent disability. For this, the committee suggested ten extensive and sweeping recommendations by passing the onus of implementing the measures on the company:

- Socio-medical care for the surviving workers and their family members.
- Aged parents and dependants of deceased workers to be supported by institutionalizing them.

- Siblings and children of workers to be given education free of cost.
- Mentally challenged children to be sent to special education schools.
- Older, mentally ill patients to be sent to psychiatric hospitals for treatment.
- Workers with infertility to be provided proper medical treatment.
- Workers and family members who have been affected physically/ mentally to be given proper medical attention and care.
- Eligible victim workers to be given re-employment or alternate employment.
- Financial assistance to be extended to other victims (former workers) towards self-employment efforts.
- Expenses of all such rehabilitation measures to be borne by Hindustan Unilever.

Upon realizing the new committee's work would not help them in any manner, the company moved a writ petition in the high court through its lawyers Satish Parasaran and Rahul Balaji on 19 October, almost a month prior to the submission of the report. The petition sought to stop the committee's work, pointing out that another high court-appointed committee had already concluded on the matter, an argument that should have been made when the committee was being formed. But the court did not budge, demanding to see the report as it was the privilege of the respondent, the Ministry of Labour, to decide whether or not to have a committee to submit its response.

Vaigai explained to me the fundamental difference between the HC-appointed committee and the Ministry of Labour's committee: the former was heavily populated with medical experts and thus focused on the medical and clinical aspects of heavy metal poisoning among the workers, whereas the latter featured more safety experts including occupational health experts, and therefore focused on occupational safety. The Ministry of Labour Committee had asked the company about the specifics of their safety procedures and emergency protocols in case of eventualities. The company was to have recorded the mercury levels of workers on a daily/weekly basis and kept moving workers out of mercury zones as soon as the body burden of mercury crossed the threshold levels. However, the factory had not been observing these protocols and the committee could pinpoint this.

As soon as the report was submitted by the Ministry of Labour in the court, Hindustan Unilever approached the Supreme Court with a prayer to not accept it. A battery of lawyers led by Mukul Rohatgi – who, three years later, would become the Attorney-General for India – and supported by leading law firm Karanjawala & Co, moved the apex court on 17 December 2011 to stall the submission of the report. With no breakthrough from the Supreme Court bench of Justice Cyriac Joseph and Justice Gyan Sudha Misra, the petition was withdrawn on 6 January 2012, a few days before the next hearing at the Madras High Court.

Thereafter, the case proceeded at breakneck speed in the Chennai courtrooms. On average, one hearing a month was held in 2012 and a dozen more in the first two months of 2013.

Then it went into limbo till early 2016, when some renewed interest came in on account of two reasons.

# 49

# KODAIKANAL WON'T

BORN TO A SCHOOLTEACHER MOTHER AND A FATHER WHO WORKED at a tyre company, Paul Polman had wanted to be a doctor and then a priest before eventually turning to economics and management after his name was not drawn in the Dutch medical school lottery. He spent twenty-seven long years at Procter & Gamble, starting as a cost analyst in 1979, becoming the managing director of its UK business and then the president of its Europe operations by 2001. He switched companies to join the rival Nestlé in 2006, as the Chief Financial Officer, later heading its business in the US. For Polman, missing out on the global CEO position of Nestlé in 2007 was a proverbial slip between the cup and the lip. When he prevailed over Manvinder Banga, the preferred insider and number two executive at Unilever in September 2008, he would become the first outsider to be hired for the top position of the $62 billion company (2021 revenue) in its eighty-year history. His appointment would even evoke a wave of disbelief among the Unilever observers.[1]

The Dutchman, who had once held priestly ambitions, soon believed that selling shampoo around the world could be a higher calling, the *Economist* describing him in a report as 'The Parable of St Paul' in its 31 August 2017 edition. About a year later, he would hang up his boots after the end of his long stint with Unilever Plc, where he had received one of the highest pay packages in the company's history.

By 2015, Polman's compensation was €10.3 million, which slipped to €8.4 million a year later, following a slowdown in growth in key markets, after India announced its demonetization policy and due to an economic crisis in Brazil. In the same year, rival company Kraft Heinz would make a bid to take over Unilever for $143 billion, an acquisition, had it materialized, could have become the fourth-largest in global corporate history.[2]

Polman's stock in social and environmental responsibility circles began soaring as high as the company's stock prices, ever since he had stepped in with one leg in Rotterdam and the other in London, followed by the announcement of the Sustainable Living Plan in 2010. The plan argued that sustainability and successful business performance should be linked, aiming to create a positive social impact. Its execution was subject to creating sustainable growth through 'purpose-led brands', cutting business costs, reducing risk and building trust with its stakeholders. The concept was Polman's brainchild, aiming to designate certain brands for taking action for people and the planet.

Not only in sustainability and environmental responsibility, Polman was different from other conventional CEOs in several other respects. In February 2015, he quietly opened a Twitter account with the handle @PaulPolman and began following Greenpeace UK, among many other green and blue channels. It probably had not occurred to him that this would soon land him into trouble over the hotly contested Kodaikanal mercury poisoning issue, which led to the unmaking of many of his predecessors and Indian executives, particularly Banga, who had lost out to Polman in the race for the CEO position.

His position notwithstanding, Polman showed genuine concern and eagerness to solve the Kodaikanal issue, even responding to a viral video that had sent shock waves on social media. The video, originally posted on YouTube on 30 July 2015, had seen an intense response on Twitter and other platforms. Featuring a twenty-eight-year-old singer–rapper from Chennai, Sofia Ashraf, who had worked in the advertising industry, the three-minute-long rap remix titled 'Kodaikanal Won't' had crossed a million views by the time it was brought to Polman's attention.

Drawing on the American rapper Nicki Minaj's hit single 'Anaconda' released a year before, Ashraf's version was trending the world over on social media. A Tamil photographer-cum-director, Rathinan Prasad, had remixed it well with some local taste and flavour – there were Bharatanatyam dancers, children dancing to Tamil folk *dappan koothu,* shots of busy streets and trains in Chennai and visuals of protesters marching on the streets holding placards against Unilever.[3]

Until this video, Prasad had been haphazardly working in movies to make ends meet. After his eleven-minute short film failed to make any waves, he had been dreaming of his big break, which was when came upon the idea for the short remix video. By 2012, he was working as a second unit director and later as an assistant director on local movie sets. After 'Kodaikanal Won't', he never looked back. He later told a journalist: 'We made the video on a shoestring budget of ₹15,000 ($200) and shot it in a day and released it online. We began to get calls from all over the world that very night. It was overwhelming.'[4]

He had roped in the local NGO Jhatkaa.org for the groovy rap video, which soon became the social media anthem for the outrage against mercury poisoning in Kodaikanal. Linked to the video was a petition to be signed on a campaign website. Using the company's logo and an image of the factory signboard, the video asked the company to 'clean up the mess', as it sternly warned that Kodaikanal would not step down until Unilever had made amends for its actions. In less than two minutes, it covered the long story of the factory and the mercury contamination at 'the princess of hill stations, Kodaikanal'.

On 6 August 2015, Polman tweeted using the trending hashtag #UnileverPollutes:

> Working actively solution kodai #UnileverPollutes for several years already Determined to solve.Need others too and facts not false emotions[5]

Written in disjointed sentences without proper punctuation, grammar and a period at the end, probably because it was typed hastily, Polman's tweet appeared to convey he was actively working to find a solution to the issue.

His remarks were also in stark contrast to Hindustan Unilever's official response to the video two days earlier, which said, 'Safety is our number one priority. Extensive studies found no harm to workers or environment in Kodaikanal,' with a link to the company's web page detailing its version of the 'facts'.[6]

Polman's tweet was a breakthrough of sort for the campaigners. With a tweet from the CEO of Unilever Plc, the parent company of Hindustan Unilever Limited, they tried to engage him further on Twitter. Jayaraman responded that 'you can verify veracity of emotions by visiting mercury-affected families. No senior exec has visited Kodai so far'. Meenakshi, going by another name, Meena Subramaniam, was the first one to catch Polman's tweet. She responded to Polman within a few minutes, saying, 'False emotions?? Get the Hg levels down to the prescribed EU norm and compensate all the poor ex workers ...' Other equally involved campaigners, such as Shweta Narayan, Saleh Mamon and many others jumped in.[7]

By then, some gears had turned at the company's global headquarters. The company's communications department and Polman's own office were not pleased with him using the #UnileverPollutes hashtag and contradicting Hindustan Unilever's stated position. Moreover, the language he had used in the tweet did not reflect well on the global CEO of the third largest FMCG company. It ran against all the branding guidelines and reputation norms set by the company. They advised Polman to refrain from responding to the groups and activists on social media, and he seemed to have decided to toe the line after that. So despite campaigners and activists trying every trick in their bag to engage him further on Twitter, Polman went into virtual 'hiding'.

All Jayaraman had managed to elicit was a response from a self-proclaimed executive coach from Naples, Florida, Sana Rupp, who wrote to him, 'Paul will solve it. I told him weeks ago to solve & they issued Unilever Human Rights Report'.

Jayaraman asked, 'If you're speaking for Unilever, fine. If not, you're skewing the pitch. Are you authorized to speak (on behalf of Unilever)?'

Rupp responded with 'I know CEO's mind-set. I don't pitch or skew, I influence! HE WILL FIX'.

But no visible or serious fixes appeared for the next two months, though Polman was understood to have asked the team to find a closure on the issue. With a lot of reluctance among the India team of Hindustan Unilever on giving in on a case they had been assiduously fighting for over a decade and a half, the mounting pressure from the global headquarters did not register immediately.

The tide swiftly began to shift when the group of fifty Goldman

Environmental Prize winners wrote to Polman on 24 September, days before he was to receive the Champion of the Earth Award at the closing ceremony of the UN Sustainable Development Goals summit in New York. Their letter started with a line, 'We, the undersigned, are winners of international environmental and human rights awards. We extend our greetings and good wishes to you on your nomination for UNEP's Champion of the Earth Award.'[8]

The letter sent to Polman's personal email address alleged that the workers had been kept in the dark about the ill-effects of mercury, and that the company had thwarted all attempts of independent and comprehensive medical examination to verify their health concerns. It also mentioned the findings of the 2011 report of the Ministry of Labour, which clearly stated that the workers of the factory had been exposed to mercury and many of them showed signs of mercury poisoning.[9]

Suggesting that the 'Minamata tragedy is being repeated in Kodaikanal,' the awardees said, 'Unilever has failed to show serious intent to solve the issue as the workers remain uncompensated, children and communities are suffering and the environment polluted'. Noting Polman's passion 'for saving forests', the letter also brought to his attention that 'the Kodaikanal factory is located within and surrounded by valuable and sub-montane evergreen forests'. It concluded by asking him to 'personally intervene to ensure that an honorable settlement is offered to workers and the contaminated environment is cleaned up to international standards'.[10] This engagement, led by Indonesian environmentalist Yuyun Ismawati, which continued till the end of December 2015, forced Polman to seriously take stock of the situation.

Following this exchange, Polman would demand that the management team of Hindustan Unilever work out a settlement, outside of the court, with the former workers without any further delay.

In the next two months, frantic activities got underway. On one level, through meetings between the lawyers of the parties – Counsel Vaigai and Counsel Balaji – and then between leaders of the ex-workers and company representatives. The discussions protracted for a while over the terms of the proposed settlement and the quantum of compensation to be paid.

With the recommendations of the Ministry of Labour report and the arguments in the courtroom, it became clear to the company that the worst outcome of the judgment could be a decision based on the provisions of the Employees Compensation Act, 1923. It could also make the company eventually liable to pay a maximum of ₹914,000 for every death and ₹1,097,000 for every permanent disability. The workers would have to go through a long process and procedure, wherein a specially constituted medical board would fix the percentage of disability for each ailing worker, take into consideration the age, last drawn wages and so on. And the statutory Employee Compensation Commissioner would make decisions on a case-by-case basis.

The global corporation, with a battery of people involved in litigation and workforce issues, was preparing to move ahead with its original plan until Polman's directive towards the end of 2015 to settle with the workers. Instantly, the team led by Dev Bajpai, Executive Director of Legal and Corporate affairs at Hindustan Unilever, began earnest efforts to start discussions with the ex-workers and their attorneys. With weeks of stretched discussions, negotiations and reconciliations under the guidance of Counsel Vaigai and Counsel Balaji, an agreement was signed on 4 March 2016 by the representatives of workers and Hindustan Unilever.

The settlement provisioned ex-gratia payments to 591 former

workers and their families towards taking care of their health and finding alternate means of livelihood.[11] The request of Hindustan Unilever to keep the details of the compensation as confidential was agreed upon by the campaigners and ex-workers. The settlement was suggested to be the second-highest compensation sum ever awarded in the annals of Indian corporate history, after the $470-million compensation for the victims of the Bhopal Gas Tragedy.

When the settlement was presented before Chief Justice Sanjay Kaul and Justice M. M. Sundresh on 9 March in the Madras High Court, the two-judge bench agreed to Hindustan Unilever's request for confidentiality and to not allow either party to disclose the quantum of compensation externally. The court also appointed advocate Suhrith Parthasarathy as the commissioner on its implementation and report back to the court on 28 March.[12]

Subsequently, the case filed in the Royal Court of Justice in London on behalf of the former workers of the company, which too had added some pressure for the settlement, was withdrawn.

This episode would finally draw the curtains to a muddy, long-drawn-out battle between hapless victims and a global corporation that began at a scrapyard in Kodaikanal in 2001 and went up to the High Court of Justice, the Queen's Bench Division in London. It was a battle that saw science, medical science, law, data and human perseverance pitted against one of the world's largest corporations in an all-consuming fight that would last fifteen years.

# PART IX

# FIGHT FOR CLEANUP

# 50

# MERCURY BALANCE

THE GREATEST CONUNDRUM THAT BAFFLED EVERYONE INVOLVED in the case was the calculation of the 'mercury balance'. The term refers to the weight of the missing balance between the total amount of raw mercury brought in by Hindustan Lever during the eighteen years of its operations and the amount used in all the finished and shipped-out fever thermometers. Where had the missing mercury disappeared? How far and wide had it travelled?

Had it spread across the Pambar Shola as mercury vapour? To the surrounding forest as discarded glass scraps and also as vapour? Or to the community nearby and to communities far away through mercury-laden glass scrap? Had it been reused by industries for making various consumables? Or had it reached the body organs of workers and the local community, inhaled and ingested through various means? It was a daunting question that had puzzled the campaigners and regulators since 2001 in the absence of any transparent accounts by the company. Rather, the company was providing different accounts through its consultants to prove that fewer quantities of mercury had escaped from the factory.

Through the multiple long-drawn-out accounts and calculations, what emerged were four different numbers – two versions given by the company through Dames & Moore, one from the local community, ex-workers and environmentalists and the fourth from the Ministry of Labour and Employment of the Government of India.

The 2001 Dames & Moore report had presented an unaccounted quantity of 559 kilograms, which, it claimed, could go up to 1,075 kilograms if the standard deviation was considered on the higher side. Its second report corrected this number to two tonnes (2,031 kg), after unearthing details of thirteen tonnes of locally procured mercury.

Through various checks and cross-verification of facts, the ex-workers and the local community demonstrated that over and above the two tonnes that the company, via its consultants, admitted to, another eighteen tonnes of mercury had been dispersed into the factory's surroundings. On hearing both sides and working out its own calculations, the Dr Rajaram Committee concluded that eleven tonnes (10,974 kilograms) of mercury had spread in the environment over eighteen years.

Mercury was lost from the factory primarily in two ways: first, through the glass waste when finished thermometers were scrapped upon not meeting the quality standards, as well as from broken thermometers at the shop floor during the manufacturing processes and from the spilled-out, overflown quantity at the filling room and other sections of the mercury area; and second, when the mercury that evaporated from the shop floor got flushed out by some three dozen exhaust fans from the mercury area, the distillation chamber and the recovery area. Inside the non-air-conditioned shop floor, mercury evaporated above an ambient temperature of 20°C.

The factory had arranged for an accounting of the incoming and outgoing quantities of mercury. As a hundred per cent export-oriented unit, the customs department had set up a post at the factory gate to check the inbound and outbound quantities through what they called 'bonding' and 'unbonding'. Theoretically, this would mean there should have been decimal-level accounting for the lost mercury. But the numbers showed a different story.

Dames & Moore had worked out the arithmetic on mercury balance in 2001, soon after the factory was shut down 'in order to estimate the total unaccounted losses of mercury over the 18 years of life of the operation'. It found that a total of 125 tonnes (125,676 kg) of mercury had been imported to the site inside containers from the US and Spain as per the customs bond register records. Over eighteen years, the factory had produced and exported 165 million (165,178,795) thermometers with the per unit content of mercury, varying from 0.66819 gram to 0.66666 gram, depending on the type and grade of the thermometer. On an average, this amounted to 110 tonnes (110,178 kg) of mercury exported through finished thermometers.[1]

While looking for the remaining fifteen tonnes of missing mercury, Dames & Moore found 9.74 tonnes (9,741 kg) of mercury present in the glass scrap stored on site; 0.28 tonne (284 kg) of mercury expended through the glass scrap disposed by the company; 2.98 tonnes (2,983 kg) that was available in the factory as raw mercury stock; and 1.91 tonnes (1,931 kg) on the shop floor under various processes of production as 'work-in-progress' mercury. Based on this, Dames & Moore reported an unaccounted quantity of 559 kilograms, which could go up to over a whole tonne (1,075 kg), if the statistical error provision of standard deviation were to be considered on the higher side.

Of the lost quantity of 559 kilograms, Dames & Moore further argued, seventy kilograms of mercury would have been lost through airborne emissions and another 170 kilograms would have remained in the soil at the factory site and in the ETP sludge kept in the factory. This computation would help find out the mercury lost to the Pambar Shola, and Dames & Moore's calculations had helped the company establish that only 300 kilograms of mercury was lost to the pristine sub-montane forests in the vicinity. The consultant tried to assert its estimate of the lost mercury in its May 2001 report by saying, 'This figure is considered to be of the correct order of magnitude based on the grassed nature of the site, limited evidence of soil erosion and comparison to the current level of mercury recognized onsite.'

Dames & Moore soon proved this figure was way off the mark.

By the time they began looking deeper into the mercury balance a few months later, Mody and Krishnan brought to the attention of the TNPCB the details of the thirteen tonnes of mercury locally procured by the company, in addition to the 125 tonnes of imports – a quantity not accounted for in the 2001 May report.

Therefore, Dames & Moore had no option but to revise the total quantity of mercury used in the factory over eighteen years as 138.5 tonnes (138,486 kg) in its second report, adding the thirteen tonnes pointed out by Mody and Krishnan. This additional mercury had turned out to be a Gordian knot for Dames & Moore – having to account in the mercury balance. But as the old adage goes, the most complex problems in the world have very simple solutions. And that's what Dames & Moore seemed to have decided as well.

With ten per cent additional mercury being added to the report – thirteen tonnes to the previously counted 125 tonnes – the consultants simply made a ten per cent correction on the usage to take care of the mercury balance. A straight but naive assumption.

In order to mask the additional mercury and to show that very little mercury had escaped by way of evaporation and waste disposal, Dames & Moore did some mind-boggling arithmetical jugglery of increasing the per-unit mercury content from 0.66

gram to 0.72 gram, an increase of 0.06 gram per unit. Exactly ten per cent addition of mercury per unit of thermometer.[2] Over the decades, the efforts to improve efficiency and streamline production processes had led to cutting down raw material inputs while manufacturing, including in the thermometer-making industry. So the per unit mercury content in fever thermometers had been falling since 1950; but as per Dames & Moore's calculations, it had actually increased by 0.06 gram.

According to the US Environment Protection Agency, the latest mercury content is significantly lower in fever thermometers. Oral and rectal thermometers in the US today contain only about 0.61 gram of mercury, not 0.72 gram or not even 0.66 gram.[3] Therefore, when Dames & Moore increased the per unit quantity, it was news to everyone.

But this did the trick for Dames & Moore and for Hindustan Lever. Using the 0.72 gram per piece calculation, it reported that 119 tonnes (119,067 kg) of mercury, not 110 tonnes of mercury calculated in the May 2001 report, had been shipped out through finished products – an increase of nine tonnes for the same 165 million pieces of thermometers.[4] Meaning, a saving of nine tonnes of mercury by an adjustment of a fraction.

With this adjustment, Dames & Moore kept the same quantity of 9.5 tonnes (9,476 kg) of mercury in the glass scrap stored on site and the 2.98 tonnes (2,983 kg) of mercury stock in the factory. However, it revised the work-in-progress mercury to 1.6 tonnes (1,605 kg) against the 1.9 tonnes (1,931 kg) found in the previous counting. Another 461 kilograms of mercury was found in the glass scrap disposed of by the company as against the 284 kilograms calculated in their previous report. In addition, another 593 kilograms was counted in the ETP sludge.[5]

Eventually, after 'correcting' the mercury balance, the agency concluded in its second report that only two tonnes (2,031 kg) of mercury were unaccounted for during the entire eighteen years of the factory's operations. But despite their best efforts, an additional 1.5 tonnes of mercury were found to be missing compared to its previous report.

To explain away the additional lost mercury, Dames & Moore insisted that about 291 kilograms could have been lost to the soil, another 105 kilograms trapped in the sediments at the factory site and beyond, including the water bodies nearby, and another 282 kilograms in the drains at the site.[6]

After making all these modifications, Dames & Moore stated that out of the two tonnes (2,031 kg) of unaccounted mercury, only 1.35 tonnes (1,353 kg) had been lost to the pristine sub-montane forests. It concluded in the 2002 report, 'Therefore, estimated offsite discharge to the Pambar Shola is approximately 1,350 kilograms.'[7] This was almost a 450 per cent increase from its own calculation of 300 kilograms a year ago. The number was further broken down to a per day estimate and the consultants reported: 'This estimate indicates unaccounted losses of about 75 kg annually over the 18 years of life of the operation equivalent to 200 gm per day or approximately 15 ml per day.'

But Mody and Krishnan were not convinced by these numbers. On an annual consumption of 7.7 tonnes of mercury, Dames & Moore had claimed a mere seventy-five kilograms of mercury vapour was escaping, which went against the proven international calculations in such cases. For them, a one per cent rate mercury vapour escape did not meet common logic. Unsettled by the adjustments and the different processes of accounting in the two reports of Dames & Moore, Krishnan and Mody scoured through the TNPCB and customs department records and the documentation of Madras Export Processing Zone (MEPZ) to verify the numbers in their ledgers and reports. What they found left them astonished: A quantity of seventeen tonnes (17,655 kg) of mercury had been lost to the environment, an average of one tonne per year and 3.36 kilograms per day when considering 305 working days in a year.

It took them a bit of common sense and logic to trace and track the documents and a little more effort to comprehend the numbers. Drawing invoices and records from MEPZ and Customs, they arrived at the per thermometer weight of 4.59 grams. Even on taking the revised 0.72 gram per thermometer mercury usage, they found that every thermometer had 15.71 per cent of mercury in it. Being an accountant himself and having worked in the company's accounting section for long, Krishnan verified this by looking at the total quantity of work-in-progress thermometers exported to the US after the factory was shut down and its declared mercury content – 1.6 tonnes (1,605 kg) of mercury out of a total quantity of 11.7 tonnes (11,740 kg).

As per a submission by the company to the TNPCB in 2002, the duo found that 290 tonnes of waste had been declared to be mercury-containing glass scrap in the shop floor area during the eighteen years of operations. If extrapolated that 15.71 per cent of the scrap was mercury, the total mercury wastage would be forty-five tonnes (45,402 kg). Krishnan then cross-checked this figure using another method. The data from the TNPCB records showed that the per piece input of mercury is one gram, of which only 0.721 gram is accounted in the final product, meaning the remaining was lost as waste – as glass scrap and escaped vapour. The remaining 0.279 gram per unit would translate to forty-six tonnes for the 165 million units produced in the factory.

Out of the forty-six tonnes, Krishnan deducted ten tonnes

(10,311 kg) of recovered and reused mercury, as submitted by the company in a letter to the TNPCB; subtracted another 15.4 tonnes (15,405 kg) as the sum total reported by Dames & Moore as glass waste on the site, meaning mercury that had gone to scrap dealers, work-in-progress mercury and the raw stock in the factory; along with yet another two tonnes (2,031 kg) of mercury considered as unaccounted in the 2002 Dames & Moore report. After removing these from the forty-five tonnes, Krishnan arrived at 17.655 tonnes of unaccounted mercury over and above what had been reported by Dames & Moore.

If the two tonnes (2,031 kg) of mercury declared by Dames & Moore as unaccounted and lost was not deducted, the total mercury disappeared through gaseous dispersal and through glass waste would be as much as 19.68 tonnes (19,686 kg). In other words, this was the total quantity of the mercury that had disappeared.

The mercury balance was the deciding factor in sensitizing authorities and people on the suspicious actions of the company and rendering its arguments meaningless. Unfortunately, however, none of the half-dozen committees set up at various times explored this issue at depth, except one. The Dr Rajaram Committee was the only body that touched upon this fact while examining various aspects related to the factory's operations.

After going through the mercury accounts and details provided by the company, its consultants and the regulatory bodies, the committee found that '10.9 tonnes (10,974 kg) of mercury has been lost to the environment'. It observed: 'On calculation it was found that the total mercury used for thermometers was 11024 kg instead of 11906 kg as stated in the balance sheet. 10% of mercury is unaccounted for, which must have been thrown to the environment.'[8]

In the absence of the TNPCB making an objective assessment of the mercury balance, the Ministry of Labour's assessment of eleven tonnes of lost mercury remains, to this day, the official account on the weight of mercury dispersed through various means during the eighteen-year period. This translates to around 610 kilograms per year. Almost two kilograms a day.

# 51

# INDIAN OR DUTCH?

UNTIL RECENTLY, THE GLOBALLY ACCEPTED MEASURE FOR RESTORING any heavy metal-contaminated site were the Dutch Standards – the golden benchmark for environmental restoration. The Dutch National Institute for Public Health and Environmental Protection had researched the human toxicological and eco-toxicological effects extensively towards the end of the last millennium before arriving at the levels that could be considered safe for the soil, water and environment.

In 2000, the Dutch government issued a soil remediation policy with intervention values indicative of serious contamination and suggested target levels. This was more than a decade after the research details were discussed at length in the Parliament in 1989 to set guideline values for restoring a site contaminated due to industrial activity or accident.[1] The research found that the normal background concentrations of mercury in soil/sediment are 0.3 microgram per kilogram and 0.05 microgram per litre in groundwater respectively. Therefore, it recommended achieving a level of at least ten micrograms per kilogram in soil and 0.3 microgram per litre in water while trying to restore a polluted site.[2] Known as the Dutch Intervention Value, it had been followed by international environmental agencies, private and public, and governments around the world ever since.

Therefore, when Dames & Moore was asked to look at the standards for remediation of the contaminated soil in the twenty-two-acre factory land, the agency could have simply recommended the Dutch Intervention Value as the restoration level.

The soil testing for its 2002 study had revealed that soil mercury levels on the site ranged from thirty micrograms per kilogram to 500 micrograms per kilogram. As a matter of fact, even some areas outside the factory site showed higher levels of mercury – twenty-six micrograms per kilogram to 110 microgram per kilogram.[3]

About sixty per cent of about 8,600 sq metres and another of 3,000 sq metres land areas within the factory site contained mercury levels up to thirty micrograms per kilogram; and yet another area of 1,800 sq metres where forty per cent of the soil contained the same high levels. Some patches within these areas showed up to 500 micrograms per kilogram of mercury – extremely dangerous for any kind of human contact.

In its estimate, Dames & Moore had found an area of 4,100 sq metres within the factory site containing 7,400 tonnes of soil, which needed to be cleaned up to eliminate 291 kilograms of mercury. For another 105 kilograms of mercury estimated to be lying outside the factory site, the consultant advised that it 'does not require remediation levels and will decrease naturally over time'.

When Dames & Moore announced its recommendation of ten micrograms per kilogram for restoring the heavily contaminated factory land and leaving the contaminated soil outside the site untouched, Mody and the local community were furious. They questioned how the company could allow the contaminated areas outside the factory site to remain untreated and how they had reached the target value of ten micrograms per kilogram when the natural background levels of mercury were only 0.3 microgram per kilogram. Their immediate demand was to restore the factory site and its surroundings to the existing levels before the factory had been set up. In other words, 0.3 microgram per kilogram or better.

To be fair, the company had abided by two of Dames & Moore recommendations in quick succession – clearing 7.4 tonnes of mercury waste from the external scrapyard and sending some 290 tonnes of mercury-laden waste for recycling to the US. And so, Mody and the community expected the same comportment on this matter. But they were proven wrong soon.

At the upper echelons of Hindustan Unilever, a few calculations would have been made before deciding not to accept this crucial cleanup standard. One could have been the cost implications of remediating 7,400 tonnes of the top soil – from a mercury content level of thirty to 500 micrograms per kilogram of soil to ten micrograms per kilogram or less. The other seemed to be geopolitical. The world over, different countries were working on their own intervention values for various heavy metals, and India was no exception. Therefore, the unspoken strategy seemed to be focused on delaying the remediation process until the Indian authorities shared their own intervention values for heavy metals. Meanwhile, there were fierce lobbying efforts by vested interest industry groups with the government to stipulate a higher target value. As a bonus, during the waiting period, a reasonable part of the mercury in the soil would have dissipated into the air and leached to deeper levels of the soil.

In fact, there were ample opportunities to get Hindustan Unilever to agree to the third, and the most important, recommendation of its consultant – remediating the factory site to the Dutch Intervention Value levels. The window of opportunity lasted until the end of 2003, when the upright, concerned bureaucrat Sheela

Rani Chunkath moved out from the helm of the TNPCB – more than a year after the Dames & Moore had made its recommendation in 2002.

The campaigners and the local community had not anticipated the strategy of Hindustan Unilever to be presented in such clear terms. At various times, the campaigners, including myself, unwittingly fell into the trap of the company. The campaigners kept arguing for a better standard than ten micrograms per kilogram, suggesting a place like Kodaikanal has natural background levels around 0.3 microgram per kilogram and the remediation standard, therefore, should be at least five micrograms per kilogram.

In a meeting on 11 October 2002 of the Hazardous Waste Management Committee, soon after the submission of Dames & Moore's second report, the local community formally raised objections to the target value, since it was way off the mark for a site abutting forests. The TNPCB asked Mody to submit documents supporting his claim that 0.3 microgram per kilogram was a more suitable target level considering the ecological sensitivity of the site. And the process of remediating the site, thus, got entangled in the red tapes of the state regulator. This was also because the priority was to decontaminate the equipment, machinery and materials lying in the factory.

The site cleanup would eventually get delayed by over twenty years. Any serious remediation measures would only start after the Government of India officially brought out its own remediation standards for polluted sites in March 2015. When the remediation standards were eventually announced by the Ministry of Environment and Forests in 2015, it turned out to be a celebratory moment for the company.

The ministry had introduced a 'screening level', below which, it did not find any potential risks to human health or the environment, and a 'response level', only above which could there be a threat to human health or the environment.[4] The screening level was 6.6 micrograms per kilogram, while the response level for mercury was fixed at thirty-six micrograms per kilogram for soil.[5] How the ministry had arrived at these arbitrary values is anybody's guess.

# 52

# NEERI AND CLAUDE ALVARES

IN 1986, A COVER STORY UNDER THE HEADLINE 'THE GREAT GENE Robbery' appeared in the now-defunct *Illustrated Weekly of India*, a magazine started by the *Times of India* group in 1923 and edited, over the years, by renowned journalists like Sean Mandy, Khushwant Singh and Pritish Nandy. The story had been investigated for months and reported by rising young environmentalist Claude Alvares, who had just finished his doctorate from the Technische Hogeschool in the Netherlands. He had exposed the efforts of international agencies to rob India of its native genetic pool of grains through the International Rice Research Institute in Manila, which was established with the support of the Ford Foundation and the Rockefeller Foundation in the sixties.

Alvares went on to set up the Goa Foundation, a civil society group in the tourist city state, along with his environmental lawyer wife, to keep fighting issues of biodiversity legally and through protests.

On learning that Alvares had been named to be part of the Supreme Court Monitoring Committee (SCMC) on Hazardous Wastes and Hazardous Chemicals in 2004, Mody felt relieved. In fact, setting up the SCMC was a landmark step by the apex court towards the end of 2003 in a milestone case by the Vandana Shiva-led Research Foundation for Science and Technology.[1] Mody had worked with Alvares during his time in Mumbai and even later. With some effort, they managed to get the Kodaikanal mercury issue included in the SCMC agenda once the case was brought to the attention of the committee in its meeting with the TNPCB on 8–9 January in Mumbai.

On its visit to the hill station in September 2004, the five-member SCMC team found 'the situation extremely serious in nature' and stated that 'there [could] be no two opinions that remediation and rehabilitation of the natural environment and of workers and others affected are both urgently required'.[2] The Committee, therefore, asked Hindustan Lever (HLL) to execute a revolving bank guarantee for ₹500 million for the TNPCB to implement remediation. To maintain an oversight on the activities, the committee recommended the reconstitution of the Local Area Environment Committee (LEAC) with independent experts and members from the local community.[3] This sent alarm bells ringing at HLL.

After the visit of the SCMC and its report coming out in ten days, HLL had realized the pitch was getting skewed in favour of the local community. Therefore, the company began working quietly on removing the plant, machinery and heavily contaminated soil from the factory floors. This was despite the TNPCB reconstituting a Working Committee and a new Local Area Environment Committee towards the end of the year.[4] To be fair, the SCMC had directed the TNPCB to seek the guidance of a national institution like Council of Scientific and Industrial Research–National Environmental Engineering Research Institute (CSIR–NEERI) for facilitating and monitoring the remediation activities. And so, NEERI was roped in to assist at the cost and management of Hindustan Lever.

NEERI started its work in January 2005 with a visit to the factory site. It began collecting samples, led by its scientists Dr Tapan Chakrabarti and Dr Mahena Patil, who would soon become experts in 'remediation of mercury-contaminated sites'.[5] After analysing the samples, the team found that about 7,358 tonnes of soil contaminated with elemental mercury required remediation, on taking the cut-off level as ten micrograms per kilogram. However, its risk assessment study arrived at a site-specific target remediation level of twenty-five micrograms per kilogram. Accordingly, it recommended techniques such as soil washing and thermal retorting to be feasible for the remediation process.[6] The soil washing would help separate the contaminated feed soil into coarse-grained and fine-grained fractions, while the thermal retorting would help segregate mercury from the fine soil. The cleaned-up coarse soil conforming to the desired standard could then be used for backfilling the site.

In case the mercury concentration in the coarse soil turned out to be greater than the target, it could then be processed in the thermal retort unit to reduce the level further. In addition, the fine soil containing higher concentration of mercury could be treated in the thermal retort unit, inside which it would be heated under a vacuum to volatilize and remove mercury from the soil.[7]

With NEERI's assessment and advice, HLL began decontaminating and moving out the machinery, upon which Mody wrote to Alvares, the SCMC and later to the new chairman of the TNPCB, R. Ramachandran, pointing out that the dismantling of machinery was being done without due process and without the presence of the local community.

In July 2005, he complained to the SCMC, alleging 'collusion between NEERI and Hindustan Lever' and subversion of the committee's order on decontamination of the machinery. Greenpeace formally approached the Government of India's Minister for Environment and Forests, A. Raja. The aggrieved ex-workers filed a police complaint against the company's management. Soon pressure grew from concerned citizens from different parts of the country and, within a few days, the SCMC convened a meeting at the TNPCB office in Chennai, which was attended by the company representatives and the local community led by Mody. After hearing all sides, the SCMC issued directives on decontamination of the machinery and remediation of the soil and appointed an Expert Committee to recommend the decontamination criteria.

The agitated local community, under Mody's leadership, asked for a detailed project report (DPR) on the protocol for decontamination of the plant and machinery and kept locking horns with the officials and chairman of the TNPCB until the Expert Committee appointed by the SCMC visited and witnessed the developments at the site. The environmentalists moved the Madras High Court by February 2006, seeking to suspend decontamination of the machinery and equipment and to direct Hindustan Lever and the TNPCB to carry out any work on decontamination only after preparing a DPR and conducting sufficient feasibility studies. The court allowed the prayer and ordered them to seek approval from the Working Committee as well.[8]

Once the TNPCB furnished copies of protocol as well as all relevant documents pertaining to the work schedule for removing contaminated material, the court allowed the work to resume and asked the company to take the local community into confidence. With this, the protracted confrontation over decontamination of the plant and machinery had come to an end.

The decontamination of equipment, machinery and materials

began a while later and was completed by May 2006. The decontaminated equipment and machinery, with apparent permissible levels of mercury content, were thereafter 'disposed of as scrap to industrial recyclers'.[9] All this was, of course, carried out under the controversial supervision and guidance of NEERI.

# 53

# FROM 25 TO 20

IN SEPTEMBER 2005, ALMOST A YEAR AFTER ITS VISIT TO THE contaminated hill station, the SCMC directed the TNPCB to constitute an Expert Committee to recommend decontamination methods and arrive at the soil remediation criteria based on a site-specific risk assessment study. When the new committee was formed and began working with the TNPCB, by the end of the year, Hindustan Lever preferred to work with the newly formed forum rather than interacting with the reconstituted Working Committee or the Local Area Environment Committee. Soon, the company and the TNPCB slowly began bypassing the two committees and the SCMC began to fade in significance.

On 28 February 2007, the NEERI submitted its report titled the 'Protocol for Remediation of Mercury Contaminated Site', listing out its suggested approach, the methodology and other technical aspects. It used the detailed risk assessment study by a UK company named Environmental Resource Management (ERM), commissioned by Hindustan Lever a year earlier, which had suggested Site Specific Target Level (SSTL) for remediation. The levels advised by the ERM were twenty-five micrograms per kilogram for child residents and twenty-nine micrograms per kilogram for children's recreational facilities – much higher than the level suggested by Dames & Moore in 2002. The ERM said it had considered and arrived at a level that could be tolerated by children, if they were to be exposed to mercury at the site in the future, by way of vegetable ingestion, dermal contact, indoor dust inhalation, outdoor dust inhalation and soil ingestion.[1]

Once the study was submitted, the state regulator asked the NEERI to obtain approval from the Expert Committee appointed upon the directions of the SCMC, and a meeting was called. At the 2 June meeting of the Expert Committee, convened to jointly review the NEERI protocol, the local community, including HWMC and LAEC, was ignored and the meeting was only attended by Hindustan Lever (by now Hindustan Unilever), the NEERI and ERM, besides the TNPCB officials and members of the Expert Committee. Once the ERM-proposed level of twenty-five micrograms per kilogram was accepted by the Expert Committee at this meeting, the clean-up criteria were more or less settled. This was despite the Expert Committee earlier recommending an average level of twenty micrograms per kilogram with a maximum allowable concentration of twenty-five microgram per kilogram at places.

As the local community kept mounting pressure on the regulator, citing the Dames & Moore recommendation, the TNPCB began vacillating in its position and wrote to the Expert Committee members that the standards accepted was twenty micrograms and not twenty-five micrograms per kilogram. And the spat would continue between the members of the committee, the NEERI and TNPCB for three months until the latter finally communicated to NEERI and Hindustan Unilever in August that 'after further clarification obtained from the members of the expert committee, it is hereby informed that after treatment of contaminated soil, the concentration of mercury shall be less than or equal to 20 mg per kg for 95 per cent of the samples analysed and only for 5 per cent of samples the maximum allowable concentration shall be 25 mg per kg'.[2]

In November, the ERM submitted its final report prepared in collaboration with NEERI titled, 'Soil Remediation at HUL Factory Site, Kodaikanal, Tamil Nadu, India – Detailed Project Report'. In a couple of weeks, a meeting was convened by the TNPCB to review the report. At the meeting, the Expert Committee, Hindustan Unilever, NEERI and the ERM decided that the TNPCB would issue 'in principle clearance' to start the basic remediation work and NEERI would be associated with the task full-time, along with the on-site ERM experts. On 7 December 2007, the TNPCB Chairman formally issued 'in-principle clearance to carry out the preparatory works in respect of the remediation at site', subject to a set of conditions.[3] And a formal permission was granted for full-scale remediation some six months after the submission of final DPR by the company in March 2008.[4]

By now, it was clear that the environmental campaigners and the local community had lost the battle for better clean-up standards. The local community had been completely sidelined in the entire process. They reminded the TNPCB about the importance of community participation as pronounced by the Supreme Court in a 2003 order. The court, citing the Rio Declaration's Principle 10, and the Section 3(2) (12) of the Environment Protection Act, 1986, had stressed the 'right to receive information and community participation with particular emphasis on hazardous materials', on collection and dissemination of information on matters of environment pollution.[5] They continued to bring up the issue, seeking clarifications. The regulator was asked to explain the basis for revising the clean-up standards to twenty micrograms per kilogram and to include community oversight to ensure transparency in remediation. Most of their suggestions were ignored by the TNPCB or responded with one-line answers.

Aggrieved and affronted, the community and the activists convened a public meeting in Kodaikanal on 9 October 2009, which condemned the ongoing covert activities of cleanup and alleged collusion between the TNPCB, NEERI and Hindustan Unilever. The meeting ended with them demanding to stop the remediation work until a public oversight committee was set up and cleanup standards rationalized. As the pressure mounted, through media reports and from environmentalists, the TNPCB once again convened a meeting of the Expert Committee, the TNPCB, Hindustan Unilever and NEERI in early January 2010, which decided that 'the Scientific Expert Committee shall review and prepare a report for fixing the threshold limit of mercury for soil remediation and constantly monitor the soil remediation work and associated activities'.[6]

The road to better clean-up was about to hit a *cul de sac* when the activists pulled a few tricks out of their hat. First, an eight-page report titled 'Double Standards' was released by the Tamil Nadu Alliance Against Mercury (TAAM) on 8 March, followed by a press conference by two filmmakers and an environmentalist – Alphonse Roy, Shekar Dattatri and Nanditha Krishna – to buttress their arguments. The third and the final step was to take up the issue directly with the environment minister, Jairam Ramesh, who was a veteran on matters of environment and sustainability.

When the local community and the environmental groups led by Jayaraman and Mody approached him, the minister readily agreed to look into the issue. He asked the secretary of his ministry, Rahul Bojja, to send a letter to the chairperson of the TNPCB thereafter. A reply came within a week, informing the minister that the apprehensions of the activists were 'unfounded'. The TNPCB also explained that the local monitoring forum, LAEC, had been dissolved by the SCMC upon setting up the Expert Committee and that permission had been granted to Hindustan Unilever for pre-remediation work at a level of twenty micrograms per kilogram for ninety-five per cent of samples and twenty-five micrograms per kilogram for five per cent of the samples in order to assess and fix the standards. Based on the sampling pre-remediation work, the Expert Committee decided to scientifically validate and substantiate the data. In the entire exchange, the TNPCB evaded direct answers to one key question – the final cleanup standards accepted by the regulator. Ramesh then asked the the Central Pollution Control Board (CPCB), which had authority over the state pollution control boards, to step in.

In September, the CPCB wrote to the TNPCB, suggesting that a criterion for mercury levels in soil ranging from five to twenty-five micrograms per kilogram, needed to be agreed upon, before taking up remedial measures; the Expert Committee along with the TNPCB needed to involve Local Area Environment Committee, Municipalities, Forest Department, Agricultural Department, Revenue Department etc, and the remedial operation could be monitored by a committee comprising TNPCB members, members of the Expert Committee and the local community.

Another letter by the CPCB to the Ministry of Environment and Forests remarked that 'much lower Site-Specific Target Level may be necessary to protect critical ecological resources and public health'. It also called for a fresh 'Risk Analysis Report to arrive at Site Specific Target Level based on risk to ecosystem integrity rather than risk to human health alone.'

Abiding by the CPCB directive for further studies and pressure from the union ministry, the TNPCB decided in favour of additional studies. In consultation with the CPCB, it identified the Indian Institute of Technology (IIT), Delhi, National Botanical Research Institute, Lucknow, and the Indian Institute of Soil and Water Conservation Research Centre, Ooty, for carrying out further studies. These institutions submitted their findings by February 2011 to the TNPCB and to the Expert Committee as advised by the CPCB. In its study, IIT Delhi recommended a site-specific clean-up standard of 22.4 micrograms per kilogram for soil remediation. The TNPCB and the Expert Committee deliberated on their findings for the next two years and made two site visits to the factory. Based on the findings of these new studies and its own further assessments, the Expert Committee arrived at a new standard of twenty micrograms per kilogram, instead of the earlier criterion of twenty-five micrograms per kilogram, by May 2013. Later, the TNPCB would return to the CPCB and seek its advice for further moves by February 2014.

For the next ten months, things remained eerily quiet because of the heat and dust raised by the parliamentary elections and the formation of the new ministry. However, the local and environmental groups kept pushing for better standards and community oversight. The issue would resurface only months after the right-wing government led by Narendra Modi assumed power in 2014. Despite a change of guard at the national level, the CPCB poked its nose into the matter, and the TNPCB had no choice but to consult it. Afterwards, the CPCB invited the local community and environmentalists for a meeting in December to discuss their concerns on the remediation standards. However, on realizing the playing field had been completely dismantled with the change of government and there were no political heavyweights on their side to push the case anymore, the environmentalists and the local community chose not to participate. Instead, they considered another option, a stronger one – or so they thought.

# 54

# THE GREEN TRIBUNAL

IN JULY 2011, JAIRAM RAMESH WAS MOVED OUT OF THE environment ministry as the Minister for Rural Development, a few months after the Wall Street Journal called him 'India's Big Green Wrecking Machine', referring to his relentless pro-environment stands that had apparently hindered industrial expansions. In his brief two-year stint, Ramesh had set off a series of trailblazing changes in the country's environmental management. One of his notable achievements was setting up the National Green Tribunal with four zonal benches. Within two months in office, he shared a draft of the National Green Tribunal Bill and enacted it in May 2010, despite large-scale resentment and heavy opposition from various quarters. The objective of the Bill and, therefore, that of the Green Tribunal, was 'effective and expeditious disposal of cases relating to environmental protection and conservation of forests and other natural resources including enforcement of any legal right relating to environment and giving relief and compensation for damages to persons and property and for matters connected therewith or incidental thereto'.[1]

In retrospect, the Indian delegation, led by its environment minister Kamal Nath, had promised at the famous 1992 UN Earth

Summit in Rio de Janeiro to 'provide judicial and administrative remedies to the victims of environmental damage'.[2] Therefore, it was the fulfilling of a two-decade-old promise, when Ramesh set up the Tribunal to make the polluters pay – the third country to do so after Australia and New Zealand. The most striking features of the Act were that the Tribunal was not bound by the cumbersome Indian Code of Civil Procedure, 1908, but instead was to be driven by the principles of natural justice, and claimed that it would dispose of all cases, as well as appeals, within six months.

After the change of guard in New Delhi in 2014, when the CPCB under the new government called a meeting, in December 2014, of concerned people, including the local community and environmentalists, the NGO representatives decided to boycott it – aware that it would not end in a favourable outcome, since the die had already been cast to pass a twenty micrograms per kilogram remediation standard. All signals pointed them towards the National Green Tribunal as the last bastion of hope.

Meanwhile, the TNPCB, in consultation with the CPCB, had advised Hindustan Unilever to go ahead with the work of a Detailed Project Report, which had been submitted by August 2015. By December 2016, permission was granted to start the preparatory work and trials for soil remediation. Permission would also be accorded soon after a writ petition filed by Jayaraman in 2006 was disposed of by the Madras High Court. The writ petition was to prevent Hindustan Lever from proceeding with remediation without detailed protocols, project reports and feasibility studies and without the approval of the Working Committee and Local Area Environment Committee constituted by the TNPCB.

In fact, when the case came up for hearing before the bench of Chief Justice Sanjay Kaul and Justice R. Mahadevan in July, the petitioner took a stand that the Working Committee and Local

Area Environment Committee were monitoring the situation and they would approach relevant forums in case of any further grievance. In a way, indicating that the petition may be withdrawn. And therefore, the bench would close the petition.[3]

The deal did not offer the prospects for a peaceful reconciliation between the company and the environmentalists. Rather, the campaigners strategized to move the National Green Tribunal after issuance of formal permission for remediation by the TNPCB. Soon after the grant of the permission, Mody moved the National Green Tribunal on 25 January 2017.

The Tribunal, after considering the matter over several hearings, by the end of April, allowed the company to proceed with the preparatory work and trial runs, which would be monitored by the Expert Committee, the TNPCB and the CPCB. The bench also directed that the Kodaikanal Municipality and the Local Area Environmental Committee (LAEC) be allowed to witness the activities on site. Further, in August, the Tribunal would enhance the LAEC with three more 'special invitees', including Mody.[4]

Accordingly, trial soil remediation started on 16 August 2017. The process carried on until November as per the provisions of the Detailed Project Report. Based on the outcome of the trial, a final remediation proposal was submitted to the TNPCB. Without wasting much time, TNPCB granted permissions in January for full-scale soil remediation up to a standard of twenty micrograms per kilogram.

In the meantime, the proceedings continued at the Green Tribunal even as the trial remediation went on at the factory site. The Tribunal asked the CPCB to obtain an expert opinion from an institute with expertise in mercury contamination, and also directed it to examine the results of the trial undertaken by the NEERI. All this was to ascertain whether the twenty micrograms per kilogram Site-Specific Target Level could be accepted as the right remediation standard or not. The Tribunal asked Hindustan Unilever to wait for its final order before starting any remediation work.[5]

In between, the most awaited 'National Programme for Rehabilitation of Polluted Sites (NPRPS)' was issued by the Ministry of Environment and Forests – to be precise, in March 2015. By its own description, it was a document to guide the assessment and remediation of contaminated sites.

The NPRPS had specified two levels – Screening Levels and Response Levels. The Response Level for mercury was the target above which there could be a threat to human health or the environment and would require some form of response to provide an adequate level of safety to protect public health and/or the environment. The NPRPS fixed this level at the revised Dutch Intervention Value of thirty-six micrograms per kilogram of soil. For agricultural, residential and recreational lands, the Screening Level, the level below which there was no potential risk to human health or the environment and needed no further investigation and assessment to establish it, was fixed at 6.6 micrograms per kilogram. A higher Screening Level of twenty-six micrograms was prescribed for commercial land and fifty micrograms for industrial land.[6]

Going by this definition, only the levels below 6.6 micrograms per kilogram can be considered safe for human health and environment, and Mody had every reason to argue for the Screening Level as the desirable standard for remediation before the Green Tribunal.

Disappointingly for Mody and the local community, the eight-member committee with four experts from the IITs in Delhi, Mumbai and Madras, and one each from NEERI, IITR, AIIMS and the Indian Council of Medical Research, after holding two meetings and considering the NPRPS levels, had concluded that the Screening Level of 6.6 micrograms/kilogram could not be treated as a remediation standard for the Kodaikanal factory site. In fact, Mody had objected to the constitution of the committee itself, alleging 'conflict of interest' for four of its eight members. He pointed out that the NEERI had received ₹3.4 million from Hindustan Unilever as consultancy fees, mostly related to the ongoing issue. The representative from IIT-Delhi was an author of a report that Mody had earlier objected to; the representative from IIT-Bombay had worked as a consultant to Hindustan Unilever; and the CSIR-IITR representative was a collaborator of the company by IITR's own admission.[7] Instead, he suggested a committee with 'neutral' experts from IIT-Hyderabad, Centre for Ornithology and Nature, Coimbatore, and a retired chemical engineer from IIT-Madras.

While the case was reaching its last leg, former Chief Justice of the Orissa High Court and a sitting judge of the Supreme Court, Adarsh Kumar Goel, replaced Justice Swatanter Kumar as the chairperson of the Tribunal on 6 July 2018. The three-member bench headed by Justice Goel did not find merits in Mody's objections, noting that the CPCB, under directions of the Tribunal, had selected the experts who deliberated the issue objectively, and furnished a unanimous report, saying, 'the mere fact of association by some of the experts will not vitiate the report and the opinion furnished by the CPCB'.[8] Rejecting Mody's plea, the bench ruled: 'At this stage, execution of remediation work should be of primary focus rather than conducting further studies, since the subject site remains contaminated for more than 20 years posing environmental and health risks.'[9] The disposal of Mody's petition by the Tribunal on 1 November 2018 cleared the way for the cleanup with a remediation standard of twenty micrograms per kilogram, against the NPRPS screening level of 6.6 micrograms per kilogram, which could have made the land suitable for agricultural, residential and recreational purposes.

Almost at the same time, IIT-Hyderabad had published a modelling study in the respected *Journal of Hazardous, Toxic, and Radioactive Waste*, which said even if remediation was immediately started and completed by 2020, the mercury levels in the soil would only marginally reduce by 2050. It suggested that 'a complete or partial clean-up of factory soil in 2020 will marginally reduce the level of contamination of forest soil by 2050 compared with a no clean-up scenario'.[10]

A law-abiding citizen with utmost faith in the Indian judicial system, Mody was left with one option. He decided to bring the issue to the Supreme Court's attention in order to finally achieve a miracle in the fight he had been part of for the last eighteen years. With his faith somewhat shattered and personal finances having dwindled, he approached the apex court on 30 January 2019.

The division bench of Justice Rohinton Nariman and Justice Vineet Saran threw away his civil appeal no. 1666 of 2019 on 5 March, effectively closing all doors to the frail senior citizen.[11] This would end eighteen years of struggle for the planet. But he refused to give up.

Mody still hoped for an outcome that could bring about better remediation of the site. As he walked out of the courtroom, he remembered the bestselling author Stephen King's words: 'Hope is a good thing, maybe the best of things, and no good thing ever dies.'

When the tired, debilitated septuagenarian returned home the next day, yet another shock awaited him. His humble cottage on St Mary's Road, as old as the factory itself, had been demolished.

# EPILOGUE

## A Poisoned Legacy

ONE OF THE KEY SPICES USED IN THE PREPARATION OF TASTY Indian dishes, including certain biryani preparations, is lichen. Known in Tamil as 'marappani', it is not cultivated on farms but collected chiefly from the wild. Lichen absorbs the aroma of wildflowers, leaves and animal scents directly from the air, which gives this rare spice its distinct flavour. As the popularity and consumption of biryani have rapidly grown in the country in recent times, so has the demand for lichen.

Some decades ago, certain traders began to approach members of a tribe called the Paliyan, who were known for gathering forest produce in the Western Ghats region of Tamil Nadu, asking them to supply lichen regularly. The Paliyan, one of the last surviving aboriginal groups of south India, are a Dravidian tribe native to the hills of Palani and its surroundings. The name Paliyan, derived from the word '*palaniyan*', means 'from Palani'. The tribe is also known as Palaiyar or Pazhaiyar. The nomadic hunter-gatherers live in small caves or hut-like structures between rocks and hunt and forage for food deep inside the forests. On average, a Paliyan family has seven members who share a room or two among themselves and with their livestock.[1] They live on wild yam, tubers, honey, bamboo rice, jujube, jackfruit, mango and such produce.

Some studies claim there are around 6,000 Paliyans scattered over the hills of Tamil Nadu. They remain one of the most exploited and voiceless peoples, who, throughout history, have been oppressed and forced to move from one place to another.[23] Another account pegs their total number at 9,500. Over the last four decades, the Paliyan population has been dwindling at an unfathomably alarming rate. Because of their scattered distribution and nomadic way of life, even social scientists have been left confounded.

Over time, however, many active gatherers among the tribe began to show symptoms of neurotoxicity and nephrotoxicity. It was evident at least among those who occasionally showed up at the Kodaikanal foothills to sell forest produce to the middlemen. Since the Paliyans largely depend on their own medicinal system – the Siddha system – and rarely visit medical practitioners or hospitals, there are no documented accounts of their symptoms. In any case, the authorities have made no efforts to explore possible links between their symptoms and mercury poisoning.

Just as there aren't enough studies on the impact of dispersed mercury on the Paliyan, there haven't been any impact studies on the Kodaikanal ecosystem either. For instance, the lion-tailed macaques found in the region still remain in the 'endangered' category of the IUCN Red List of Threatened Species since the last update in 2020, based on technical reports from researchers at the Centre for Wildlife Studies and the Sálim Ali Centre for Ornithology and Natural History.[4] A report has suggested that the total global population of 4,000 lion-tailed macaques could decline by twenty per cent in the next twenty-five years due to a variety of reasons, mercury poisoning being one of them.

More commonly found relatives of *homo sapiens* than the lion-tailed macaques in the mercury-affected Pambar Shola region – the Kodaikanal Wildlife Sanctuary and the nearby Berijam forests – are the Nilgiri langurs, bonnet macaques and black-footed grey langurs, all facing threat to survival. The leopard and tiger, two of the five surviving species of big cats, once frequently sighted in Tiger Shola, perhaps due to the abundance of their prey species such as the spotted deer (chital), sambar, blackbuck, black-naped hare, Indian wild boar, Indian porcupine, common langur and Indian peafowl,[5] are now 'vulnerable' in the region.

The sloth bear that feeds on fruits, ants and termites, listed as 'vulnerable' on the IUCN Red List, has almost disappeared from the area, mainly Bear Shola, because of the damage to its habitat, most severely in the last two decades. The Asiatic elephant, commonly reported in the area until recently, too, has mostly disappeared.[6]

Other hoofed mammals under threat in the region are the Indian bison, barking deer (sambar) and the wild dog, the latter of which is in the Red List's endangered category. Also known as whistling dog, red dog or mountain wolf, a large number of the 2,500 surviving dogs live in the region and their headcount has been declining.[7]

The Bombay Natural History Society (BNHS), which had been conducting bird ringing in Kodaikanal and its surroundings since 1970, recorded ninety-four species of rare birds in the Kodaikanal Wildlife Sanctuary. Most of the high-altitude endemic birds of the Western Ghats that were previously seen in these sholas,[8] have stopped visiting the region presently. For instance, the Nilgiri pipit, has decreased in number in the locale and the frequency of sightings of the Indian rufous babbler has plummeted drastically. Generalist bird species from the middle and lower elevations such as the plum-headed parakeet, brahminy kite, black kite, Tickell's blue flycatcher, chestnut-headed bee-eater, red spurfowl, red-vented bulbul and common hawk-cuckoo have moved to higher-altitude areas, where they could be competing with habitat-specific endemic birds.[9]

Bird and animal sightings in the region have been steadily declining in the recent years – both in the number of species and the frequency of their sightings. The clearing of forest cover for cultivation, the consequent reduction in rainfall and rise in temperature have had a severe impact on the local climate, and therefore, on the animal and avian visits. Kodaikanal's popularity as a tourist hill station and an industrial town has also had a damaging effect on the region's ecosystem. As the cover of industry and tourism has broadened, human settlements have intruded upon large tracts of land around the hill ridges and reduced the sensitive forest-land area. But more acute than all these was the imbalance created by the spread of mercury in the sensitive sholas that would have destroyed many and forced many other endemic species to move deeper into the wild or to other nearby regions.

Indeed, the consequences have been palpable on the region's flora and fauna. A revised survey of the local wildlife stated: 'Many species of animals such as the bear, tiger, and the Nilgiri tahr, Nilgiri langur and Asiatic elephant have disappeared. So have many species of reptiles, amphibians and fishes.'[10] In fact, not only the larger fauna, even the butterflies, cicadas, dragonflies and damselflies have begun to disappear.

Due to the lack of scientific studies on the impact of heavy metal poisoning on the flora and fauna in the region, it is difficult to ascertain the precise contribution of mercury emission and mercury waste disposal from the thermometer factory, in addition to the mercury waste dump in the forest areas until 2001, to the depletion of the sensitive ecosystem; however, even with the present evidence, it is reasonable to deduce that the impact is considerable. It is clear that the effects of the mercury dispersed and dumped in the forest areas until 2001 have caused a devastation of a catastrophic degree in Kodaikanal.

At this point, any discerning reader would wonder what prevented science from establishing the extent of damage caused by Hindustan Lever's mercury dispersal in Kodaikanal. Yes, despite ample anecdotes of large-scale devastation on the flora and fauna, there haven't been many noteworthy impact studies. In this regard, an exception is some of the remarkable research work carried out on Kodai Lake to understand the bioaccumulation of mercury in fish, and on lichens and mosses in the adjacent areas of the factory. Nevertheless, if the steady mercury dispersal is a fact and the bioaccumulation in lichens, mosses and fish has been proven incontrovertibly, isn't it fair to say the ecosystem of the area would also be indisputably impacted, causing a debilitating effect on the flora, fauna and humans?

For a long time, studies had established beyond doubt that elemental mercury absorption by plant leaves led the trail to humans. A peer-reviewed study on mercury toxicity in plants published in the *Botanical Review* found that some of the mercury emitted into the atmosphere is absorbed by leaves and migrated to humus, the organic component of soil, through fallen leaves. Besides, airborne mercury contributed significantly to the mercury content of crops and reached humans, too.[11] The high levels of mercury dispersal into the atmosphere leads to reduced photosynthesis in leaf foliage, thereby contributing to the stunted growth of plants and devastation of forests. The *Botanical Review* study concluded that 'mercury replaces magnesium, the central atom of chlorophyll, and prevents photosynthetic light harvesting in the affected chlorophyll molecules, resulting in the breakdown of photosynthesis process itself.'[12] In line with this finding, a recent UNEP-funded study found serious impact on the physiological activities of plants in the region because of increased mercury presence in the air, particularly during daytime.

The study supported by the UNEP's Global Mercury Observation System (GMOS) established that the daytime total gaseous mercury (TGM) concentration in Kodaikanal was strongly modified by solar radiation, evaporation, rainfall and seasonal changes.[13]

A 2019 modelling study by IIT Hyderabad carried out a mass balance analysis, showing that the main source of mercury in the uncontaminated forest areas shifted over time from atmospheric deposition to direct inputs (waste dumps) and mercury runoff from the HLL factory.[14] Of late, other studies linking the factory's impact on the ecosystem have emerged. Many more are underway and several research groups are on the ground investigating. This makes demonstrating the impact of mercury dispersal in the area – on the ecosystem in general and on specific target species populations, including human beings – through science significantly relevant. Scientific community is hopeful that many breakthrough studies of mercury impacts on the Kodaikanal ecosystem are yet to come out, similar to the cat brain study that has come out in 2020 from a team in University of Saskatchewan (USask), Canada, on the Minamata case.

Who could have comprehended and summarized all of this better than Paul Polman when he responded to the Goldman Environment Award winners in September 2015, suggesting that in order 'to diagnose mercury-related illnesses, it is essential to establish the mercury exposure levels above which someone's health is likely to be impaired'.[15] He was merely asking to establish scientifically that the mercury exposure levels in Kodaikanal were beyond the safe levels and harming humans. That could be why he admitted to the Goldman Prize winners the company's omissions two decades earlier, before instructing the India unit to settle for an 'undisclosed sum' of recompense with its ex-workers. It could also be why he tried to expedite the process to remediate the twenty-two-acre factory plot, which remained contaminated with extremely dangerous levels of heavy metal for almost four decades.

Polman knew well that it had been irrefutably proven that mercury bioaccumulates in organisms at the top of the food chain – fish and alligator in the aquatic ecosystem; tiger, leopard and lion among the wild fauna; hawks, eagles, falcons and other raptors in avifauna; and in human beings. Mercury accumulated in tissues passes from organism to organism until it accumulates in the organs of the species at the crown of the food chain, causing irreparable damage to them, including genetic alterations. In certain cases, it can even endanger the survival of the entire species.

In cases like this, it would not be inaccurate to assume that in the absence of scientific evidence astutely collected by close monitoring, assessment and analysis over a period of time, the justice would be delayed and denied to people and the natural environment. As of today, Kodaikanal continues to lag behind in the scientific evidencing regard.

To elaborate, there had been no corroborative studies linking the dwindling population of raptors or of the carnivorous predator animals in the Palani Hills region to the incessant mercury dispersal for almost four decades – two decades of ongoing factory operations and another two of non-operational time. The same is the case for many disappearing predators, dwindling insect populations and shrinking flora.

Shockingly, there haven't been any studies, either epidemiological or etiological, on the impact of mercury toxicity on the human population in the region – beyond the limited epidemiological study conducted by Hindustan Lever on the factory workers.

It is no coincidence that many of the sub-sholas of Pambar Shola – such as Bear Shola and Tiger Shola – were named after animals that used to abound in the area, and the signature animals have been missing in the respective sholas, of late. If the flora and fauna have been depleting and disappearing in these sholas, can it be attributed only to the influx of tourists, or can it also be ascribed to the changes in the fundamental nature of the ecosystem due to the increased presence of chemical materials such as mercury? If a site is pumped with twenty tonnes of toxic elemental mercury continuously for more than eighteen years, leading to the gaseous metal filling the surrounding air with amounts greater than 2,600 times of what is normal, wouldn't it impact the plant and animal population of that habitat?

The poisoning of the Kodaikanal region remains a disaster of catastrophic proportions in the absence of needful and timely intervention. The case now features on a long list of similar tragedies caused by the negligence of corporations. The queen of hill stations has been left in the shadow of Unilever's toxic legacy, with little hope that the heavy metal poisoning of land, air, people and wildlife will ever be properly remediated. It took fifteen years of campaigning to have HLL settle with the workers whose lives it had endangered. Even so, the tonnes of mercury dispersed in the town will continue to affect generations of people living in Kodaikanal.

The local community continues to hold out hope that Unilever will come forward to acknowledge its full responsibility and take the necessary steps to ensure that Kodaikanal is once again truly safe for its inhabitants.

# NOTES

## Prologue

1. Quoted in an email from Paul Polman to Yuyun Ismawati on 25 September 2015, Balifokus, Indonesia.
2. *8.0 Statements and Physical Examinations of Alleged Victims*, Report of the Committee Constituted by the Ministry of Labour and Employment, Government of India, vide order No: C-18019/08/2011 ISH.II dated 9 September 2011 for submission to the Madras High Court in the writ petition 8291/2006.
3. 'Few Individual Testimonies about Health Problems', *The Indian People's Tribunal Report*, headed by Justice S. N. Bhargava, Indian People Tribunal on Environment and Human Rights, June 2003, pp. 8–16.
4. Ibid.
5. *8.0 Statements and Physical Examinations of Alleged Victims*, Report of the Committee Constituted by the Ministry of Labour and Employment, dated 9 September 2011.

## 1. Watertown

1. Stephen B. Sulavikm, *Adirondack of Indians and Mountains, 1535–1838*, Cooperstown: Purple Mountain Press, 2007.
2. D. H. Janzen, 'Tropical Blackwater Rivers, Animals, and Mast Fruiting by the Dipterocarpaceae', *Biotropica*, July 1974, Vol. 6, No. 2, pp. 69–103.
3. W. P. Duncan and M. N. Fernandes, 'Physicochemical characterization of the white, black, and clear water rivers of the Amazon Basin and its

implications on the distribution of freshwater stingrays (Chondrichthyes, Potamotrygonidae)', *PanamJAS,* 2010, Vol. 5, No. 3, pp. 454–64.

4. 'A Combined Customer List,' The University of Tennessee Press. Available: https://utpress.org/download/9781572334915/Appendix_A_Combined_Customer_List.pdf. Retrieved on 10 August 2020.
5. 'Chesebrough-Pond's Ltd, Unilever Art', Archives and Records Management. Available: http://unilever-archives.com/Record.aspx?src=CalmView.Catalog&id=GB1752.EFL%2FCP. Retrieved on 10 August 2020.

## 2. Chesebrough-Pond's

1 Hugh Chisholm (ed), 'Vaseline', *Encyclopaedia Britannica,* Vol. 27 (11th ed.), Cambridge: Cambridge University Press, 1911, p. 946.
2. *Standard Oil Co. of New Jersey v. United States,* US Conlawpedia. Available: https://sites.gsu.edu/us-constipedia/standard-oil-co-of-new-jersey-v-united-states-1911/. Retrieved on 13 August 2020.
3. 'Our Heritage, A story of skincare breakthroughs over more than 150 years, Pond's', About Pond's. Available: https://www.ponds.com/us/en/about-ponds.html. Retrieved on 13 August 2020.
4. 'Chesebrough-Pond's USA, Inc.', Updated on 31 August 2020, Encyclopedia. Available: https://www.encyclopedia.com/books/politics-and-business-magazines/chesebrough-ponds-usa-inc. Retrieved on 13 August 2020.

## 3. The Death of Clarence Borel

1. Clarence Borel, Plaintiff-appellee, v. Fibreboard Paper Products Corporation et al., defendants-appellants, National Surety Corporation, intervenor-appellee, 493 F.2d 1076 (5th Cir. 1973) *Justia US Law.* Available: https://law.justia.com/cases/federal/appellate-courts/F2/493/1076/4552/. Retrieved on 31 May 2020.
2. Ibid.
3. Ibid.

4. Sally Kuykendall, 'Skewed Studies: Exploring the Limits and Flaws of Health and Psychology Research,' ABC-CLIO, Santa Clara, California.
5. Ibid.
6. Jack Lewis, 'The Birth of EPA', *EPA Journal*, November 1985, US Environmental Protection Agency. Available: https://archive.epa.gov/epa/aboutepa/birth-epa.html. Retrieved on 2 June 2020.
7. Ibid.
8. Ibid.
9. Clean Air Act Amendments, *ScienceDirect*. Available: https://www.sciencedirect.com/topics/engineering/clean-air-act-amendments. Retrieved on 10 August 2020.
10. Bruce Miller, 'Federal regulations and impact on emissions, Fossil Fuel Emissions Control Technologies,' 2015 *Science Direct*. Available: https://www.sciencedirect.com/topics/engineering/clean-air-act-amendments. Retrieved on 31 May 2020.
11. 'Evolution of the Clean Air Act', US Environmental Protection Agency. Available: https://www.epa.gov/clean-air-act-overview/evolution-clean-air-act. Retrieved on 31 May 2020.
12. 'Mercury Pollution and Enforcement of the Refuse Act of 1899: Hearing Before a Sub-committee of the US Congress House Committee on Government Operations,' Conservation and Natural Resources Subcommittee.
13. EPA History: Clean Air Act of 1970/1977, US Environmental Protection Agency. Available: https://www.epa.gov/history/epa-history-clean-air-act-19701977. Retrieved on 2 June 2020.
14 Dichlorodiphenyltrichloroethane (DDT) is an insecticide used in agriculture, and polychlorinated biphenyls are industrial products or chemicals.
15. Phil Wisman, 'EPA History (1970-1985),' November 1985, US Environmental Protection Agency. Available: https://archive.epa.gov/epa/aboutepa/epa-history-1970-1985.html. Retrieved on 2 June 2020.

## 4. Kodaikanal

1. Rudyard Kipling, *Something of Myself: For My Friends Known and Unknown*, New Delhi: Asian Educational Services, 1997.
2 Capt. B. S. Ward, 'Memoir of the Vuragherry and Kunnandaven Mountains', *Madras Journal of Literature and Science*, October 1837, Vol. 6, p. 280; Nirmal Tej Singh, *Irrigation and Soil Salinity in the Indian Subcontinent: Past and Present*, Cranbury, NJ: Lehigh University Press.
3. Capt. B. S. Ward, 'Memoir of the Vurraghery and Kunnundevan mountains', *Madras Journal of Literature and Science*, October 1837, Vol. 6, p. 280. Available: https://www.biodiversitylibrary.org/item/176523#page/13/mode/1up. Retrieved on 6 June 2020.
4. K. S. Jayaraman, 'Protests at Indian solar observatory refit', *Nature,* 1999, Vol. 400, p. 606. Available: https://www.nature.com/articles/23109. Retrieved on 2 June 2020.

## 5. Silver Screen to Quicksilver

1. John Waterbury, *Exposed to Innumerable Delusions: Public Enterprise and State Power in Egypt, India, Mexico, and Turkey*, New York: Cambridge University Press, 1993.
2. Helen Mary Jacqueline, *Dynamics of industrial growth in Tamil Nadu: A structural and spatial analysis*, PhD Thesis, Department of Economics, Madurai Kamaraj University, 2012. Available: https://shodhganga.inflibnet.ac.in/bitstream/10603/133392/11/11_chapter%205.pdf. Retrieved on 2 June 2020.
3. Ibid.

## 6. Palani Hills and Pambar Shola

1. Premalatha S., Sanil R. and Franklin Charles Jose, 'Shola trees in the upper Nilgiris of Western Ghats', *Journal of Basic & Applied Biology* 3(3&4), 2009, pp. 97–102.

2. Zai Whitaker, 'Remembering Bob and Tanya, saviours of the Western Ghats' sky islands', *Firstpost,* 18 October 2020. Available: https://www.firstpost.com/living/the-zai-whitaker-column-remembering-bob-and-tanya-saviours-of-the-western-ghats-sky-islands-8916621.html. Retrieved on 28 October 2020.
3. 'About Us', Vattakanal Conservation Trust. Available: https://www.vattakanal.org/. Retrieved on 28 October 2020.
4. Joseph Satish Vedanayagam, 'Engaging Religion in the Fight for Environmental Justice: Jesuits and Conservation in the Palni Hills of South India', Environment & Society Portal, Rachel Carson Center for Environment and Society, *Arcadia*, Summer 2019, No. 24.
5. 'Palni Hills', Vattakkanal Conservation Trust, Archived at Wayback Machine. Available: http://www.vattakanalconservationtrust.org/Home/activities/palni-hills. Retrieved on 28 October 2020.
6. 'Pambar shola: A Biodiversity Treasure Trove under Threat', Greenpeace Archives. Available: https://archive.is/20070619150805/http://www.greenpeace.org/india/campaigns/toxics-free-future/toxic-hotspots/kodaikanal-tamil-nadu/pambar-shola-a-biodiversity-t#selection-805.0-805.56. Retrieved on 30 October 2020.
7. Palani Hills Threatened Plants, Marcus Sherman, *Flickr Album*. Available: https://www.flickr.com/photos/marcus334/albums/72157633090525857/. Retrieved on 30 October 2020.
8. K. M. Matthew, *The Flora of the Palani Hills, South India,* Tiruchirapalli: Rapinat Herbarium, St Joseph's College, 1999.

## 7. Made in India

1. R. Kannan, *MGR: A Life*, Gurgaon: Penguin Random House India, 2017.
2. URS Dames & Moore, *Environmental Site Assessment and Preliminary Risk Assessment for Mercury, Kodaikanal Thermometer Factory, Tamil Nadu, India*, Summary Report prepared for Hindustan Lever Limited, 24 May 2001. Available: https://kodaimercury.org/backdoor/wp-content/uploads/2015/08/Annexure-1-URS-Dames-More-2001.pdf.

3. URS Dames & Moore, *Environmental Site Assessment and Risk Assessment for Mercury HLL Thermometer Factory Site, Kodaikanal, Tamil Nadu, India*, 8 May 2002.
4. Report of the Committee, constituted by Ministry of Labor and Employment, Government of India, vide order No.C-18019/08/2011 ISH.II dated 9 September 2011 to examine the technical and rehabilitation issues raised in the write petition no. 8291/2006 before the High Court of Madras, 9 November 2011.
5. Atul Dev, 'The Unending Fallout of Unilever's Thermometer Factory in Kodaikanal', *Caravan*, 18 August 2015. Available: https://caravanmagazine.in/vantage/unending-fallout-unilever-thermometer-factory-kodaikanal. Retrieved on 14 August 2020.
6. URS Dames & Moore, *Environmental Site Assessment and Preliminary Risk Assessment for Mercury*, 24 May 2001.
7. Ibid.

## 8. A Ticking Time Bomb

1. 'About Us', Bombay Natural History Society. Available: https://www.bnhs.org/. Retrieved on 12 August 2020.
2. Ian Lockwood, 'On the danger list', *Frontline*, August 2003, Vol. 20, No. 16, pp. 2–15.
3. 'Declaration of Areas as Critical Tiger Habitats in the three Tiger Reserves of the State, Tamil Nadu', *Government Gazette Extraordinary*, Part II – Section 2, 13 August 2012.

## 9. The Mercury Dump Yard

1 Atul Dev, 'The Unending Fallout of Unilever's Thermometer Factory in Kodaikanal, *Caravan*, 18 August 2015. Available: https://caravanmagazine.in/vantage/unending-fallout-unilever-thermometer-factory-kodaikanal. Retrieved on 2 June 2020.

2. Navroz Mody, 'Mercury in the Mist: Portrait of a corporate crime', *Sanctury Asia*, August 2003.

3. Anusha Parthasarathy, 'The Nity Gritty', *Hindu Metro Plus*, 17 October 2013. Available: https://www.thehindu.com/features/metroplus/the-nity-gritty/article5243995.ece. Retrieved on 2 June 2020.
4. 'Activists expose Hindustan Lever's illegal Mercury waste dumps in Kodaikanal', Press Release by Greenpeace & PHCC, 28 February 2001. Available: https://www.geocities.ws/priyaflorence/pr17.htm. Retrieved on 14 March 2022.

## 10. Liquid Metal Everywhere

1. Nityanand Jayaraman, 'Unilever's Mercury Fever', *Indiatogether.org*, October 2001. Republished with permission from *Corpwatch.org*. Available: http://www.indiatogether.org/environment/articles/unilever.html. Retrieved on 2 June 2020.
2. Ibid.
3. Email dated 7 March 2001 from Debasis Ray, Corporate Communications Manager, Hindustan Lever Limited to Nityanand Jayaraman with the subject line: YOUR QUERIES ON THERMOMETER FACTORY, 7 March 2001.
4. 'Our Corporate Purpose', Unilever Annual Review 2000 and Summary Financial Statement, p. 1. Available: https://www.unilever.com/Images/2000-unilever-annual-review-part1_tcm244-424108_en.pdf. Retrieved on 13 August 2020.
5. 'HLL orders comprehensive audit & review at thermometer plant, suspends operation for the time being'. Press Release by Hindustan Lever Limited, 8 March 2001.
6. 'Lever, Clean up, Don't Cover up'. Press Release by Palni Hills Conservation Council, United Citizens Council of Kodaikanal, Greenpeace and Toxics Link, 9 March 2001.
7. 'Tamil Nadu groups launch alliance against Mercury and Lever.' Press Release by Tamil Nadu Alliance Against Mercury, 12 March 2001.
8. Proc No: HWM/4280/TNPCB/2001-01 dated 23 March 2001, Tamil Nadu Pollution Control Board, Chennai.
9. Ibid.
10. DO Lr No: HWMM/BC/MERC/KODK/2001 dated 19 March 2001

by TNPCB to Hindustan Lever Ltd, 123 GN Chetty Road, T Nagar, Chennai.

11. 'Hindustan Lever admits to Dumping of Mercury-containing Wastes.' Press Release by Greenpeace, 23 March 2001.
12. 'Greenpeace India seeks apology from HLL', *Times of India*, 23 March 2001.

## 11. Greenpeace vs Hindustan Lever

1. URS Dames & Moore, *Environmental Site Assessment and Preliminary Risk Assessment for Mercury*, 24 May 2001.
2. Ibid.
3. Proc. No. HWM/12391/D1/DGL/MERCURY dated 9 May 2001, Tamil Nadu Pollution Control Board, Chennai.
4. URS Dames & Moore, *Environmental Site Assessment and Preliminary Risk Assessment for Mercury*, 24 May 2001.
5. Jayaraman, 'Unilever's Mercury Fever', *Indiatogether.org*, October 2001, Republished with permission from *Corpwatch.org*. Available: http://www.indiatogether.org/environment/articles/unilever.html. Retrieved on 2 June 2020.
6. Sarah Hiddleston, 'Poisoned ground', *Frontline*, 24 September 2010. Available: https://frontline.thehindu.com/cover-story/poisoned-ground/article30181769.ece. Retrieved on 20 October 2020.
7. Navroz Mody, 'Mercury in the Mist: portrait of a corporate crime', *Sanctuary Asia*, August 2003.
8. 'Hard Talk with Niall Fitzgerald, Chairman, Unilever Plc', *BBC News 24*, 21 August, 2001.
9. Mody, 'Mercury in the Mist', *Sanctuary Asia*.

## 12. Christopher Martin Colorant

1. Justice Bhargava, *The Indian People's Tribunal Report*, p. 9.
2. Nahla Nainartiruchi, 'Medicine man', *Hindu*, 8 November 2013. Available: https://www.thehindu.com/features/friday-review/history-and-culture/medicine-man/article5329791.ece.

3. Justice Bhargava, *The Indian People's Tribunal Report*, pp. 9–10.
4. Ibid., p. 10.

## 13. Urine Samples

1. Dr Mohan Isaac and Arun Praveen, *Report of Preliminary Assessment done by Community Health Cell, Bangalore, of persons exposed to Mercury in Kodaikanal*, Community Health Cell (CHC), Bangalore, 2002.
2. Justice Bhargava, *The Indian People's Tribunal Report.*
3. Advertisements inviting employees for health checks up in *Dinamalar* and *Dinamani*, 2 April 2001.
4. *A study presented by HLL team on workers in the HLL thermometer factory in Kodaikanal*, Community Health Cell (CHC), Bangalore, 2001.
5. T. Rajgopal, H. V. Ravimohan and P. Mascarenhas, 'Epidemiological surveillance of employees in an Epidemiological surveillance of employees in a mercury thermometer plant: An occupational health study', Hindustan Lever Limited, India, *Indian Journal of Occupational and Environmental Medicine*, April 2006, Vol. 10, No. 1.

## 14. The Indian People's Tribunal

1. *Memorandum of Settlement arrived at Under section 12(3) of the Industrial Disputes Act,* 1947, Department of Labour, Government of Tamil Nadu.
2. *9.3 Rehabilitation and Healthcare Requirements of the Victims*, Report of the Technical Committee constituted by the Ministry of Labour and Employment, Government of India in connection with the Writ Petition No 8291 of 2006 in the Honorable High Court of Madras, Directorate General Factory Advice Service and Labour Institutes Ministry of Labour & Employment, 9 November 2011, p. 124.
3. TNN, 'Greenpeace Wants Probe into Kodaikanal Mercury Pollution', *Times of India*, 30 June 2002. Available: https://timesofindia.indiatimes.com/Greenpeace-wants-probe-into-Kodaikanal-mercury-pollution/articleshow/14589307.cms. Retrieved on 9 September 2020.

4. Michael L. Lewis, *Inventing Global Ecology: Tracking the Biodiversity Ideal in India, 1947-1997* (Series in Ecology and History), Illinois: Ohio University Press, 2004.
5. Ananth V. Krishna, *India Since Independence: Making Sense of Indian Politics*, New Delhi: Pearson Education India, 2011.
6. Tarunabh Khaitan, 'Dealing with Discrimination', *Frontline*, 10 May 2008. Available: https://frontline.thehindu.com/the-nation/article30196011.ece. Retrieved 16 August 2020.
7. Justice Bhargava, *The Indian People's Tribunal Report.*

## 15. The Salt-to-Salon Empire

1 Alice Morse Earle, *Home Life in Colonial Days*, Massachusetts: Berkshire Traveller Press, 1898. Available: http://www.gutenberg.org/files/22675/22675-h/22675-h.html.
2. Ibid.
3. 'Unilever Art, Archives and Records Management', Unilever. Available: https://www.unilever.com/about/who-we-are/our-history/unilever-archives.html. Retrieved on 1 September 2020.
4. 'An Indian Journey, HUL 75 Years Special Issue, Doing Well by Doing Good,' Hindustan Unilever Limited, Corporate Communications Department, 165/166 Backbay Reclamation, Mumbai, pp. 7–13. Available: https://www.hul.co.in/Images/hul_75years_special_issue__tcm1255-447470_en.pdf.
5. 'Unilever Art', Archives and Records Management, Unilever.
6. 'History and Background of the Unilever Company', UKEssays, 1 January 1970. Available: https://www.ukessays.com/essays/commerce/history-and-background-of-unilever-company-commerce-essay.php. Retrieved on 31 August 2020.
7. 'Our History 1920–29', Unilever. Available: http://www.unilever.com/about/who-we-are/our-history/1920-1929.html. Retrieved on 2 September 2020.
8. The event is recorded in the Gazetteer of India (Maharashtra State, Greater Bombay District, Volume II, published by the Government of Maharashtra); *An Indian Journey, HUL 75 Years Special Issue*,

Doing Well by Doing Good, Hindustan Unilever Limited, Corporate Communications Department, 165/166 Backbay Reclamation, Mumbai, pp. 8–11. Available:https://assets.unilever.com/files/92ui5egz/production/5adee4ae34e4573926212ee0bee9b8271e388600.pdf/hul---75-years-special-issue.pdf.

9. 'Company History – Hindustan Unilever', Moneycontrol. Available: https://www.moneycontrol.com/stocks/company_info/company_history.php?sc_did=HU. Retrieved on 1 September 2020.

## 16. T. Thomas and Lever's Desi Overtures

1 *Unilever Reports & Accounts*, 1956. Available: https://www.unilever.com/Images/1956-annual-report_tcm244-509318_1_en.pdf. Retrieved on 2 September 2020.
2. Simon Williams and Ruth Karen, *Agribusiness and the Small-scale Farmer: A Dynamic Partnership for Development*, London: Routledge, 1985.
3 'The Gift of Hope & Other Stories', HUL 75 Years Special Issue, pp 14–23. Available: https://www.hul.co.in/Images/hul_75years_special_issue__tcm1255-447470_en.pdf.
4. Ibid.
5. Ibid.

## 17. Mother Teresa and Asha Dan

1. 'Asha Daan – The gift of hope', Planet & Society, Hindustan Unilever Limited. Available: https://www.hul.co.in/sustainable-living/Copy_of_case-studies/asha-daan-the-gift-of-hope.html. Retrieved on 1 September 2020.

## 18. Fair & Lovely to Dove

1. Sohini Das and Sayantani Kar, '40 years ago...and now: Nirma girl endears, but brand's seen better days', *Business Standard*, 6 November 2014.

2. A. S. Ganguly, 'From Challenges to Opportunities', HUL 75 Years Special Issue, *Doing Well by Doing Good.* Available: https://www.hul.co.in/Images/hul_75years_special_issue__tcm1255-447470_en.pdf. Retrieved on 2 September 2020.
3. Quoted in 'In Remembrance: Vincent Lamberti '47, '51 PhD', Obituaries, *Yale Alumni Magazine*. April 2014. Available: https://yalealumnimagazine.com/obituaries/1326. Retrieved on September 2, 2020.
4. John Crudele, 'Unilever Sets Deal for Pond's', *New York Times*, 2 December 1986. Available: https://www.nytimes.com/1986/12/02/business/unilever-sets-deal-for-pond-s.html. Retrieved on 5 September 2020.

## 19. The ₹100 Billion Company

1. Ruth Kassinger, *Build a Better Mousetrap: Make Classic Inventions, Discover Your Problem Solving Genius, and Take the Inventor's Challenge*, Hoboken, NJ: John Wiley & Sons., 2002.
2. S. M. Datta, 'From Strength to Strength', HUL 75 Years Special Issue. Available: https://www.hul.co.in/Images/hul_75years_special_issue__tcm1255-447470_en.pdf.
3. Ibid.
4. H. R. Machiraju, *Merchant Banking: Principles and Practice*, New Delhi: New Age International, 2007.
5. 'Corporate Governance, Mergers & Demergers', HUL Annual Report 2011-12. Available:https://www.hul.co.in/Images/mergers-and-demergers_2011-12_tcm1255-436392_en.pdf. Retrieved on 4 September 2020.
6. Datta, 'From Strength to Strength', HUL 75 Years Special Issue, pp. 28–33.
7. 'Lakme by Leo Delibes, From the Montreal Opera', *NPR Music*, NPR.org, 11 May 2007. Available: https://www.npr.org/2007/05/11/10112052/lakme-by-leo-delibes. Retrieved on 4 September 2020.
8. Robin Abreu, 'Proposed merger of HLL, Brooke Bond Lipton to be India's largest consumer-goods company', *India Today*, 15 May

1996. Available: https://www.indiatoday.in/magazine/economy/story/19960515-proposed-merger-of-hll-brooke-bond-lipton-to-be-india-largest-consumer-goods-company-833184-1996-05-15. Retrieved on 4 September 2020.

9. 'Foods & Refreshment, Annapurna', Hindustan Unilever Limited. Available: https://www.hul.co.in/brands/food-and-ink/annapurna.html. Retrieved on 5 September 2020.
10. 'Annapurna', Hindustan Unilever Limited, Available: https://www.hul.co.in/brands/foods-refreshment/annapurna/.html. Retrieved on 16 March 2022
11. Datta, 'From Strength to Strength'.
12. '3:4 Ratio Announced For HLL, Ponds Merger', *Business Standard*, 17 March 1998. Available: https://www.business-standard.com/article/specials/3-4-ratio-announced-for-hll-ponds-merger-198031701020_1.html. Retrieved on 5 September 2020.
13. Ibid.

## 20. The Banga Era

1. PTI, 'Everstone takes over Modern Foods, eyes Rs 1,000-cr turnover', *Business Standard*, 1 April 2016. Available: https://www.business-standard.com/article/pti-stories/everstone-takes-over-modern-foods-eyes-rs-1-000-cr-turnover-116040100971_1.html. Retrieved on 6 September, 2020.
2. Hindustan Unilever Factsheet, 2017-2018. Available: https://www.hul.co.in/Images/hul-factsheet_tcm1255-537653_en.pdf. Retrieved on 2 September 2020.
3. V. Kasturi Rangan and Mona Sinha, 'Hindustan Unilever's "Pureit" Water Purifier', *Harvard Business School Case Study*, 28 March 2011.
4. 'HUL's efforts in health and hygiene have reached over 150 million people in India', *Business India Social Responsibility*, 13 February 2020. Available: https://businessindia.co/csr/huls-efforts-in-health-and-hygiene-have-reached-over-150-million-people-in-india. Retrieved on 5 September, 2020.
5. John Lancaster, 'Building Wealth by the Penny in Rural India, a Sales

Force in Saris Delivers Soap, Social Change', *Washington Post*, 14 March 2006.

6. 'Unilever Sustainable Living Plan India Progress 2018', Unilever. Available: https://www.hul.co.in/Images/pdf_27may_uslp-india-report-2018_tcm1255-537316_1_en.pdf. Retrieved on 4 September 2020.
7. 'Project Prabhat - Developing local communities: Case Studies', Hindustan Unilever Limited, Available: https://www.hul.co.in/sustainable-living/Copy_of_case-studies/developing-local-communities-with-project-prabhat.html. Retrieved on 7 September 2020.
8. Ibid.

## 21. Size 30

1. 'Sharp Focus on FMCG, M. S. Banga, Chairman – 2000-2005', *Doing Well by Doing Good*, HUL 75 years of Special Issue, 2009, Hindustan Unilever Limited, pp. 38-43.
2. Govindkrishna Seshan and Satish Sarangarajan, 'Power brands, the new FMCG mantra', *Rediff.com*, 15 November 2005. Available: https://www.rediff.com/money/2005/nov/15spec.html. Retrieved on 5 September 2020.
3. 'Antitrust: Commission fines producers of washing powder €315.2 million in cartel settlement case', Press Release by the European Commission, Brussels, 13 April 2011. Available: https://ec.europa.eu/commission/presscorner/detail/en/IP_11_473. Retrieved on 7 September 2020.
4. Reuters, 'Unilever raises stake in Indian unit to 67 per cent', 5 July 2013. Available: https://in.reuters.com/article/us-unilever-openoffer/unilever-raises-stake-in-indian-unit-to-67-per cent-idINBRE9630Q320130704. Retrieved on 6 September 2020.
5. 'GlaxoSmithKline Consumer Healthcare Limited merges with Hindustan Unilever Limited', Press Release by Hindustan Unilever Limited, 1 April 2020. Available: https://www.hul.co.in/news/press-releases/2020/glaxosmithkline-consumer-healthcare-limited-merges-with-hindustan-unilever-limited.html. Retrieved on 6 September 2020.
6. 'Unilever Sustainable Living Plan Launch', 15 November 2010,

Hindustan Unilever Limited. Available: https://www.hul.co.in/Images/unilever-sustainable-living-plan-launch_tcm1255-463864_en.pdf. Retrieved on 12 September 2020.

7. *Unilever Sustainable Living Plan India Report*, 2019, Hindustan Unilever Limited. Available: https://www.hul.co.in/Images/unilever-sustainable-living-plan---hul-summary-of-progress-2019_tcm1255-551089_1_en.pdf. Retrieved on 6 September 2020.

## 22. An Unexpected Ally

1. Eleanor Lawrence, 'Microbial Mercury Mop', *Nature*, 5 January 2000. Available: https://doi.org/10.1038/news000106-8.
2. *Co-ordinated Research Projects (CRP) Annual Report of Activities and Statistics for 2002*, August 2003. Research Contracts Administration Section, Department of Nuclear Sciences and Applications, International Atomic Energy Agency. Available: http://cra.iaea.org/cra/documents/2002-annual-report.pdf. Retrieved on 6 September 2020.
3. PTI, 'Closed Unilever factory source of Mercury Pollution', *Deccan Herald*, 17 January 2004. Available: https://web.archive.org/web/20140222041628/http://archive.deccanherald.com/Deccanherald/jan172004/n9.asp. Retrieved on 24 August 2020.
4. M.V. Balarama Krishna, D. Karunasagar and Dr J. Arunachalam, 'Study of mercury pollution near a thermometer factory using lichens and mosses', National Centre for Compositional Characterisation of Materials (CCCM), Department of Atomic Energy, India, *Environmental Pollution 124*, 2003, pp. 357–360.
5. Ibid.
6. Ibid.
7. Ibid.
8. Excerpts from the *Report from SCMC visit to Tamilnadu*, dated 20–22 September 2004, Supreme Court Monitoring Committee On Hazardous Wastes, Reproduced by Greenpeace on 21 March 2005 under 'Kodaikanal, Tamil Nadu'. Available: https://wayback.archive-it.org/9650/20191118115508/http://p3-raw.greenpeace.org/india/

en/news/bahut-ho-gaya-greenpeace-and1/kodaikanal-tamil-nadu/. Retrieved on 9 September 2020.

9. M. Horvat, Z. Jeran, Z. Špirič, R. Jaćimović and V. Miklavčič, 'Mercury and other elements in lichens near the INA Naftaplin gas treatment plant, Molve, Croatia', *Journal of Environmental Monitoring*, Vol. 2, No. 2, pp. 139–144.
10 B. V. Elsevier, *Environmental Pollution*, Available: https://www.journals.elsevier.com/environmental-pollution. Retrieved on 9 November 2020.

## 23. Lichens Full of Clues

1. Krishna, Karunasagar and Arunachalam, 'Study of mercury pollution near a thermometer factory using lichens and mosses', *Environmental Pollution* 124, 2003, pp. 357–60.
2. K. Bridgen and Ruth Stringer, 'Atmospheric dispersal of mercury from the Hindustan Lever Limited thermometer factory, Kodaikainal, Tamil Nadu, India, using Lichen as a bio-monitor, Greenpeace Research Laboratories', Technical Note 04/2003, November 2003.
3. Robert Anderson, 'Who's Smiling Now', *Frontline*, 24 June 2000; 'Smiling Buddha: 1974', India's Nuclear Weapons Program, Nuclear Weapon Archives. Available: http://nuclearweaponarchive.org/India/IndiaSmiling.html. Retrieved on 6 September 2020.
4. K. S. Jayaraman, 'How to be an investigative science journalist', *SciDevNet*, 30 March 2013. Available: https://www.scidev.net/global/communication/practical-guide/how-to-be-an-investigative-science-journalist-1.html. Retrieved on 6 September 2020.
5. PTI, 'Closed Unilever factory source of Mercury Pollution', *Deccan Herald*, 17 January 2004. Available: https://web.archive.org/web/20140222041628/http://archive.deccanherald.com/Deccanherald/jan172004/n9.asp. Retrieved on 24 August 2020.
6. Ibid.
7. Ibid.

## 24. Mercurial Fish

1 URS Dames & Moore, 'Introduction, Section 1', *Mercury Levels in Sediments and Fish in Kodai Lake, Environmental Site Assessment and Risk Assessment for Mercury HLL*, 8 May 2002.
2. Ibid.
3. URS Dames & Moore, 'Table 5-11', *Mercury Levels in Sediments and Fish in Kodai Lake*, 8 May 2002.
4. Ibid.
5. URS Dames & Moore, 'Table 7, Total Mercury Concentration in Soil/ Sediment/Lichen/Water samples, North Site, including Kodai Lake, *Mercury Levels in Sediments and Fish in Kodai Lake*, 8 May 2002.
6. Ibid.
7. Ibid.
8. URS Dames & Moore, 'Table 8, Total Mercury Concentration in Soil/ Sediment/Lichen/Water samples, South of Site, including Kodai Lake, *Mercury Levels in Sediments and Fish in Kodai Lake*, 8 May 2002.
9. URS Dames & Moore, 'Table 5-11', *Mercury Levels in Sediments and Fish in Kodai Lake*, 8 May 2002.

## 25. The DAE Returns

1. M. V. Karunasagar, Balarama Krishna, Y. Anjaneyulu, J. Arunachalam, 'Studies of mercury pollution in a lake due to a thermometer factory situated in a tourist resort: Kodaikkanal, India', *Environmental Pollution*, 2006, Vol. 143, No. 1, pp. 153–58.
2. Ibid.
3. Ibid.
4. Ibid.
5. Ibid.
6. Ibid.

## 26. The Huckleby Family Tragedy


1. Martin Walon, 'Mercury in Food: A Family Tragedy', *New York Times*, 10 August 1970.
2. Ibid.
3. A. Curley, V. A. Sedlak, et al, 'Organic Mercury Identified as the Cause of Poisoning in Humans and Hogs', *Science*, 1971, Vol. 172, No. 3978, pp. 65–67.
4. Russel D. Snyder and Don F. Seelinger, 'Methylmercury poisoning, Clinical follow-up and sensory nerve conduction studies', Department of Neurology, University of New Mexico, School of Medicine, Albuquerque, New Mexico, USA, *Journal of Neurology, Neurosurgery, and Psychiatry*, 1976, Vol. 39, pp. 701–04.
5. 'As we live and breathe: the challenge of our environment.' *National Geographic*, 1971, National Geographic Society, Special Publications Division, Washington, D.C.
6. Robin Hill Gardens, 'Who Remembers Ernestine Huckleby?' Available: https://blog.bolandbol.com/2007/05/30/who-remembers-ernestine-huckleby/. Retrieved on 18 June 2020.
7. Snyder and Seelinger, 'Methylmercury poisoning, Clinical follow-up and sensory nerve conduction studies', *Journal of Neurology, Neurosurgery, and Psychiatry, 1976,* pp. 701–04.


## 27. Barton Booth and the Black Pills


1. Thomas Dormandy, *The Worst of Evils: Man's Fight Against Pain, a History*, New Haven: Yale University Press, 2006.
2. Dr Lydia Kang and Nate Pedersen, *Quackery: A Brief History of the Worst Ways to Cure Everything*, New York: Workman Publishing, 2017.
3. Jeremy Manier, 'For Lincoln, ancient cure worse than his malady', *Chicago Tribue,* 17 June 2021. Available: https://chicagotribune.com/news/ct-xpm-2001-07-17010770220-story.html. Retrived on 19 March 2022.
4. Richard M. Swiderski, *Quicksilver: A History of the Use, Lore and Effects of Mercury*, Jefferson: McFarland & Company Inc., 2008.

5. Ibid.
6. Ibid.
7. 'Tibetan Medical and Astro-Sciences Institute, Men-Tsee-Khang.' Available: https://www.men-tsee-khang.org/index2.html. Retrieved on 2 September 2020.

## 28. The Mystery of Minamata Bay

1. H. A. Walon, 'Did the Mad Hatter have mercury poisoning?', *British Medical Journal (Clinical Research Edition)*, 1983.
2. David Edelstein, 'Burton's 'Alice': A Curious Kind Of Wonderful,' *NPR.org,* 4 March 2010. Available: https://www.npr.org/2010/03/04/124244102/burtons-alice-a-curious-kind-of-wonderful. Retrieved on 1 September 2020.
3. S. J. Withrow and D. M. Vail, *Withrow and MacEwen's Small Animal Clinical Oncology* (4th ed), St. Louis, MO: Elsevier, 2007.
4. Shabnum Nabi, '*Toxic Effects of Mercury*', New Delhi: Springer, 2014.
5. Lee T. Ostrom, A. Cheryl and Wilhelmsen, '*Risk Assessment: Tools, Techniques, and Their Applications*' (Second Edition), New York: John Wiley and Sons Inc., 2012.
6. M. Harada, 'Minamata Disease: Methylmercury Poisoning in Japan Caused by Environmental Pollution', *Critical Reviews in Toxicology*', Vol. 25(1), 1995, pp. 1–24.
7. Ibid.
8. George, S. Timothy. '*Minamata: Pollution and the Struggle for Democracy in Postwar Japan*', Cambridge: Harvard University Press, 2001.
9. Jun Ui (ed), *Industrial pollution in Japan,* The University of Okinawa, United Nations University Press, 1992.
10. Katherine Montague and Peter Montague, *Mercury*, Oakland, CA: Sierra Club, 1971.
11. Ibid.
12. Ashley K. James, Susan Nehzati, Natalia V. Dolgova, Dimosthenis Sokaras, Thomas Kroll, Komyo Eto, John L. O'Donoghue, Gene E. Watson, Gary J. Myers, Patrick H. Krone, Ingrid J. Pickering, and Graham N. George, 'Rethinking the Minamata Tragedy: What Mercury

Species Was Really Responsible?', *Environ. Sci. Technol.*,Vol. 54 (5), 2020, pp. 2726–2733.

13. UN Environment Program, Minamata Convention on Mercury. Available: http://www.mercuryconvention.org/. Retrieved on 21 June 2020.

## 29. Alois Alzheimer

1. Antonio Tagarelli, Anna Piro, Giuseppe Tagarelli, Paolo Lagonia and Aldo Quattrone, 'Alois Alzheimer: A Hundred Years after the Discovery of the Eponymous Disorder,' *Int J Biomed Sci,* June 2006, Vol. 2, No. 2, pp. 196–204.
2. Alois Alzheimer, *Alzheimer's Disease International.* Available: https://www.alz.co.uk/alois-alzheimer. Retrieved on 22 June 2020.
3. Robert Siblerud, Joachim Mutter, Elaine Moore, Johannes Naumann and Harald Walach, 'A Hypothesis and Evidence That Mercury May be an Etiological Factor in Alzheimer's Disease', *Int J Environ Res Public Health*, 2019, Vol. 16, No. 24, p. 5152.
4. Ibid.
5. Tetsuya Takahashi et al, 'Methylmercury Causes Blood-Brain Barrier Damage in Rats via Upregulation of Vascular Endothelial Growth Factor Expression', *PLoS One*, January 2017.
6. Tetsuya Takahashi and Takayoshi Shimohata, 'Vascular Dysfunction Induced by Mercury Exposure', *International Journal of Molecular Sciences*, 2019.
7. Giuseppe Genchi, Maria Stefania Sinicropi, Alessia Carocci, Graziantonio Lauria and Alessia Catalano, 'Mercury Exposure and Heart Diseases', *Int J Environ Res Public Health*, January 2017, Vol. 14, No. 1, p. 74.
8. G. Bjorklund, V. Stejskal, M. A. Urbina, M. Dadar, S. Chirumbolo and J. Mutter, 'Metals and Parkinson's Disease: Mechanisms and Biochemical Processes', *Current Medicinal Chemistry*, 2018, Vol. 25, No. 19, pp. 2198–214.

## 30. Fish Eats Mercury, Man Eats Fish

1. Michael B. Parsons and Jeanne B. Percival, *'A brief History of Mercury and its Environmental Impact'*, Geological Survey of Canada, Mineralogical Association of Canada Short Course 34, Halifax, Nova Scotia.
2. *Mercury Emissions from Coal-fired Power Plants, The Case for Regulatory Action*, Northeast States for Coordinated Air Use Management 101 Merrimac Street Boston, Massachusetts 02114, October 2003.
3. *Mercury Study Report to Congress*, Volume I: Executive Summary, December 1997, Office of Air Quality Planning and Standards and Office of Research and Development, US. Environmental Protection Agency.
4. UN Environment, Artisanal and Small-Scale Gold Mining (ASGM), Available: https://web.unep.org/globalmercurypartnership/our-work/artisanal-and-small-scale-gold-mining-asgm. Retrieved on 20 July, 2020.

## 31. Almaden to New Almaden

1. M. Garcia Gomez, et al, 'Exposure to mercury in the mine of Almaden', *Occupational and Environmental Medicine*, Vol. 64(6), 2006, pp. 389–95.
2. Ellen Czaika and Bethanie Edwards, 'History of Mercury Use in Products and Processes', *Mercury Science and Policy at MIT,* 15 January 2013. Available: https://mercurypolicy.scripts.mit.edu/blog/?p=367. Retrieved on 1 September 2020.
3. Ibid.
4. U.S. Geological Survey, 'Mercury', *Mineral Commodity Summaries*, January 2020. Available: https://pubs.usgs.gov/periodicals/mcs2020/mcs2020-mercury.pdf. Retrieved on 17 July 2020

## 32. Fever Thermometers, Lights and Bulbs

1. Interstate Mercury Education and Reduction Clearinghouse (IMERC), 'IMERC Fact Sheet Mercury Use in Batteries', December 2018. Available: http://www.newmoa.org/prevention/mercury/imerc/factsheets/batteries_2018.pdf. Retrieved on 21 July 2020.
2. Ibid.
3. Ibid.
4. E. G. Pacyna, J. M. Pacyna, K. Sundseth, J. Munthe, K. Kindbom, S. Wilson, P. Maxson, 'Global emission of mercury to the atmosphere from anthropogenic sources in 2005 and projections to 2020', *Atmospheric Environment*, 2010, Vol. 44, No. 20, pp. 2487–499.
5. IMERC Fact Sheet Mercury Use in Lighting, December 2018.
6. Supra.

## 33. 'Dump for a Dump'

1. Permission to export Mercury bearing waste to M/z Bethlehem Apparatus Co, Pennsylvania USA, vide Lt No: HWM/27566/93-1, TNPCB letter dated 12 March 2003.
2. 'Bethlehem Apparatus in Hellertown, Pennsylvania'. Available: http://www.bethlehemapparatus.com/. Retrieved on 2 September 2020.
3. PTI, 'India Sends Hazardous Waste Back to US', *Times of India*, 17 April 2003. Available: https://timesofindia.indiatimes.com/india/India-sends-hazardous-waste-back-to-US/articleshow/43609694.cms. Retrieved on 27 August 2020.
4. Ibid.
5. PTI, 'Dump for a dump, from India to U.S.', *The Statesman*, 17 April 2003.
6. Raja Simhan T. E., 'HLL mercury waste to leave for NY on May 7, *Hindu BusinessLine*, 4 May 2003. Available: https://www.thehindubusinessline.com/todays-paper/tp-news/article28912604.ece. Retrieved on 27 August 2020.
7. 'Part 263-Standards Applicable to Transporters of Hazardous Waste', Electronic Code of Federal Regulations, US Government

Publishing House. Available: https://www.ecfr.gov/cgi-bin/text-idx?node=pt40.26.263&rgn=div5. Retrieved on 27 August 2020.

8. Simhan, 'HLL mercury waste to leave for NY on May 7'.
9. Saritha Rai, 'Hazardous Waste Is Shipped From India to U.S. Recycling Plant', *New York Times*, 7 May 2003. Available: https://www.nytimes.com/2003/05/07/world/hazardous-waste-is-shipped-from-india-to-us-recycling-plant.html. Retrieved on 6 June 2019.
10. Ibid.

## 34. Direct Actions

1. L. J. Bunin, 'Reconceptualising Radical Environmentalism: Greenpeace's Campaign to Ban the Burning of Toxic Waste at Sea', *New Political Science,* 1997, Vol. 19, No. 3, pp. 75–88.
2. PTI, 'Greenpeace to monitor Periyar waters', *Times of India*, 21 November 2002. Available: https://timesofindia.indiatimes.com/city/thiruvananthapuram/Greenpeace-to-monitor-Periyar-waters/articleshow/28990384.cms. Retrieved on 10 September 2020.
3. 'Hindustan Lever Limited Reports and Accounts, 2002,' *Annual Report,* 2002. Available: https://www.hul.co.in/Images/annual-report-2002_tcm1255-436198_en.pdf. Retrieved on 30 August 2020.
4. 'Greenpeace Confronts HLL at its own AGM: Address Your Pending Liabilities in Kodaikanal,' Press Release by Greenpeace India, 13 June 2003.
5. 'Thermometer plant acted responsibly, says Banga', *Hindu BusinessLine,* 14 June 2003.
6. Indian People Tribunal *Report on Kodaikanal,* Press Release by Hindustan Lever Limited, Mumbai, 14 June 2003.
7. 'HLL's Denials Persist Along Expected Tracks: The Truth is Out', Press Release by Greenpeace India, 15 June 2003.
8. Ibid.

## 35. Rainbow Warrior in Mumbai

1. Michael Brown and John May, *The Greenpeace Story*, London: Dorling Kindersley Limited, 1989, pp. 12–13.
2. 'Rainbow Warrior Sails into Grand Welcome; However, Greenpeace Activists Not allowed to Disembark from the ship', Press Release by Greenpeace India, 6 December 2003. Available: https://wayback.archive-it.org/9650/20200405171611/http://p3-raw.greenpeace.org/india/en/news/rainbow-warrior-sails-into-gra/. Retrieved on 9 September 2020.
3. Ibid.
4. Bridgen and Stringer, *Atmospheric dispersal of mercury from the Hindustan Lever Limited thermometer factory*, November 2003.

## 36. Shareholder Activism

1. M. S. Banga, 'Reinventing Distribution, 2004 AGM Speech', Speech by Chairman of Hindustan Lever Limited. Available: https://www.hul.co.in/Images/agm_speech_2004_reinventing-distribution_tcm1255-434445_en.pdf. Retrieved on 12 September 2020.
2. 'Greenpeace spooks HLL AGM; Demand Public Apology for Kodaikanal Mercury', Press Release by Greenpeace India, 4 August 2004. Available: https://wayback.archive-it.org/9650/20200405061357/http://p3-raw.greenpeace.org/india/en/news/greenpeace-spooks-hll-agm-dem/. Retrieved on 29 August 2020.
3. Sumitra Nair, 'Film production goes beyond ordering, catering and lighting: Miriam Joseph', *The Week*, 13 January 2019. Available: https://www.theweek.in/leisure/society/2019/01/13/film-production-goes-beyond-ordering-catering-lighting-miriam-joseph.html. Retrieved on 30 August 2020.
4. 'Greenpeace spooks HLL AGM; Demand Public Apology for Kodaikanal Mercury', Press Release by Greenpeace India, 4 August 2004. Available: https://wayback.archive-it.org/9650/20200405061357/http://p3-raw.greenpeace.org/india/en/news/greenpeace-spooks-hll-agm-dem/. Retrieved on 29 August 2020.

## 37. From Boardrooms to TV Studios

1. 'On the Kodaikanal Mercury Issue' with Sreenivasan Jain, *NDTV*, 8.30 p.m., 29 June 2004.
2. Hindustan Lever Limited, Reports and Accounts, 2003. Available: https://www.hul.co.in/Images/annualreport2003_tcm1255-436199_en.pdf. Retrieved on 30 August 2020.
3. Vishakh Unnikrishnan, '45 dead, 600 poisoned: HUL finally responds to mercury poisoning victims', *Catch News*, 2 July 2015. Available: http://www.catchnews.com/india-news/48-dead-600-poisoned-hindustan-unilever-finally-responds-to-mercury-poisoning-victims-1435723835.html. Retrieved on 10 September 2020.
4. 'Poison case puts Polman's green boasts on the line, Nicci Smith in Kodaikanal', *Sunday Times*, 26 April 2015. Available: https://www.thetimes.co.uk/article/poison-case-puts-polmans-green-boasts-on-the-line-5fsrscj02nl. Retrieved on 8 November 2020.
5. Michael Skapinker and Scheherazade Daneshkhu, 'Can Unilever's Paul Polman change the way we do business?' *Financial Times,* 29 September 2016. Available: https://www.ft.com/content/e6696b4a-8505-11e6-8897-2359a58ac7a5. Retrieved on 10 September 2020.

## 38. 'Make it a Green Peace'

1. Brown and May, *The Greenpeace Story*.
2. Ibid.
3. Brown and May, *The Greenpeace Story*; Chuck Davis, *The Greater Vancouver Book: An Urban Encyclopedia*, Vancouver: Linkman Press, 1997.

## 39. Phyllis Cormack, Edgewater Fortune, Cannikin

1. Robert Hunter, *'Warriors of the Rainbow, A Chronicle of the Greenpeace Movement from 1971 to 1979'*, Western Australia: Greenpeace with Fremantle Press, Fremantle, 1971.
2. Brown and May, *The Greenpeace Story*, p. 12.

3. Ibid., p. 14.
4. Ibid.
5. '1971-Cannikin, Accomplishments in the 1970s: Lawrence Livermore National Laboratory'. Available: https://web.archive.org/web/20050217061020/http://www.llnl.gov/50th_anniv/decades/1970s.html. Retrieved on 15 September 2020.
6. Brown and May, *The Greenpeace Story*, p. 15.
7. Sally Eden, 'Greenpeace,' *New Political Economy*, 2004, Vol. 9, No. 4, pp. 595–610.

## 40. Love Canal

1. 'Hooker Electrochemical Claim Deed to Board of Education'. Available: https://upload.wikimedia.org/wikipedia/commons/2/2c/Hooker_Electrochemical_Quit_Claim_Deed_to_Board_of_Education.pdf.
2. 'The Antitoxics Movement, Environmental History', Global Warming Causes, 2 May 2020. Available: https://www.briangwilliams.us/environmental-history/the-antitoxics-movement.html. Retrieved on 12 September 2020.
3. Headline No. 1: Love Canal timeline, *Niagara Gazette,* 26 July 2006. Available: https://www.niagara-gazette.com/news/local_news/headline-no-1-love-canal-timeline/article_a049cccd-77a1-5692-a824-706a200b927f.html. Retrieved on 12 September 2020.
4. Ibid.
5. Greenpeace Testimony before the US Environmental Protection Agency: Review of aft Permit for Ocean Incineration Aboard M/T Vulcanus, 31 August 1982; Greenpeace Testimony before the US Environmental Protection Agency on the Proposed Designation of the North Atlantic Incineration Site, 14 April 1983.
6. 'The Anti-toxics Movement', *The Environmental Movement in Ireland,* Springer, 2008. Available: https://doi.org/10.1007/978-1-4020-6812-6_8. Retrieved on 10 September 2020.
7. Ibid.

## 41. 'The Poison Gas Is Spreading!'

1. R. Varma and D. R. Varma, 'The Bhopal Disaster of 1984', *Bulletin of Science, Technology & Society*, 2005, Vol. 25, No. 1, pp. 37–45.
2. Sreekanth Khandekar and Suman Dubey, City of Death, *India Today*, 31 December 1984.
3. Varma and Varma, 'The Bhopal Disaster of 1984'.
4. Ibid.

## 42. Birth of the *Rainbow Warrior*

1. Interview with Michael Niman, author of *People of the Rainbow: A Nomadic Utopia*; John Tarleton, July 1999. Available: http://www.johntarleton.net/niman.html. Retrieved on 2020.
2. Brown and May, *The Greenpeace Story*, p. 53.
3. Ibid., p. 54.
4. Ibid., p. 113.
5. Catherine Field, '"Third team" in Rainbow Warrior plot,' *New Zealand Herald*, 30 June 2005. Available: https://www.nzherald.co.nz/nz/news/article.cfm?c_id=1&objectid=10333480. Retrieved on 17 September 2020.
6. Brown and May, *The Greenpeace Story*, pp. 113–14.
7. Ibid., p. 117.
8. Rainbows and Warriors, An interview with Steve Sawyer by Fred Steward, *Marxism Today*, November 1985, p. 20. Available: http://banmarchive.org.uk/collections/mt/pdf/85_11_20.pdf. Retrieved on 18 September 2020
9. Ibid.

## 45. Mody, Mohamed and Krishnan

1. WP No. 8291 of 2006 before the High Court of Madras by *Ponds Hindustan Lever Limited Ex-Mercury Employees' Welfare Association vs Hindustan Unilever, State of Tamil Nadu and Others*.

2. Ibid.
3. Interim Order dated 29 June 2007 by the High Court of Madras in the WP No.8291 of 2006 between *Ponds Hindustan Lever Limited Ex-Mercury Employees' Welfare Association vs Hindustan Unilever, State of Tamil Nadu and Others.*
4. Dr P. N. Vishwanathan, *Report - Thermometer Factory, Hindustan Lever Ltd, Kodaikanal,* 2-A, Way Line, Lucknow-226001, March 2001.
5. 'Kodaikanal Mercury Factory – Contamination Response, India, Press Release by Hindustan Unilever, 20 June 2018. Available: https://www.hul.co.in/news/2018/kodaikanal-mercury-factory/. Retrieved on 23 March 2022.
6. Sarah Hiddleston, 'Poisoned ground', *Frontline*, 24 September 2010. Available: https://frontline.thehindu.com/cover-story/poisoned-ground/article30181769.ece. Retrieved on 20 October 2020.
7. Ibid.
8. Ibid.
9. Annexure 8, Report of S. K. Dave of the site visit and clinical evaluation of ex-employees of Kodaikanal, Report of the Committee of Experts appointed under the directions of the Honorable High Court of Judicature of Madras in Writ Petition No. 8291/2006, Submitted in 2006 to the High Court.
10 T. Rajgopal, H. V. Ravimohan, P. Mascarenhas, 'Epidemiological surveillance of employees in an Epidemiological surveillance of employees in a mercury thermometer plant: An occupational health study', Hindustan Lever Limited, India. *Indian Journal of Occupational and Environmental Medicine* – April 2006, Vol. 10, Issue 1.
11. Editorial Board, *Indian Journal of Occupational and Environmental Medicine*, Official Publication of Indian Association of Occupational Health (IAOH). Available: https://www.ijoem.com/editorialboard.asp. Retrieved on 13 October 2020.
12. Supra.
13. Ibid.
14. Ibid.

## 46. 'Elementary Mercury'

1. Profile of Tom van Teunenbroek, Ministry of Infrastructure and Environment, The Netherlands, Nanosafety Research and Legislation in European Union: Future Activities. Available: https://www.linkedin.com/in/tom-van-teunenbroek-46633745/?originalSubdomain=nl. https://na.eventscloud.com/file_uploads/bfa9a9b84080eef3ef5a5e51008f367a_vanTeunenbroek.pdf. Retrieved on 12 October 2020.
2 Tom van Teunenbroek, *A Review of the Occupational Health Surveillance of Employees of the Kodaikanal Thermometer Plant of Hindustan Lever Ltd*, TNO Milieu Energie En Procesinnovatie, Number 01/05/201, 28 May 2001.
3. van Teunenbroek, *A Review of the Occupational Health Surveillance of Employees at the Kodaikanal Thermometer Plant of Hindustan Lever Limited - Final Report*, Rotterdam, 1 October 2003.

## 47. Counsel Vaigai

1. Annexure 8, Report of S. K. Dave of the site visit and clinical evaluation of ex-employees of Kodaikanal. Report of the Committee of Experts appointed under the directions of the Honorable High Court of Judicature of Madras in Writ Petition No. 8291/2006. Submitted in 2006 to the High Court.
2. Brian J. Koos, D. Lawrence, M. D. Longo, 'Mercury toxicity in the pregnant woman, foetus, and newborn infant: A review,' *American Journal of Obstetrics and Gynecology*, 1 October 1976, Vol. 126, No. 3, pp. 390–409.
3. 'Justice Bhargava, *The Indian People's Tribunal Report*, p. 13.
4. Annexure 8, 'Report of S. K. Dave of the site visit and clinical evaluation of ex-employees of Kodaikanal', Report of the Committee of Experts appointed under the directions of the Honourable High Court of Judicature of Madras in Writ Petition No. 8291/2006. Submitted in 2006 to the High Court.
5. Report of the Committee of Experts appointed under the directions of the Honourable High Court of Judicature of Madras in Writ Petition No. 8291/2006. Submitted in 2006 to the High Court.

6. Ibid.
7. *Point-Counterpoint – A Detailed and Referenced Counter to Unilever's Arguments Against a Thorough Clean-up*, Chennai Solidarity Group, kodaimercury.org, 15 April 2016. Available: http://kodaimercury.org/point-counterpoint-a-detailed-and-referenced-counter-to-unilevers-arguments-against-a-thorough-clean-up/. Retrieved on 13 October 2020
8. Hiddleston, 'Poisoned ground'.
9. Ibid.
10. Ibid.

## 48. Sleeping Lion

1. Order by the Ministry of Labour and Employment, Government of India, Order No. C-18019/08/2011-ISH.II dated 9 September 2011.
2. Ibid.
3. Analysis and Recommendations, 9.2 Compensation Requirements, Report of the Technical Committee constituted by the Ministry of Labour and Employment, Government of India in connection with the Writ Petition No. 8291 of 2006 in the Honorable High Court of Madras, Directorate General Factory Advice Service and Labour Institutes, Ministry of Labour and Employment, 9 November 2011, p. 120.

## 49. Kodaikanal Won't

1. David Jones and Mark Potter, 'Unilever names Nestle's Polman as CEO, shares leap', *Reuters*, 4 September 2008. Available: https://in.reuters.com/article/us-unilever/unilever-names-nestles-polman-as-ceo-shares-leap-idUSL44874120080904
2. Ibid.
3. 'Kodaikanal Won't,' Jathaka.org, July 30, 2015. Available: https://www.youtube.com/watch?v=nSal-ms0vcI.
4. Parshathy J. Nath, 'How the Kodaikanal Won't video went viral', *Hindu*, 5 August 2015. Available: https://www.thehindu.com/news/national/

tamil-nadu/how-the-kodaikanal-wont-video-went-viral/article7500019.ece.

5. Paul Polman's tweet with hashtag #UnliverPollutes, 8.27 am, 6 August 2015 from Twitter for iPad. Available: https://twitter.com/paulpolman/status/629124033716559873?lang+en. Retrieved on 24 March 2022
6. Unilever's tweet, 8.30 am, 4 August 2015 from Twitter Web Client, Available: https://twitter.com/unilever/status/628581316972388352. Retrieved on 24 March 2022.
7. Responses to Paul Polman's tweet with hashtag #UnliverPollutes. Available: https://twitter.com/paulpolman/status/629124033716559873?lang+en. Retrieved on 24 March 2022.
8. Email by Yuyun Ismawati and others to Paul Polman, Chief Executive Officer, Unilever Plc, dated 24 September 2015.
9. Ibid.
10. Ibid.
11. 'HUL & former employees of Kodaikanal factory sign settlement', Press Release by Hindustan Unilever Limited, 9 March 2016. Available: https://www.hul.co.in/news/press-releases/2016/hul-former-employees-of-Kodaikanal-factory-sign-settlement.html.
12. Order of the High Court of Judicature, Madras dated 9 March 2016 in WP Nos. 8291 of 2006, 23748 & 23749 of 2011 & WP Nos. 9228, 9236 of 2006; 40 of 2013 and 7761 of 2006.

## 50. Mercury Balance

1. URS Dames & Moore, 'Environmental Site Assessment and Risk Assessment for Mercury HLL', 8 May 2002.
2. Ibid.
3. 'Mercury Thermometers', US Environmental Protection Agency. Available: https://www.epa.gov/mercury/mercury-thermometers. Retrieved on 18 October 2020.

4 URS Dames & Moore, 'Mercury Balance, Environmental Site Assessment and Risk Assessment for Mercury HLL Thermometer Factory Site, Kodaikanal, Tamil Nadu, India', 8 May 2002.

5. Ibid.
6. Ibid.
7. Ibid.
8. *Report of the Technical Committee Constituted by the Ministry of Labour and Employment*, Government of India, in connection with the Writ Petition No. 8291 of 2006 in the Honourable High Court of Madras, Directorate General Factory Advice Service and Labour Institutes Ministry of Labour and Employment, 9 November 2011, p. 115.

## 51. Indian or Dutch?

1. The Netherlands Government Parliamentary Proceedings, Ministry of Housing, Spatial Planning and the Environment (VROM), Lower House of Parliament, 1988–1989, No. 5.
2. Circular on target values and intervention values for soil remediation, Dutch Target and Intervention Values, 2000 (the New Dutch List), Ministry of Housing, Spatial Planning and the Environment (VROM), pp. 2–51. Available: https://www.esdat.net/environmental%20standards/dutch/annexs_i2000dutch%20environmental%20standards.pdf. Retrieved on 20 October 2020.
3. 5.3 'Mercury Distribution on Site, Environmental Site Assessment and Risk Assessment for Mercury HLL Thermometer Factory Site.
4. 'Volume II-2.1-b Screening and Response levels, Guidance document for assessment and remediation of contaminated sites in India, Volume II – Standards and checklists', National Program for Rehabilitation of Polluted Sites in India, 1st Edition, March 2015, Ministry of Environment and Forests, Government of India.
5. Ibid.

## 52. NEERI and Claude Alvares

1. Order dated 14 October 2003 and further proceedings on Writ Petition (C) No.657 of 1995, Research Foundation for *Science, Technology and Natural Resource vs Union of India & Ors.*

2. Report of the Visit of the SCMC to Tamil Nadu, 20–22 September 2004, Supreme Court Monitoring Committee (Ref: SC CWP 657 of 1995). Available: http://www.sipcotcuddalore.com/downloads/scmc_tn_visit.pdf. Retrieved on 21 October 2020.
3. Ibid.
4. Tamil Nadu Pollution Control Board Proceedings No. HWM/27566/D1/DGL /Mercury Vol 18-2 / dated 14 December 2004.
5 Dr Tapan Chakrabarti, 'Setting-up of a risk based remediation goal at a mercury contaminated site in Kodaikanal (TamilNadu)' *National Networking Workshop on 'Contaminated Sites: Subsurface Investigations and Remediation*, 12 and 13 July 2018, New Delhi.
6. Dr Tapan Chakrabarti, Mahena P. Patil, A. Deshkar and Atul Narayan Vaidya, 'Setting-Up of a Risk Based Remediation Goal at a Mercury contaminated site in India', *IWWG International Waste Working Group, Specialized Session C*, October 2007. Available: https://www.wtert.net/paper/1047/setting-up-of-a-risk-based-remediation-goal-at-a-mercurycontaminated-site-in-india.html. Retrieved on 21 October 2020.
7. *8.0 Feasibility Studies on Soil Washing and Thermal Retorting*, Protocol for Remediation of Mercury Contaminated Site at HLL Thermometer Factory, Kodaikanal, National Environmental Engineering Research Institute, Nehru Marg, Nagpur-440020, February 2007.
8. WP No. 4686 of 2006 *Nityanand Jayaraman vs Union of India* before the High Court of Court of Judicature at Madras.
9. Kodaikanal, India – The Facts, Unilever. Available: https://www.unilever.com/sustainable-living/what-matters-to-you/kodaikanal-india.html. Retrieved on 21 October 2020.

## 53. From 25 to 20

1. Former HLL Mercury Thermometer Factory, Kodaikanal, Tamil Nadu, India: Site Specific Target Levels, ERM, 2006.
2. TNPCB Letter No. T14/TNPCB/HWM/F.27566/HLL/DGL/07 dated 20 August 2007 to T. Chakrabarti, NEERI, and the Factory Manager, M/s HLL, Kodaikanal.

3. TNPCB Letter No. T14/TNPCB/HWM/F.27566/HLL/DGL/2007 dated 7 December 2007 from N. Sundaradevan, Chairman, TNPCB to the Factory Manager, M/s HLL, Kodaikanal.
4. TNPCB Letter No. T4/TNPCB/HWM/F-27566/DGL/2008/Dated: 19 June 2008 from R. Ramachanan, Member Secretary, TNPCB, to Factory Manager, Hindustan Unilever Ltd, Kodaikanal.
5. Order of the Supreme Court of India on *Research Foundation for Science Technology and Natural Resource Policy vs Union of India and others.* Writ Petition No. 657 of 1995, dated 14 October 2003.
6. Minutes of meeting of Scientific Experts Committee (SEC) and TNPCB officials on Remediation of Mercury contaminated soil at M/s Hindustan Unilever Ltd, Thermometer Factory Premises, Kodaikanal, dated 9 January 2010.

## 54. The Green Tribunal

1. The National Green Tribunal Act, 2010 (No 19 of 2010), National Green Tribunal, 2 June 2010. Available: https://greentribunal.gov.in/sites/default/files/act_rules/National_Green_Tribunal_Act,_2010.pdf. Retrieved on 23 October 2010.
2. James Brooke, 'The Earth Summit; Delegates From 4 Nations Warm to a High-Profile Role: Global Powerbroker', *The New York Times,* 12 June 1992. Available: https://www.nytimes.com/1992/06/12/world/earth-summit-delegates-4-nations-warm-high-profile-role-global-powerbroker.html. Retrieved on 23 October 2020.
3. Order on WP No. /4686/2006 *Nityanand Jayaraman vs Union of India & Others,* before the High Court of Judicature, Madras, 12 July 2016.
4. Order on Original Application No. 211/2018 (M.A. No. 1011/2018, M.A. No. 1125/2018 & M.A. No. 1341/2018) (Earlier O.A. No. 22/2017) (SZ), *Navroz Mody vs Union of India & Ors* before the National Green Tribunal Principal Bench, New Delhi.
5. Ibid.
6. 'Volume II–2.1-b Screening and Response levels, National Program for Rehabilitation of Polluted Sites in India, Guidance document for

assessment and remediation of contaminated sites in India Volume II – Standards and checklists', 1st Edition, Ministry of Environment and Forests, Government of India, March 2015.

7. Order on Original Application No. 211/2018 (M.A. No. 1011/2018, M.A. No. 1125/2018 & M.A. No. 1341/2018) (Earlier O.A. No. 22/2017) (SZ), *Navroz Mody vs Union of India & Ors* before the National Green Tribunal Principal Bench, New Delhi.
8. Ibid.
9. 'NGT Rejects "Conflict of Interest" Charge, Clears Way for Kodaikanal Mercury Remediation,' *News18,* 19 November 2019. Available: https://www.news18.com/news/india/ngt-rejects-conflict-of-interest -charge-clears-way-for-kodaikanal-mercury-remediation-1934609.html. Retrieved on 31 October 2020.
10. A. Qureshi, and K. Subhavana, 'Multimedia Mercury Cycling in a Legacy Contaminated Tropical Montane Forest (Kodaikanal, India) and Implications for Monitoring and Assessment of Future Contaminated Regions,' *Journal of Hazardous, Toxic, and Radioactive Waste,* 2002, Vol. 24(4).
11. Order on Civil Appeal No: 1666 of 2019, *Navroz Mody vs Union of India* on 5 March 2019, In the Supreme Court of India, Civil Appellate Jurisdiction.

## Epilogue

1. K. Shenbaham, 'Culture and lifestyle of Paliyan tribes at Palani hill, Dindigul district', *International Journal of Humanities and Social Science Research,* February 2016, Vol. 2, No. 3, pp. 37–40.
2. Ibid.
3. V. Selvakumar, 'The Paliyars and Shiva Temples of the Caturagiri Hills, Virudunagar District, Tamil Nadu, South India and the Caturagiri Vazhinadaiccindu', *International Journal of Research in Humanities and Social Sciences,* 2018, Vol. 5, No. 2, pp. 60–73.
4. Wilson Thomas, 'Habitat loss puts lion-tailed macaque in IUCN endangered list for the sixth time', *Hindu,* 25 September 2020. Retrieved on 28 October 2020.

5. C. Arivazhagan, R. Arumugam and K. Thiyagesan, 'Food Habits of Leopard (Panthera Pardus Fusca), Dhole (Cuon Alpinus) and Striped Hyena (Hyaena Hyaena) in a Tropical Dry Thorn Forest of Southern India', *Journal of Animal Ecology*, May 2005, Vol. 64, No. 4, pp. 439–50.
6. A. R. Rahmani, M. Z. Islam and R. M. Kasambe, *Important Bird and Biodiversity Areas in India: Priority Sites for Conservation (Revised and updated)*, Bombay: Bombay Natural History Society, Indian Bird Conservation Network, Society for the Protection of Birds and BirdLife International U.K., 2016, pp. 1992 + xii.
7. Nilgiri Marten Martes gwatkinsii, D. Mudappa, D. Jathana and T. R. S. Raman, The IUCN Red List of Threatened Species 2015, Martes gwatkinsii (errata version published in 2016). Available: https://www.iucnredlist.org/species/12847/86161239. Retrieved on 8 November 2020.
8. Rahmani, Islam and Kasambe, '*Important Bird and Biodiversity Areas in India*', 2016, pp. 1992 + xii.
9. Ibid.
10. Ibid.
11. M. Patra, and A. Sharma, 'Mercury Toxicity in Plants', *The Botanical Review*, 2000, Vol. 66, No. 3, pp. 379–422.
12. Ibid.
13. R. Karthik et al, 'Temporal variability of atmospheric Total Gaseous Mercury and its correlation with meteorological parameters at a high-altitude station of the South India', *Atmospheric Pollution Research*, 2016, pp. 1–10.
14. A. Qureshi and K. Subhavana, 'Multimedia Mercury Cycling in a Legacy Contaminated Tropical Montane Forest (Kodaikanal, India) and Implications for Monitoring and Assessment of Future Contaminated Regions', *Journal of Hazardous, Toxic, and Radioactive Waste*, 2020, Vol. 24, No. 4, 05020002.
15. Email to Mrs Ismawati from Paul Polman on Friday, 25 September 2015, 1:03 p.m.

# ACKNOWLEDGEMENTS

FOR A LONG TIME, THE PEOPLE OF KODAIKANAL AND ITS surroundings have wanted to express their deep anguish at the unprecedented disaster that was thrust upon their lives and their serene habitats. This book is a result of my mission to give vent to their and my own anguish at the catastrophe and, needless to say, concern for the lives and locales it so gravely impacted.

Millions of people around the world have succumbed to or have been suffering the heinous effects of mercury exposure, many of them oblivious that the culprit behind their declining health is mercury. To them I express my heartfelt sympathies. Numerous species of flora and fauna have also suffered the devastating effects of the poisonous liquid metal, with many becoming extinct or near-extinct.

The individuals to whom I owe gratitude are too many to name. Nonetheless, this is my humble attempt.

The people of Kodaikanal have been a source of steadfast inspiration to write this book. I thank the numerous workers of the Pond's/Hindustan Lever mercury thermometer factory with whom I closely interacted during my stint at Greenpeace and beyond. Thanks also to the many residents of the hill station who shared with me invaluable anecdotes about the insidious devastation.

Raja Mohamed, Gopal Krishnan and Mahendra Babu, the

three ex-workers of the factory who went on a mission to organize their former colleagues and began a fight against a gigantic global corporation that lasted for almost fifteen years. Their support and cooperation lent meaning to my job at Greenpeace. Thanks especially to Krishnan for the endless sessions during which we worked and re-worked the mercury balance calculations until fully satisfied; to Mohamed for introducing me to many ex-workers and members of the local community; and to both for remaining in touch with me to this day.

Thanks to Navroz Mody and Selvi Meenakshi, the duo that launched the attack against the company by representing the local community, and in 2002–04 helped me quickly learn about the issue in depth through many meetings in their humble cottages. Both deserve great appreciation for their dedication and courage, Mody specifically for his relentless fight against the company, despite his poor health and personal challenges. I do not exaggerate when I say that he deserves national recognition for his efforts.

The community that fought the big fight, in fact, transcends the hill station. The newly formed Tamil Nadu Alliance Against Mercury and many other organizations, in the state and nationally, had joined forces with Greenpeace and the ex-workers at various stages of this protracted fight. While the individuals associated with the struggle are too many to name, the person who has been spearheading it to date is Nityanand Jayaraman, who had supported me during my Greenpeace days and briefly during the writing of the book. He and his team are keenly following the remediation work currently ongoing at the factory site. I wish them strength as they continue the fight to save our ecosystems.

Those from Greenpeace who supported me either in the campaign or during the course of writing this book, sometimes in both cases, are Nirmala Karunan, Ganesh Nochur, George Mathen

(Appupen), Samir Nazareth, Adarsh Vashney, Shailendra Yashwant, G. Ananthapadmanabhan, Malini Morzaria, Ruth Stringer, Casey Harrell, David Santillo, among others. Annie Leonard, presently co-Executive Director of Greenpeace USA, declined to participate in the book, presumably because her Indian border entry restrictions are still in place. Nonetheless, I thank all of them for their contributions.

I would also like to thank all the scientists and doctors who I interviewed for the book, some of whom I have known since my Greenpeace days. I specifically acknowledge the frankness of Dr J. Arunachalam and Dr M. V. Balarama Krishna, both from the Department of Atomic Energy's National Centre for Compositional Characterization of Materials (NCCCM), Hyderabad, and thank them for their multiple research studies to demonstrate the increased presence of mercury in the Kodaikanal ecosystem – which aided me immensely.

Dr K. S. Jayaraman played a key role in shaping the contours of the campaign through his PTI despatches – first by means of a news report on the DAE study, subsequently with another despatch while sending 300-odd tonnes of mercury waste back to the US. He deserves a special mention here. I also acknowledge the support of the journalists M. R. Subramani, T. E. Raja Simhan and George Iype, among others. The Tamil channel Sun TV deserves praise for supporting me and covering the daring act of sneaking into the Tuticorin port to stream the despatch of mercury waste in 2003, and also for their coverage of the issue multiple times thereafter.

Vaigai Ramamurthy fought an unparalleled decade-long legal battle for the ex-workers and their families. She was kind enough to read through sections of the manuscript and offer valuable legal perspectives in many instances. I thank her and her team wholeheartedly. Other lawyers who helped me in the course of writing this book include Suhrith Parthasarathy, appointed as a commissioner by the Madras High Court to implement the settlement, and J. S. Kannan, a Chennai-based lawyer who secured for me a plethora of government, regulatory and court documents through RTI channels. I also acknowledge the support of Satyajit Sarna & Associates for carrying out a legal review of the manuscript.

Teesta Guha Sarkar, my publisher at Pan Macmillan India, directed the structure and composition of the book. She and Isha Banerji, my editor, have helped make this book what it is today. Besides the duo, I am also thankful to my ever-dynamic agent Anish Chandy who was quick to recognize the potential of the book and placed it with the right publisher.

I was prompted to write *Heavy Metal* by a great friend, the founder-CEO of the elderly care startup Winage, Dr Arun Varma. Over uncountable conversations, he challenged me to start writing the book and continues to inspire me to continue with my writing adventures. As the first reader of the manuscript, he added immense value to it by whittling and fleshing it out in equal measure. Along with Bharat Kumar, formerly with the US Consulate in Chennai, he gave me precious feedback that helped refine the book. I offer them my sincere gratitude.

Finally, thanks are due to my mother, my wife Geetha Pillai, my son Tejus and my dog Snowy for being with me on this journey.

# INDEX